C000195293

HOUSE BUYING, SELLING & CONVEYANCING with BUYING BARGAINS AT PROPERTY AUCTIONS

House Buying, Selling & Conveyancing by Joseph Bradshaw, revised and updated by Margaret Bradshaw © 2001 Law Pack Publishing Ltd.

Buying Bargains at Property Auctions by Howard R. Gooddie © Howard R. Gooddie

Law Pack Publishing Limited
76-89 Alscot Road
London SE1 3AW

www.lawpack.co.uk

Printed in the Great Britain

ISBN: 1-902646-87-8

All rights reserved.

Crown copyright forms are reproduced with the permission of the Controller of Her Majesty's Stationery Office.

Important facts

This Law Pack book contains the information and instruction for buying and selling registered and unregistered houses without a solicitor. This book is for use in England or Wales; it is not suitable for use in Scotland or Northern Ireland.

The information it contains has been carefully compiled, but its accuracy is not guaranteed, as laws and regulations may change or be subject to differing interpretations.

Neither this nor any other publication can take the place of a solicitor on important legal matters. As with any legal matter, common sense should determine whether you need the assistance of a solicitor rather than rely solely on the information and forms in this Law Pack book.

We strongly urge you to consult a solicitor if:

- you do not understand the instructions or are uncertain how to complete and use a form correctly;

- what you want to do is not precisely covered by the this book.

Exclusion of Liability and Disclaimer

This book is sold with the understanding that neither the authors nor the publisher are engaged in rendering legal advice. If legal advice is required, the services of a solicitor should be sought. The publisher and the authors cannot in any way guarantee that the forms in this book are being used for the purposes intended and, therefore, assume no responsibility for their proper and correct use.

Whilst every effort has been made to ensure that this Law Pack book provides accurate and expert guidance, it is impossible to predict all the circumstances in which it may be used. Accordingly, neither the publisher, authors, retailer, nor any other suppliers shall be liable to any person or entity with respect to any loss or damage caused or alleged to be caused directly or indirectly by what is contained in or left out of this Law Pack book.

Contents

HOUSE BUYING, SELLING & CONVEYANCING

BUYING BARGAINS AT PROPERTY AUCTIONS

HOUSE BUYING, SELLING & CONVEYANCING

Introduction

It isn't true that only those who have gone through a long, expensive and involved training can possibly understand the intricacies of house buying, selling and conveyancing.

Anyone can set up as, and take on the title of Estate Agent. No qualifications or licences are required.

Traditionally, trained and qualified solicitors have done conveyancing. Not because their training qualified them to do it, but because a nineteenth century government, grateful for their support in collecting some taxes, gave them a legal monopoly of conveyancing for a fee. That leaves doing a conveyance for no fee, which means that you can do a conveyance for yourself or anyone else for whom you wish to do a favour. The only skills required are reading, writing and an ability to count your money.

People do far more for themselves than ever before. From painting and decorating to car maintenance, people are having a go themselves. And it isn't only practical things that are tackled.

A few years ago, the technicalities for obtaining a divorce were simplified and a little later the government withdrew the provision of legal aid for parties to divorces which were not defended. The increasing popularity of divorce and the bankrupting nature of solicitors' fees for doing the transaction have between them produced thousands of do-it-yourself divorcees who have done their own divorces, and saved themselves over £500 by expending a little time and effort.

Moreover, during the process of doing their own divorces, people have found that what hitherto they thought was a thoroughly legal process is only judicial insofar as a judge has to give a nod over their papers, and all the rest is an administrative matter.

Nowadays, transferring a house from one owner to another is done, in most of England and Wales, by filling in simple forms – that is the legal side of it.

In this book, I hope to show that housing transactions have even less of the law about them than divorce actions. Nowadays, transferring a house from one owner to another is done, in most of England and Wales, by filling in simple forms – that is the legal side of it. The bit that can be complicated is when you are using monies from the sale of

3

one house to pay for the purchase of another. But that is not a legal problem, it is a business transaction. You don't hare off to a fully-trained legal man when you are trading up-market from a Bentley to a Rolls; settling the HP on one and taking out a new loan on the other. You no more need to know the relevant housing Acts of Parliament inside out when you buy a house than you need to know the Road Traffic and Consumer Credit Acts when buying or selling a car. Whether it is a house or car that is being dealt with, you need to know about honesty and fair dealing and if you meet up with someone who sells you an unroadworthy car or seriously misrepresents a property to you, the laws are there to punish the offender; it is then that you really need a lawyer – a good one.

You no more need to know the relevant housing Acts of Parliament inside out when you buy a house than you need to know the Road Traffic and Consumer Credit Acts when buying or selling a car.

Just because wrongdoers can be punished under Acts of Parliament, this does not mean to say you should not be prudent within your competence. If you are considering buying a car that has done a fair mileage, you put it through some stringent tests, and if you are not sure about it, but are still interested, at a price, you get a qualified mechanic to give you a report on it. If you want to make sure there is no Hire Purchase on it, go to the local Citizens' Advice Bureau (don't ring, there's a form to fill in) and for little more than the cost of a stamp they will check it out for you. So there you are, the legal owner of a bigger and better car, and you need know no more law at the end of the transaction than at the beginning. But look at what you have accomplished: you have satisfied yourself that the car is what it is cracked up to be and checked that the person offering it for sale owns (has good title to) it. 'Ah!' you say, 'houses are not like cars. Surely it's more complicated, and doesn't the rule caveat emptor (let the buyer beware) apply in full force to a housing transaction? Isn't the whole business a splendid opportunity for scoundrels to practise their wicked ways?'

My answer is: certainly houses are not like cars. Cars can be stolen; repainted; engine and number plates swapped. You can't very well shift a whole house. As for 'let the buyer beware', in its application to housing it is, in the main, a reference to the purchaser making sure that the vendor has good title (can prove he owns and has the power to sell) and as you will learn from these pages, you obtain this assurance by sending a simple form (no fee payable) to the Land Registry.

Most Land Registry forms mentioned can be found on the Land Registry website, www.landreg.gov.uk, where they can be filled out and printed off (but, currently, not saved, so check before printing) –

others from law stationers – still others from the Inland Revenue Stamp Office.

No solicitor has a better method than that given here; and if, when you last bought a house, any precautions were taken to make sure that you did get vacant possession before the money was handed over (and vice versa when you sold) the odds are that it was you who did the legwork. Solicitors rely on the general law, together with the basic honesty of the absolute majority of house-owners on these practical points. On the legal point of proving ownership, where the ownership is registered, they rely on the state-backed guarantee provided by Her Majesty's Land Registry. I invite you to do the same.

HM Land Registry was established at the end of the nineteenth century, the Land Transfer Act which set it up having finally made its way through Parliament after centuries of attempts had failed. If you read what the sponsors of the Act had to say in its support you will see that they intended to make dealing in land as simple as dealing in, to use their nineteenth century words, 'stock and chattels'. To that end the Land Registry was established, and of course someone has to pay for its upkeep. Who better than those who benefit. The public? Today, the buyer of the average house pays nearly a hundred pounds to the Registry – but who has had the dealing simplified for him? The lawyer.

It is ironic that an Act passed nearly a century ago to benefit the general public, at a time when most people had left school at eleven years of age or earlier, has been made to appear so complicated that the vast majority of house buyers and sellers, who will have had at least eleven years of schooling, are being persuaded to pay solicitors to do something they could well do for themselves. It tells us something, either about our education system or about the lawyers' propaganda machine; I think it is the latter. Indeed, the propaganda is so effective it has even convinced lawyers themselves that they really are protecting their clients from a thousand and one things that can go wrong.

Since 1984, governments have laboured mightily to bring about competition in the conveyancing business. According to the Council for Licensed Conveyancers there are now approximately 750 licensed conveyancers in the UK (including both fully and limited licensed) to compete with more than 38,000 lawyers. So throughout we will refer to fee-taking conveyancers as solicitors, under the generic surname of Skinner.

I have done my own little survey. I put this question, 'What do you think a solicitor does for you that you could not do for yourself?' Invariably the answer is, 'All those searches'. This answer is usually spoken with such reverential awe, it seems that ordinary trusting people have come to believe that every time they buy a house their solicitor has worked his way through reference after reference, file after file, and book after book in office after office and cellar after cellar, emerging with the scrolls into the light of day, covered in dust and with a cold wet towel round his head.

In reality, the searching consists in sending off a few forms, which have ready-printed questions, to the authorities who answer them for you. If you really find this difficult to believe, at least have a look at the said forms. When you see them, I am sure you will agree that of all the forms you have ever had the misfortune to struggle with, those used in housing transactions suffer least from officialese and gobbledegook. If you have already bought or sold a house, you will have found that the only thing about the whole transaction which struck you as truly professional was the sheer size of the bill at the end of it. It doesn't matter whether your conveyance was done by qualified solicitors or their clerks, you got the same job done and the same breathtaking bill.

If you have already bought or sold a house, you will have found that the only thing about the whole transaction which struck you as truly professional was the sheer size of the bill at the end of it.

Another thing that really seemed to puzzle the respondents to my survey was: how did one manage to use the money from the sale of Flitsville for the purchase of Newsville; when it is well known that you have to actually flit from Flitsville before you get your money for it? As you will learn, it can be done when you can get all the parties or their representatives together at the same time. But where that is not possible it is done by the simple expedient of taking a bridging loan for a few days. The interest is at about 3 per cent over base rate, so on £30,000 the charge is a mere £10.46 per day with a minimum of £15, plus an arrangement fee which will depend on the moneylender you go to. To bridge a day, you can even leave your furniture in the van overnight and get bed and breakfast somewhere. Because those who cut out estate agents can choose their own buyers and control the pace, they seldom need a bridging loan and never need to give four or five thousand pounds to the chain-breakers.

Conveyancing can appear to be very lucrative for solicitors. Of course, like everybody else they have big expenses nowadays. Office rents are not cheap, secretaries demand a living wage; they also require central heating and are not prepared to type on any old PC. Solicitors have also been known to defend the high cost of conveyancing on the ground that it subsidises the pitifully low rates of pay they receive for work in some criminal courts. Whether solicitors, given their costly overheads, are doing conveyances as cheaply and efficiently as they could, the fact remains that house owners are increasingly coming to the conclusion that lawyers' shops are situated in a market they cannot afford to patronise.

Indeed, many people with young growing families are aching to move house but are deterred by the high costs. The older end, having seen it all before, cannot face the anxieties generated by the selling and conveyancing system. To them, the opportunity to do their own and cut out the middlemen, has proved a godsend.

Over the years I have, as a property owner, conveyed shops, offices, houses and the like for myself – nothing has ever gone wrong. Never have I regretted my choice, and neither have I ever met any other person who does their own conveyancing who has any regrets. Sorting out the problems that house buyers and sellers have has convinced me that it would have been far better for many of them had they tackled the job themselves from the beginning.

Transferring property is nowhere near as difficult as it has been made out to be, but that does not mean to say that the technical work can be done by a two-year-old chimpanzee suffering from brain damage. If in a few of the pages that follow it seems rather complicated, take courage and keep going, remembering it's all new to you. It might even be shock that is stopping your brain functioning; shock at the simplicity, and shame as you realise how in the past you have been so easily persuaded that it was all so fantastically difficult.

Though it is hoped that this book makes an interesting and useful read in itself, it is intended to be kept at the learner Estate Agent's and Conveyancer's elbow for reference as he picks his way through buying and selling and conveyancing for himself.

On the way he will notice that strategies and tactics are given so that purchasers pay less and vendors get more. This inherent paradox can only make life more interesting all round where both vendor and purchaser have invested in the book. So if you spot from your opposite number's tactics a fellow reader, keep the knowledge to yourself, turn back to the book and check up on how to cope. Why let the professionals have all the fun? Do the job yourself and take a pride in it!

A word about forms

One word of warning regarding form numbers, which this book refers to frequently. These numbers come from a variety of sources. All Land Registry forms and Land Charges Department forms are numbered by the Land Registry and the numbers are used by all law form publishers. The same principle applies to Inland Revenue forms. There are also forms which are produced by commercial firms that use the name and number of the originating party, such as the local search forms.

However, other forms are given their number by the publisher of the form and, frequently, different publishers use different numbers. Plus, over the years solicitors have got used to using general conveyancing expressions. For example, 'preliminary enquiries' and 'enquiries before contract' are the questions to be asked in writing before exchange of contracts; the publishers will name and number them according to their own preference. So when asked to answer preliminary enquiries if you are selling, do not be surprised to find that the form has a different name. In the old days, the buyer's solicitors sent these to the seller's lawyers; they still do if they do not have to accept the Sellers Property Information Forms.

The various Property Information Forms. These were introduced in a vain attempt by the legal profession to create a seller's property information pack and the idea was that the seller's solicitors would complete and send these to the buyer or his solicitors, along with a local search, draft contract, title information and so on. The scheme was not overly popular. Some solicitors still follow the procedure but almost never will the seller pay for and volunteer a local search certificate, while other solicitors prefer to use the printed enquiries or even their own from their word processor, etc.

Do not be surprised to find that when you sell your home you may be asked to volunteer replies to Property Information Forms, or you may be sent the buyer's solicitor's preferred version of preliminary enquiries. When you buy your new house, do not be surprised if you are sent replies to Property Information forms, or are invited to send in your preliminary enquiries. This confusion simply represents the distinction between solicitors who prefer the old way and those who prefer the new.

A similar confusion in names and numbers applies to the requisitions on title, questions posted by the buyer to the seller's solicitors after contracts have been exchanged.

One final word of warning: a number of these forms is due to be changed or supplemented at the time of going to print. This includes the local search form Con29, which will be divided; from October 2001, there will be two forms (one optional) with some changes in the numbering. There will also be a form for water company searches that will probably come in at the same time. Various other search forms are due to be introduced at some indeterminate stage in the future.

1 Buying

First of all, you must find something to view. Answering estate agents' and private vendors' advertisements in local papers is one obvious way, and touring round finding 'For Sale' boards is another. But there are also the not so obvious, such as placing your own advertisements in newspapers and even shop windows in the locality you have decided is the one for you. There is also the direct approach of knocking on doors and asking 'Is this house for sale?' to which you might be lucky enough to get the answer, 'No, but that one over there is.' In any case, such an approach can often lead to a useful conversation about the area and its qualities and problems.

Having found a house to view, your main consideration is: can I make a home here?

When you have viewed a number of houses within a short period of time it is sometimes, at the end of the day, difficult to remember which had what – the address alone is not always sufficient to bring the memories flooding back. So try to pick on some salient feature – the more ridiculous the better, such as 'the one with the surly butler', 'the one with the circular pink mirrors on the bathroom walls', 'the one to suit mother-in-law', etc., and make a note accordingly on the particulars if you have got some from an agent. Why not take your video camera (though the owners might think you are a burglars agent, or worse a reporter!)? Remember, when viewing property to which you have been introduced by an agent, that he gets his commission from the vendor – he owes very little, if any, duty to a purchaser. The higher the price he gets for the vendor, the more his commission, but he's got to be a bit of a dullard if the only reason he is sticking out for the extra couple of hundred pounds is because it will push his commission from £500 to £505.

Having found a house to view your main consideration is: can I make a home here? I suggest that there are two additional criteria to which you should pay attention. The first is already at the back of your mind: is it structurally sound? The second sounds a bit daft when you haven't yet bought, but old hands who have often been moved up, down and across the country for one reason or another will testify to its importance: will it be easy to sell if ever I need to move? We will look at each in turn.

Whether you can make a home in the house you are about to view is a highly personal question. Nevertheless, there are a few points that are common to many people. For instance, if you are getting on in years you have to consider whether children screaming at all times of the day and night are easily tolerated. Even if you are young, you might well find other peoples' kids too much to bear. A new, neat and tidy development where there is just a bunch of nice newly-married couples but very few children, is no guarantee of a quiet life for those who want one. Noisy, late-finishing house-warmings, followed by every conceivable sort of party, followed by slamming of car doors can disturb the sleep just as effectively as the screaming children the newly-weds will soon produce!

If you are buying a semi or terrace (town/mews/cottage style) house, get to know as much as you can about who will be doing what at the other side of that joint and party wall, and if the vendors have the television, radio or CD player going full blast when you call, have it switched off and listen. When there are neighbours' drives that you look out over, try to make sure there will not be a boat or caravan blocking your view.

If vendors don't mention why they want to sell and where they are moving to, ASK!

Vendors who insist on viewing 'strictly by appointment' often do so because they want to manipulate the situation – for example, if they have at one side a neighbour who takes his bagpipe band off every weekend in his caravan, while the young mariner at the other takes his boat and yapping dog away at the same time, who can blame such a vendor for insisting on weekend viewing? And it's a certainty that any vendor, if questioned, will only vouchsafe that the neighbours are quiet people who keep themselves to themselves, but are of sterling worth if called upon in a crisis. And if they think you have an inkling that a band next door is trying to perfect its line-up and gets it all together on Mondays, Wednesdays and Thursdays, they will laugh that off with: 'Oh, it's quite lively, we quite enjoy it – keeps us young you know. Actually we've heard that they are splitting up – pity really'.

If you are a non-gardener or simply can't find the time for Britain's major hobby, don't be persuaded to buy just because the garden looks so well established, so neat and tidy already, and only appears to need a minimum of maintenance. All gardens need constant attention if they are to look as though they need no attention. A shower of rain just after you have viewed can germinate a thousand weeds.

Any objection from any member of your family should be listened to before you finally decide. Teenagers might say of an open-plan house that there is nowhere for them to go. Open-plan houses seem to suit the very young and the very old, but situations near rivers don't suit either. They are too wet for non-swimmers and too damp for the arthritic.

Before you go out viewing, it is a good idea to get into your head what hectares, yards, feet and metres look like. When told a room is 20 feet by 14 feet or 6 metres by 3 metres, can you visualise it in your mind? Is the bath at your present abode of such a size that you can enjoy a long, lazy soak in it? Whether it is or not, measure it, and use the size as a comparison. Will your furniture fit? If it will, fine. If it won't then you have to choose – furniture or house.

Having made your first visit during the week, make your second at the weekend (or vice versa), so as to get a different perspective of the neighbours and the neighbourhood.

Having made your first visit during the week, make your second at the weekend (or vice versa), so as to get a different perspective of the neighbours and the neighbourhood. Park your car some distance away and walk – you will see a lot more of the district that way.

With a bit of luck, there will be heavy rain before you move in, so while you round to look for damp, and you never know, there might have been a burst pipe or a fire to ruin the decorations. Even if contracts are signed you may still say 'You didn't tell me about this lot. To be fair you must put it right', but that very much depends on the contract, as you will see from chapter 8.

You are not really entitled to make these subsequent visits, (but why should the sellers object?), and maybe the first thing you must really persuade yourself of is that though you are going to the house to poke around in somebody else's private domain, you must not be embarrassed about it. The vendors knew you and others were likely to do this from the moment they thought about putting the house on the market, and they have had ample time and opportunity to hide any dirty linen and to empty the cupboard of skeletons.

A lot can be learned while walking up the path. A gate that is falling to bits isn't a very good introduction. Is the path itself cracking and subsiding? Is the drive likely to help or hinder when you have a flat battery? Will icing cause problems in the winter? Can you see any cracks in the stucco or brickwork? If there is a lot of zig-zag cracking around the windows and doors they are signs of old or new subsidence. If the cracks have been filled in some time ago and have not re-appeared, all is no doubt well.

All houses subside a little after being built and it usually expresses itself in no more than cracked plaster. But if the cracks have been filled and parted again, or worse still, bricks have cracked vertically, there is real trouble, as there is if a wall is starting to lean or taking on the shape of a saucer. You don't need to start digging around the foundations, or paying a surveyor to do so to know that this one is not for you – unless it can be bought for the price of the land.

While still walking slowly up the garden path, have your first look at the down-pipes, roof and chimney if there is one. Have another look up from the back garden later, and if it is a tall house bring along your binoculars so that you can inspect the chimney-stack and pot. A swift look at the TV aerials in the vicinity will tell you about TV reception. If there are a lot of tall fancy ones about, reception is likely to be poor.

Damp

Once again, you are looking to see if the structure is doing the thing that a house is supposed to do: shelter you from the elements. Damp is the indicator of most structural problems in a house. Water tries to get in from the top, ends, sides and bottom. As if that were not enough, we bring it in via pipes, and builders use thousands of gallons of water in the building of a house. Houses are built of such things as bricks, mortar and wood, all of which are porous, and the soil in Britain seldom dries out, so the fabric of a British house is always damp to some extent. It is when that dampness passes an unacceptable level that things begin to rot and owners have to start paying out.

Houses are built of such things as bricks, mortar and wood, all of which are porous, and the soil in Britain seldom dries out, so the fabric of a British house is always damp to some extent.

Blocked, overflowing gutters and cracked downpipes can be a source of water which will penetrate in sideways, as also can badly pointed chimney stacks. Driving rain can find its way in through cracks round doors and windows. Otherwise, sideways penetration of water is very rare as modern houses are almost certainly constructed with two outside walls roughly two inches apart and pinned together by metal wires or straps. The two inch gap, called a cavity, forms an insulation barrier ensuring that water can penetrate only as far as the cavity and no further. However, in the building process careless builders have been known to drop mortar down the cavity and allow it to accumulate on the ties.

In this case the mortar build-up can form a bridge to convey water from the outer to the inner wall. If you are buying a house in the course of construction take your torch to have a look and tell the foremen if you find his brickies are laying up problems, as well as bricks, for the future. Once a house is completed and there is no internal evidence of damp from this cause you can be pretty sure there is none. If you really want to be sure, there is only one way to find out and this applies to much else – take the house down brick by brick!

In all modern, indeed in nearly all houses, there will be a damp-proof course. This is needed because the ground in Great Britain is nearly always damp, the brickwork in the foundations will soak it up, and it will quickly spread round the house. A damp-proof course is a water-tight skin of some sort.

The old system was to set slates on the third or fourth brick course above the ground, and below the level of the floor joists. Slate does not bend and the slight movements of a house can, over time, fracture parts of the slate course. For many years now, builders have used mineral felt or plastic sheet, both of which are flexible and can cope with anything but a really radical structural movement. What it can't cope with is the owner who piles soil up against the wall to a height above the course.

Count to the third or fourth course of bricks and you will see the slate or black, bituminous material protruding a little somewhere along the line. Once you have found the height follow the line right round the house to see if your vendor has been silly. If he has, pay really particular attention to the plaster, skirting board and any other woodwork on the opposite side of that patch inside the house and give general attention to the whole of the ground floor woodwork if there are wooden floors, because damp does spread. If no real damage has been done, removal of the offending material from the outside wall is imperative. This done, check to make sure that the air bricks are clear and if the damp is only slight it will soon disappear.

And here it is worth making a general point about 10-, 20-, 30- or even life-time guarantees and it is this: it's easy for the firm to give the guarantee, but who will guarantee that the firm will still be in business if ever you need them?

What can be done when the damp course is damaged or the house was built without one? You could get a builder to go round the house knocking out a brick at a time and inserting a damp course as he goes. It might work – it will certainly be expensive. There are firms who specialise in various, what can loosely be described as 'patent systems'. You can find them in the Yellow Pages and they will usually give a free estimate. Some of these systems have a good success rate. Most firms will give some sort of long guarantee. And here it is worth making a general point about 10-, 20-, 30- or even life-time guarantees and it is this: it's easy for the firm to give the guarantee, but who will guarantee that the firm will still be in business if ever you need them?

So that's the base and sides dealt with; what about the roof? The most common form of construction for residential property is a pitched roof, covered either with slates or tiles. It is often difficult to gain access to roof space, but if you have any doubts about the construction, it is best to cope with the difficulty now. In the case of an old house, it is reasonable to assume that any fault in the construction itself will have developed already and your external examination will have told you whether the roof is bowing or not. If it is and has been bowed or buckled for a number of years and there is no internal evidence of damp it is probably all right. However, if you decide to have a look in the roof space, take a good torch with you but keep switching it off to see if any daylight is coming in because of missing, broken or drifting slates or tiles. While you are up there you can check on insulation of ceiling, tanks and pipes, and if there is none or it isn't done up to modern standards, you have found another bargaining point or two.

Recent decorations can provide internal evidence of damp. Vendors do titivate their houses up ready for sale; and they also, sometimes, do it to cover up evidence. If you suspect this has happened, see if you can borrow a damp meter from your friendly DIY shop, but be careful that you are not tracing the run of a water pipe or drain and mistaking it for damp. The instructions that come with the meter will tell you about all that.

Flat roofs need special attention

If a pitched roof covered in slate or tile goes wrong, the replacement of a few slates or tiles will, more often than not, solve the problem. But the only remedy for a badly damaged flat roof is often the complete replacement of the covering. The most usual coverings are lead, asphalt roofing felt and sometimes zinc, and it is important that roofs be laid to a proper fall so that water does not gather in any depressions. If you can see any such pools then trouble is on its way – sooner or later.

As the covering is exposed to heat in one season and cold in another and sometimes both on the same day, and its expansion and contraction rate is not equal to the boards on which it is laid you can often see the skeleton impression of the boarding showing through the covering. Now, that boarding should run at right angles to the gutter; if it is parallel to the gutter, water will gather in the depressions, which will have nothing on the depression that will settle over you when you get the builder's quotation (avoid estimates) for the repairs. Felt roofs last about ten years, asphalt up to 30 years. Evidence of downward damp can be seen on ceilings, upstairs walls and chimney breasts. The fault can often be located and dealt with by climbing a ladder and cleaning out the gutter. Where there are stains all round the upper walls, unless you are getting a real bargain, it might be as well to try elsewhere.

It is not always easy to examine floors, particularly when they are covered with lino or carpets. A vendor refusing to let you have a careful look might give grounds for suspecting his: 'Oh, the floors are all right, you can take my word for it.' It is particularly desirable to have a thorough examination made if there are any indications of springiness, such as ornaments rattling, when you walk across the floor, or you suspect that it is rotting joists that are allowing the floor to part company from the skirting board. The floor into a bay window is the favourite place for the rot to set in and by an outside door is runner up. If your vendor tells you that you can have every confidence in it, ask him to jump up and down on it for awhile, after all he knows the way round his cellars better than you do.

Timbers can be affected by dry rot, wet rot, beetle or woodworm. Dry rot is insidious. It is a fungus and it glories in finding a bit of damp wood to set up business in. It gets down between the fibres of wood and dries the wood out. Dry-rotted wood looks as if it has been dehydrated to a brown cracked appearance and crumbles to dust at a touch when in an advanced stage of development. Unfortunately, the damage is well under way before there is any external manifestation of it as mentioned above. But the conditions under which it thrives can be spotted: damp, smelly, unventilated corners.

Wet rot gets going when the wood becomes so saturated that the fibres break apart, weakening the wood. It tends to happen at the end of timbers (hence the attention to skirting board gaps) where water can get in between fibres, but of course, it can occur elsewhere; around sink, bath and WC wastes are likely areas. Depending on how far the wet rot has gone it can be cured, often quite inexpensively, by replacing the rotted timber and rectifying the fault that caused it. Take a strong torch with you into the cellar (if there is one), because the floor joists are more likely than not to be nicely exposed for your inspection. Poke around with a strong penknife – if you can slide it into the wood at right angles to the run of the grain you've found something.

The third ill that can affect timbers is beetle or woodworm. Woodworm is the caterpillar of the beetle. The flying beetle alights and injects her egg into timber and flies away until she is ready for a repeat performance. The egg develops into a worm which, feeding on the life-giving juices of the timber, transforms itself into a beetle in the image of its mother, and burrows out into the light of day leaving behind it a tunnel in the wood and a little pile of sawdust beside it. Which all goes to show that if you simply go round, no matter how meticulously, squirting things into the worm holes, you can't be sure you have got all the little beggars; that is why you need a specialist firm in to say whether the beetle is still active, and if it is, to give you a quote for pressure spraying the timbers.

To find out if the worm has been active enough to cause real danger, the penknife test is used. As with the wet and dry rot, badly affected timber can be replaced and your decision must be based on the amount of repair required; so if you find evidence of wood rot of any kind, call in one of the specialist firms who will give you a quotation and offer a guarantee. If the problems have been discovered early enough the cost need not be ruinous.

There are a lot of solid floors about nowadays, so if such a floor has parted from the skirting board the supporting fill has re-arranged itself and that is why settlement has taken place – it can be rectified, but make sure there is no zig-zagging on the outer wall because in that case the foundations might be rearranging themselves too.

Electrics

Another point to cover is the electrical system. A sure sign of wiring that has had its day is the plug with round pins. The whole house needs re-wiring. In older houses during your inspections of the roof space and cellar, look out for any wires that pass across the joists. If you see two element wires twisted together and festooned along you can be pretty sure some re-wiring is necessary to bring the electrical system up to modern standards of efficiency, and above all, safety.

The area electricity board will be only too glad to make a visual inspection without charge and they will give a free quotation for any work required. If for any reason the supply is cut off, as it no doubt will be, if there is to be any gap between the time when the vendor leaves and you move in, no re-connection will be made if the whole system is not up to standard.

Decorations

Decorations can cover a multitude of sins, and are, of course, like sin, a matter of personal preference.

Costs of decorating can be high particularly if you have tall ceilings, with fancy cornices or moulding. The rooms might look immaculate but always take the precaution of lifting a picture off the wall to find out if pale patches will remain when the vendor has gone. Incidentally, whether you re-decorate because you dislike the colour scheme or because the place is a dirty tip, the cost will be pretty much the same, although, if the wallpaper is already peeling off it might be cheaper!

Plumbing

We've dealt with unwanted water getting into the house and causing damp – now we will have a look at the water that we do want in the house. If you are to get your water from a well, you will need someone to tell you if the well is sufficiently deep to avoid pollution of the water by any drains that might be or become defective. A well must also be situated at a reasonable distance from any possible source of contamination. In fact, before you go any further, a few words with the local authorities would be in order – they might already know the situation and have costly plans for the owner or his successor.

Find the tap at the highest point and try the pressure. Also try the hot water pressure to the bath – you don't want to wait all day for the bath to fill. Neither do you want to spend all day pulling on the WC plunger, so drop a piece of paper into the pan and see if you can send it on its way with one shot, and while you are about it note if the pan or the washbasin is cracked.

When you walk round the garden and find a portion that is squelchy or there is an ominous line of subsidence in the driveway it might be that the vendor is a bit of a stinker and is not levelling with you. However, you can square him up by getting a firm in to test the drains. If they use the water pressure system, they could cause damage so get the vendor's written permission first – as a matter of fact, if the firm has anything about them they will have a standard form intended to indemnify themselves, so have a word with them to make sure it isn't amended to land you in the ...

I would like to instruct vendors not to read the next paragraph, but if they can't resist reading I implore them not to draw any guidelines from it to help them with their sales!

Central heating systems need examining. Ask to see last year's receipts for the fuel used. If it is a system such as gas, ask if it has been regularly serviced.

Central heating systems need examining. Ask to see last year's receipts for the fuel used. If it is a system such as gas, ask if it has been regularly serviced. Find a radiator at the highest point in the house and as you turn the air-release screw hold a lighted match to it. If you set up a lighted gas jet it isn't because gas has got into the system, it is the product of some corrosion that has started. It might only need some anti-corrosion fluid putting in the system – on the other hand that might not be sufficient. In any case, all the more reason to have a careful look round for leaks particularly at joints. Leaks also tend to make nasty stains on carpets.

If you remember most of the tips given above, a vendor will not notice how much you are noticing. A glance takes in that the electric socket on the skirting board has square holes, and the same glance tells you that the floor is well up to the skirting board, and as you walk over to the bay to admire the view your ears tell you that the presents from Blackpool and Malaga on the sideboard are not doing a clog dance accompanied by castanets. And while you are admiring the view, you might as well test the window to see if it opens.

Surveys

There might seem to be a lot to look at, but houses are big things and cost big money. You can't expect to get satisfaction if you buy one with the same nonchalance as when you buy a new light bulb.

Can you rely on a lender's surveyor's report thinking: 'Well, he will tell me if there is anything wrong with it'? Well, he will and he won't. His job is to tell the building society whether the land and buildings thereon (as the saying goes) is good enough security for the money they are thinking of lending you to assist you in your purchase. He has no obligation to you, so he will not stick his neck out telling you that the structure is perfectly sound, but you can be sure that he will let the building society know if the foundations or the roof are in danger of collapse, and that whereas they think they are getting a desirable residence as security, there is the distinct probability that in a year's time all that would be left for them to get their money back on would be a plot of land covered in rubble. (Incidentally, it does not necessarily work quite like that. When a borrower defaults, the building society does take and sell the property. In the extremely rare case where they do not raise sufficient money to cover the defaulter's indebtedness, and their own and their agents' and solicitors' costs, then the defaulting borrower can still be sued for the balance).

A vendor of a property less than ten years old is apt to say that it is guaranteed by the National House Building Council (NHBC). Well, not quite! What a builder gets for his purchaser is a ten-year cover. It is sometimes called a 'ten-year structural warranty', but this is inaccurate. It covers more than just the structure, particularly for homes registered for cover since 1 April 1999. Since 1988 the scheme has been known as 'Buildmark'.

You require the balance of the period of cover to be transferred to you, but NHBC and builders do not require it. Add a clause to the contract saying the vendor will assign it to you (using a form CS12, or HB12).

Don't think that buying a recently-built house means that you will get a repair-bill-free ten years – you won't.

The protection which NHBC gives is in two sections. Firstly, the builder's obligations and secondly NHBC's insurance cover. Under the first section, the builder has to put right at his own expense any defects which arise as a result of his failure to comply with the NHBC minimum standards of workmanship and material and which are notified to him in writing during the first two years of the house's life Don't think that buying a recently-built house means that you will get a repair-bill-free ten years - you won't. A house owner is not relieved of his normal maintenance responsibilities, and the agreement does not cover normal wear and tear, or normal shrinkage. Some items such as fences, white goods and lifts are not covered at all.

Under the second section, cover is in three main parts. Firstly, against loss of deposit in the event of the builder's insolvency between exchange of contracts and completion. Secondly, against the costs of repairs that result from the builders insolvency or failure to meet an arbitration award or judgement which arise during the period up to two years from the date of the NHBC certificate. Thirdly, the cost of more serious items which arise during the third to tenth years from the date of the certificate (Please note that the 'certificate' is also known as the 'Ten Year Notice'). There is a fourth element of cover is NHBC is the building control authority in place of the local council. This covers costs of putting right breaches of the statutory building regulations.

The NHBC cover saves you from the consequences of basic bad building and that's about it. That is to say, broadly, the cover is for such items as subsidence or settlement, and other major structural defects due to non-compliance with standards, such as collapse or serious distortion of joists or roof structure, chemical failure of material affecting the load-bearing structure.

Since 1 April 1999, the cover has been expanded and includes, amongst other things, double glazing, defective flooring, defective flues and wet applied plaster. It also includes insurance against the cost of cleaning up contamination of the plot on which the house stands, if a statutory clean-up notice is served on the owner.

If you are a second or subsequent buyer, you cannot claim on the NHBC for defects which the first purchaser reported to the builder, nor defects which were visible, on reasonable inspection, (whatever that is) at the time of purchase.

During its existence, the National House Building Council has done sterling service for the owner-occupier, particularly the original purchaser from a builder, in raising minimum standards of building and finish. If you are thinking of buying a newly built house, see if the builder is on the NHBC Register. If he isn't, it might be that he has been kicked off. If he has there may be problems with obtaining cover regardless of the fact that he may have hung on to the documents. On the other hand he might be a splendid, upright, entrepreneurial character who knows what he, like his father before him, is about and is determined not to have any 'pen-pushers' telling him what to do. Ask some of his previous buyers. They'll soon tell you how good he is. Mind you, he might be the salt of the earth, but he will never sell his house to anyone wanting to raise a loan on it and a cash buyer will never sell it to anyone wanting to raise money to aid the purchase. Fact is the absence of an NHBC Certificate for a new house renders it un-saleable unless something similar is in place, which enjoys market recognition. Generally, this means insurance or the benefit of one of the other schemes recognised by the Council of Mortgage Lenders. See next section.

So, the old hands will prefer to buy a house that is six or seven years' old, where any weak spots have had time to show.

You will see from the necessarily brief description given above some of the things the NHBC is and isn't. When you are in any deal which involves the ten-year structural warranty, write off to their Council and get just as much information as you can. While we are dealing with newly built houses, it is as well to ask a vendor of a second hand house whether he intends moving into one. Builders' dates for completion are seldom kept and can often be weeks, or even months, wide of the mark. Also, find out if you are likely to be tagging yourself into a chain and how long it is.

Given the climate in England and Wales, and the rarity of a long summer drought, the NHBC guarantees given in the past three or four years could well have expired before we experience a drying out of sub-soils, thus testing the foundations and possibly starting some nasty movements in many a dream home. So, the old hands will prefer to buy a house that is six or seven years' old, where any weak spots have had time to show.

All the above might seem like a great song and dance production number, and if you employ a surveyor to make a full inspection of the property that is exactly what the vendor will tell you he or she did. Surveyors are responsible and can be held for cash damages at law if they put it down in writing that a house is sound, but experience proves otherwise. For example, when you move in together with a grand piano and a host of can-can dancing friends for a house-warming party and the floor is not strong enough to support the revelry, the surveyors could have to pay for new timbers for the floor, and wooden legs for you and your friends. So surveyors have to be very cautious, otherwise they don't get their insurance renewed. The premiums are high in any case and that, and the interminable time surveyors spend looking at property to make sure they are safe, is reflected in their bills. It is also reflected in their reports, which are sometimes splattered with gems of ambiguity.

If you opt for anything less than a full structural survey (very costly), all you will get are such masterpieces as 'from a head-and-shoulders inspection through the loft aperture the roof timbers appeared to be sound', or this page filler: 'the kitchen tiles are of a somewhat dated design'.

However don't buy the idea that a full structural survey is a kind of insurance. If after you move in, you spot things that the surveyor missed, don't think that a polite letter saying, 'Dear Mr. Tape, please will you send me £2,000 to pay for repairing the woodrot that you did not warn me about' will take any tricks. It won't. It is not easy to sue for professional negligence, which is not the same as getting it wrong. You (on your own) have to prove that the surveyor (backed by his professional association and his insurance company, even into the House of Lords) did not use the level of skill and care that one would normally expect a qualified person to use. Not easy!

Why pay for the survey when you will later be paying insurance premiums for a policy that covers that danger?

A house which has been standing 50 years may be ready for a face-lift, but it isn't likely to fall down tomorrow, and though the finish on recently-built houses might not be of the best, it is ridiculous to be frightened of what our builders have produced by the hundreds of thousands for private buyers. And there is always the National House Building Council guarantee. In any case, let's face it: when did you ever see a house fall down? Paying for a survey is often looked on as a form of insurance. You or your vendor should easily have spotted if there is serious subsidence already, so why pay for the survey when you will later be paying insurance premiums for a policy that covers that danger?

CML Handbook

This is perhaps as good a place as any to make one cardinal observation. There are - in the estimation of solicitors and the banks, building societies and other organisations that lend money to aid a purchase - right ways and wrong ways of doing things.

Buying a new house from a builder who is the salt of the earth - as honest as the day is long sort of thing - who cannot offer NHBC or similar protection (see section 6.6 of the Handbook noted below) is something you are perfectly at liberty to do if you are not borrowing their money, but do not be surprised to find you may have trouble selling later.

There are other issues of a more technical nature, which will be referred to in the coming chapters; if you want to know what they are, have a look on the Internet. Or ask a ten-year-old child to do it for you. (Perhaps the kid that got the new video working!) Much of this 'lore' (not 'law') was published in 1999 as the Council of Mortgage Lenders Handbook for England and Wales. You can find it at www.cml.org.uk. Check for updates though; it has been changed on several occasions since first published.

Put the question: is it a good investment, in so far as I will be able to realise it without too much anguish, if ever I need to?

Try to read Part I of the Handbook; it tells you what all the solicitors you will deal with ought to be doing. Part II sets out the special requirements of some of the main CML Members. If you are buying and your lender is not named in the handbook, ask them if they are members, and what their Part II requirements are. Then follow them to the letter! The CML Handbook is not the final word on what to do, but be warned - you can ignore all or any of it if you wish, if you are not borrowing money to aid the purchase, but if you gloss over some of the problems discussed in the Handbook, you may find you will have trouble selling later, or will be put to expense that perhaps your seller should have incurred when you bought the house.

Six good questions

You can usefully look a vendor straight in the eye and ask him a few pertinent questions, the answers to which could determine whether you should spend further time and money on the project.

1 Is the property freehold? If it isn't, what is the ground rent and how long has the lease to run?

2 Does the owner have to pay any maintenance charges to anyone apart from builders, decorators, etc., to whom he himself has given specific orders?

3 Is the road and main drain taken over by the council or do the frontagers have to club up every now and then to have them repaired?

4 If you are in a business or profession can you put up your brass plate and can your spouse hang out the washing or are there any restrictions?

5 Has anyone got the right to traipse across any part of your property? Ever?

6 If there is any evidence (extra cookers, sinks, etc.) of more than one family living in the property, what guarantee is there that they will all move out, thus ensuring that you get full vacant possession on completion?

7 Has the property ever been flooded or faced serious risk of flooding?

In case you are thinking of making alterations, ask if the vendor happens to know if there are any restrictions in the deeds on this point, and if there aren't, whether there are any restrictions imposed by the local authority – such as a preservation order. A vendor might not declare all that he knows at this point, but don't worry too much as we have other ways of making him talk as you will learn later.

Think long and carefully about buying a house which will only fit your requirements if you make a number of structural alterations. Such alterations invariably cost more than the number you first thought of. It's the etceteras and extras that are costly. In any case, if you are buying a house on an estate, it will be a property of a certain class and by improving it you risk bringing it out of that class and making it difficult to sell, if and when you decide to move again.

This is the third criterion you must have in mind when you go viewing. Put the question: is it a good investment, in so far as I will be able to realise it without too much anguish, if ever I need to? You might think that, compared with similar properties, the one you are looking at is a snip. It no doubt has to be, to attract a viewer at all! You don't want to be in that vendor's situation ever, so you would be wise to avoid buying a house situated near any of the following: a fish and chip shop, a take-away cafe, a hospital, a public house, a church, a garage or repair shop, a fire station, or a public lavatory. All the foregoing, and a few more beside, can be anything from a nuisance to a serious disadvantage; even if you happen to be deaf and have no sense of smell, others are not so afflicted. Any Estate Agent who knows anything at all, knows that such badly-located properties should only be put on the market at the height of a house-selling boom when, literally, anything will sell.

At the first whiff of any rumour about plans for any kind of non-residential development round about where you live, get together with your previously independent and apathetic neighbours and protest loud and long at any hint of intrusion by such property-price-debasers into what has previously been such a highly respectable area; unless, that is, you stand to make a vast profit because the property under discussion is your very own. In such a case, the protesters are dog-in-the-manger reactionary luddites opposed to all forms of progress which public spirited individuals (you) are slaving away trying to introduce.

Sometimes it takes ages to find a property that comes up to scratch and suits your requirements; sometimes it's a case of beginner's luck. In either case remember you are not the only bargain-hunter around, and the race goes to the swift. Don't go groggy when the finishing line is in sight – be ready with your own pack of conveyancing forms.

2 New houses

For young people buying their first house, a brand new one has what can only be called a strong romantic attraction. Here they will make their attempt to create a home. Builders know what attracts – note how they advertise homes for sale, when what they are trying to sell is a plan, and more often than not, a half-finished house. But when the house is finished the starry-eyed home-makers move in, secure in the knowledge that no one has been born, lived, loved, divorced or died in it. The aura of the past will not seep out of the brickwork. The dead hand of the past will not push them into outdated ways of living. It will all be new! It is all brave! But as in all romances, beauty is in the eye of the beholder – desire overpowers reason, and faults and blemishes are ignored. Another great attraction of a newly-built house is that it promises to be repair-free for a number of years – if anything goes wrong it is likely to be because of a fault in manufacture for which someone else is responsible, and not wear and tear which falls to the user to put right.

There is also the National House Builders' certificate, or one of the other schemes, the benefits and restrictions of which we have already noted. With this protection you have the warranty against ruinous subsidence, but some would say you can do without running the risk of a nightmare experience of subsidence in the first place. If you get subsidence from any other reason than climate it has to be because of bad building and that means solicitors, barristers and courts for you.

From an investment point of view, it is often the case that the last house to be completed on a development is the best buy.

From an investment point of view, it is often the case that the last house to be completed on a development is the best buy. The romantic ideas and repair-free attraction of brand new houses militate against the resale of a house on an unfinished development. A vendor can have for sale a house to which he has added a number of refinements, is offering a fair list of extras and be only asking the same price as the builder is for a brand new house, yet the vendor has to search high and low for a buyer while the developer is signing buyers all the while, and he signs them up on a take-it-or-leave-it basis. Builders and their Skinners know how to take advantage of a situation where desire overpowers reason.

The developer appoints a solicitor who acts for him in the sale of each of the houses on the development. Except for the address or plot number, the contract and transfer (there are one or two things you need to know about contracts and transfers – all will be revealed in later chapters) are identical for all. It is almost unheard of for any purchaser's Skinner to persuade the developer's Skinner to change any detail in the contract or transfer. Lay person conveyancers get to see the papers with their own eyes, and if they see anything they don't like can take it up with the builder face to face – whereas the Skinnerhood is deskbound and at best will only write a letter.

Builders and their agents will often try pressurising you into signing a contract when a house has a substantial amount of work to be done on it, or even when the building has not been started. In such a case, you need to be very desperate, trusting or foolish to sign up unless, at the very least, the contract is made subject to the house being completed in accordance with a set of plans, a specification, your surveyor's approval or – pretty weak but it is better than nothing – an existing show house. The less of the house you can see when you sign the contract, the greater the risk. This is because the sale agreement will generally confer on the builder the right to change materials of construction and the design. Not necessarily to any material degree in his estimation, but it may be important from your standpoint!

Also try to tie the developer down to some kind of completion date. Houses are built in the open air, by people who are relying on others for supplies of material to arrive according to the hopes and dreams of a deviser of a critical path analysis, which pleased its creator when he put it on paper. But his Creator might send flood, storm, tempest, lightning and thunderbolt to thwart his plans, and deep down the developer knows about that. So, we are introduced to the almost meaningless phrases that abound in house sale and purchase transactions; a proviso for completion will be a slight variant on the well worn 'will use his best endeavours to complete the house with all due expedition'.

Sometimes builders will ask for stage payments. That is to say they will require a proportion of the purchase price to be paid when say, the footings are in, followed by more money at window sill height, more when the roof is on, and a final payment on completion. This method can be costly, particularly if you are taking a mortgage, because at each stage the building society surveyor has to have a look, and you have to pay him a fee, and as soon as the stage payment is advanced you start paying repayments on the loan, even though you might not move into the house for many a month. It's a risk.

First-time buyers

Some builders advertise as though there are some terms, prices, mortgages and services special to buyers of their houses. There are not. It is all put on the price of the house. The only help for first-time buyers is the government Home Loan Scheme. So tell the builder you will do your own conveyance, get your own mortgage, pay cash – so how much discount for relieving them of all that worry? You could get a pleasant surprise provided you promise not to tell your new neighbours!

Last-time buyers

Now it's your turn. A plethora of advice to those about to retire pours forth from accountants, solicitors, estate agents, travel agents, stockbrokers, banks and building societies, all of whom claim to offer financial services.

Financial services hate stillness. Their motto is: Let's get them churning their money in my churn, and some of it will stick to the sides for me.

The death of a spouse, or your retirement, are not sufficient reasons to move house.

The death of a spouse, or your retirement, are not sufficient reasons to move house. It might be that you would save money on rates and heating in a smaller house, but just look at what the move will cost you. No matter where you live, you will pay some rates and heating bills. It could take you donkey's years to recoup the expense of moving.

If it's the cost of upkeep that bothers you, get down to your Citizens Advice Bureau (CAB) and find out what practical help is on offer from local charity organisations for someone like you who has spent a lifetime fighting and working for the country.

Elderly people sometimes fear a disabling fall and are attracted to living complexes where wardens, either resident or on call, can get an ambulance for them. The same reassurance could be gained by installing in one's present home a radio call signal; speak to the CAB or Help the Aged about it.

There is also the Department of Social Security. At long last the government is realising that though houses might be privately owned, they are part of the national stock of housing and wealth, and to those who can't cope financially, help should be given. Though less and less as time goes by.

Don't forget when doing your sums, to ask yourself a few 'comfort' questions:

- You have a garage of your own. Could you tolerate sharing? Is there a parking place for every resident and their visitors?

- You have, at worst, only had one wall through which noise could seep. Could you tolerate noise from the sides, above, below, and across the landing?

- When the sun shines you can sit in your own garden chair in your own garden, a few feet from your own door. Will you be able to do that?

- You have your own place for your own dustbin. Will the new compare favourably?

- You can choose your own odd-job man and your own time for the job to be done and indeed, whether to have it done this year or at all.

Those who have never occupied a home under a lease usually only fully realise what they have committed themselves to when the bills come in.

Part exchange

Find out 'what's the discount for cash?' It can be considerable. If you and the combined high-powered salesmanship of the local estate agency could not find a buyer for your house, neither can the builder … not at the price you were asking. So consider knocking your asking price down by the combined amount of the cash discount and the agent's fees and get the house sold yourself. You can then bargain with anybody anywhere and from then on get your sums right about how much your new house actually cost you and how much profit you made on the last one. No builder will be upset by the tactics recommended here. His advertisement drew you to the site, he has sold a house and that is what he wants … the sooner the quicker!

There are a lot of risks in buying and selling, but in order to get anything done one has to take some risks. The art is in drawing the line between acceptable and unacceptable risks and each person will decide for himself where that line is to be drawn when buying a new house, or for that matter in any of the other transactions outlined in this book.

3 Sell first or buy first?

If you have never bought a house before, then the question answers itself. But if you are an owner who needs to move to a larger or smaller house, or needs to get away from the neighbours or in-laws, or needs to raise some money by buying a cheaper house, which way round you work is crucial. The decision has to be made in the light of both your personal needs and resources, and the general state of the housing market at the time.

You can, of course, go out viewing properties, and when you see one that suits you, say 'Yes, I will buy this when I have sold my own.' And you might drag the vendors on for ages while you screw the last penny out of your sale. On the other hand, the vendor of your dream property may have read this book too, and the answer will be 'I'll give you x number of weeks.' How many times have you heard of 'chains' breaking down. How many times have you seen the silly 'sold subject to contract' slips pasted onto and then taken off For Sale boards? Greed, slipshod estate agents and lawyers' bad timing are the usual causes.

Since the mid-1930s there has been a drift upwards in prices, but the movement goes in fits and starts: so spot the rising market and you can safely buy first, and be pretty sure of selling your own house swiftly and profitably. You can always tell when the housing market has reached its bottom and is about to rise. Similarly, you get a very clear signal that a boom is within six months or so of petering out: the mass media will tell you. When they make headlines out of the fact that young people are being priced out of the market, and when they have stories about people making fortunes in a few years out of houses, the market is at the top. Nevertheless, so as not to miss the bus, new buyers join in, and so keep the pot boiling a little longer. But the bus was just about to pull up at a compulsory stop.

On the other hand, when, on your telly, you see a lugubrious man standing in front of an agency For Sale board, which has obviously taken root, and he tells you that he has not had sign, sound nor smell of a viewer for over eighteen months, then the market is about to pick up.

Houses adjacent to petrol stations, hotel car parks, fire stations and the like should always be sold when the market is on the boil, if they are to get sold at all.

Apart from such problem cases, do not be afraid that after a boiling market prices will crash – they never have. What happens is that those overpriced houses that have been overhanging the market waiting for prices to rise get taken off. Only the rubbish remains. So if there is no other reason for a move than your fancy for a different sort of house – wait for a slack time. Patiently read the advertisements, and go viewing until you find something that suits you exactly. Then, if your house is presented and priced in the manner hereinafter prescribed you will sell it, because at this point the market having been slack a while, only the rubbish remains for you to compete with. You will thus avoid being pressurised by the frenetic mood that prevails at the height of a boom in the housing market. The vendor of the house you want to buy will be delighted to see you and allow you plenty of leeway. Your buyer will only have a choice between rubbish and yours. Deposits are paid on signing contracts, traditionally 10 per cent, but when moneylenders are competing for business and are offering mortgages of more than 100%, negotiate a deposit to suit your circumstances.

February, March and April are the best months to sell. But life goes on 365 days a year. There are always some buyers about. Even Christmas can be good if a couple of your neighbours make you a present of having 'For Sale' boards planted in their gardens. Take advantage of their viewers who know all about their houses from the agent's particulars, so might drive past them, but if you have your own board – which will only cost you a few pounds, will knock on your front door, even if it is only to ask your price. Don't keep them on the doorstep in such poor weather – invite them in to discuss it.

4 Estate agency

Insurance companies, building societies and brokers of all kinds have put together strings of house-selling shops, and distorted the business out of all recognition, but they still trade on the folk-memory of the personal service that independent estate agents took many years to establish in the minds of home owners.

Branch office after branch office has been opened. Every city and town centre is stuffed with them. Their numbers have increased out of all proportion to the increase in owner-occupied houses. Many offices are lucky to sell more than one house per week. Each office is staffed with a couple of receptionists who try to look busy for seven days a week, waiting for victims to give themselves up. The person who knows what estate agency is now about (possibly a chartered surveyor, more likely an insurance man) oversees a number of offices and can be called on the mobile on the golf course or in bed, when required.

If your name is Feather, and not Bold, and you give yourself up to an agent, the receptionist will make an appointment for the representative to call and 'survey' and value your house. It will no doubt happen on the same day as you applied. That's the last time you'll see any greased lightning in this transaction. Agents always have spent more of their own time and money on getting in houses for sale than in selling them, because as you have already read, houses sell themselves – eventually, if you will let them.

Estate agents say they...

(a) Make a survey of the house to be sold.

(b) Make a valuation.

(c) Prepare a set of particulars.

(d) Commission a photograph.

(e) Circularise the particulars using their computers and network of associated agents.

(f) Draft advertising and arrange for it to be displayed in their own monthly circular and in the press.

(g) Display a full-colour photo of your house in their shops.

(h) Negotiate with interested parties.

(i) Offer you and your purchaser a full range of financial services including using the money from one house to buy another.

(j) Liaise with your solicitor.

(k) Charge you according to their percentage scale, only if the house is sold.

Now for The Facts...

(a) **Survey:** if it were a written structural survey that you could pass on to the prospective purchaser, that would be OK, but you won't get that. You are selling. What do you want with a survey? You check for subsidence every time you open a door or window. You check the drains every time you pull the plug, and if you haven't fallen through the floorboards into the cellar lately, the woodwork is good enough to be going on with, and you know without any help from them. Of course, if counting the number of rooms and jotting down their sizes is a survey, you get that. Big deal.

(b) **Valuation**: when you have read chapter 8, you will be entitled to put the letters FBSPV (Fellow of the Bradshaw School of Property Valuers) after your name.

(c) **Particulars**: if you can't go through your own house with a notebook and pencil, who can?

(d) **Photographs**: have you seen some of them? You've no doubt got better ones in your own album.

(e) **Lists, computers and networks of agents**: your milkman, who sees your Sale board every day, has more up-to-date news about who's looking for a house such as yours than any agent sitting in front of a computer 50 miles away. Having been a potential buyer, you will know what a fat lot of use the stuff is and it is nearly certain that your buyer will come from within 25 miles.

As far as matching people to houses, what has been your experience when you were looking for a house? New buyers come on the market every day, as they sell their own houses, having decided to get married, divorced or take promotion, all of which can necessitate a move.

People drop off the lists when they get fixed up. You know how long they keep on sending you particulars after you have found a house. Sometimes they keep coming from an agency through whom you have just bought.

(f) **Monthly magazine**: more junk mail. Newspapers: you will read the chapter on advertising and learn how much expenditure of time and expertise that requires. Do you think that what the agent does in this regard amounts to much?

(g) **Shop window**: this is about the only thing that agents have that you can't have for yourself, and so 'anything you can do I can do better' doesn't apply. In this respect, Property shops are worth considering because they do the display job at a fraction of the cost. Very few people buy houses they first saw displayed in an agency. The agency has already paid the rent, so putting up your photo costs next to nothing. If this is what works, why do they go in for all that costly advertising in the press, buying boards, paying signwriters to look after them, putting them up and taking them down, why not just use their own shop window (no prizes for even a polite answer)? Shop windows are used as much for attracting new vendors as for anything else. But the pictures are of houses they have not sold. If they can't sell those, how can they sell yours?

(h) **Negotiating** with a buyer usually amounts to persuading you to bring your price down and in getting you to wait till the buyer sells his house.

(i) **Financial services** means: there are so many agencies at it nowadays that selling commissions are not enough to keep them all going, so they have to look for other sources of revenue. So they try to sell you and your purchaser insurances, mortgages, and if things go badly enough, chain-breaking and bridging loans, so as to grab the commission amounting to thousands of pounds. This is where they come into their own, and yours as well, if you give them half a chance.

Using the money from one house to buy another: the estate agent to whom you left it leaves it, in turn, to the solicitor, who in turn will often leave you with the problem of a bridging loan or a costly chain-breaking scheme.

(j) **Liaison with your solicitor**: this amounts to the agent writing to your solicitor saying 'this is one of ours' and eventually, if ever, 'here is our commission bill'.

(k) **Advertising**: Historically, estate agents have written the most appallingly ambiguous rubbish when advertising the charming, deceptively spacious family property, in which, in real life, you can't swing a cat. Nowadays, this can be a criminal offence and so the agents will ask you to validate their claims and that can make you a criminal as well! They do the same when advertising briefly about their charges. 'No sale – no charge' sounds good enough, but it might mean that all you get is a mention of your house to anyone who enquires for a property such as yours. 'Free advertising' might mean: we put a few lines about it in our monthly bulletin which is given out to callers and distributed to the Skinners' waiting rooms where it takes its chance among a pile of magazines and other junk.

So after a little run-of-the-mill 'advertising' you will be expected to pay for your share of their full-page adverts, of which anything up to a quarter can be taken up in publicising their own outfit.

Now here's a little gem of business sense for you: If your name is Feather and you have been persuaded to use an agency and a Skinner, at least gird up your loins to write a letter to Skinner, Hand and Glove incorporating the following: 'do not pay the agent's commission out of the sale monies, but forward their account to me and I will deal with it'. You will then have some bargaining power if you have come to the conclusion that you have not had value for the money claimed, or charges have been made that you never agreed to.

Agency agreements do need looking at and studying before you sign; see what the agreement says about selling yourself or later through another agent. Don't be afraid to say to the representative, 'Leave it with me for my granddad or grandson, solicitor or nerve specialist to have a look at it'. Then calculate the likely bill, and ponder (a) to (k) above. Looked at in the cold light of day, the list of things agencies claim to do for you does not amount to much. Certainly not to the enormous commissions that get spirited away out of the price you get for your house.

If your local branch of Dick, Turpin & Co. only put a board in your garden and a picture in the shop window and then start charging for adverts, you can get that from a property shop at a fraction of the price.

Middlemen: estate agents, solicitors, building societies, insurance people, and all the rest who are trying to amass a fortune as swiftly as possible out of the housing market, have needs of their own. From your own workplace you know that you do things not only for your customers, but to keep the organisation going and see to your own creature comforts.

Trips abroad, cameras and other valuable prizes are offered on a local and regional basis to the 'representative of the month' by agency chains. The winners are those who get the most 'instructions' (houses for sale). Competition is keen, not only within the firms, but between agencies. Blows have been struck when a representative of one agency has gone poaching from another. Do not get caught in the crossfire. You could find yourself in court, at best as a witness, and at worst, as a losing defendant who is refusing to pay two commissions because rival agencies are claiming to have been the effective cause of your sale.

When you are dealing
with these middlemen,
recognise that much
of the advice you get
from them is not only
what they think is best
r you, but what is best
for them.

So when you are dealing with these middlemen, recognise that much of the advice you get from them is not only what they think is best for you, but what is best for them. For instance, they want to deal with as few people as possible for as much money as possible. Solicitors and agencies plead professional ethics as a reason for not treating with more than one potential buyer – what miserable pleaders they are. An agency chooses a buyer with a house for sale so that it can swell the number of houses on its books – that buyer is not necessarily the best for you.

5 The moneylenders

Bridging loans

You may have seen a house you particularly want, but have to exchange contracts quickly before you can organise your sale, or perhaps having made an acceptable 'subject to contact' offer to buy and having accepted an acceptable 'subject to contact' offer to sell, and your purchaser has withdrawn at an embarrassingly late stage in the pre-contact game.

What are the options? One is obviously to lose your intended purchase, but bridging loans offer one way forward if you can afford to pay two mortgages - that on the house you wish to sell and that on the house you wish to buy.

If you are tempted to do this, ask yourself a question and make sure you get an honest answer. How quickly will your house sell and will you really get what you want for it? If you get it wrong and you still bridge, month after anxious month can pass before you get rid of your old home. One good tip is have the house you wish to sell structurally surveyed and if you are recommended to get specialist reports on the boiler, the electricity or whatever, get them. You will soon find out of there is a 'nasty' hiding under the floor boards that might have an adverse impact on your ability to sell, or to sell at the price you want or even need.

House exchanges

If you are buying a new house from a builder, you may find the builder will offer to take your own house in part exchange. They normally insist you buy a house with a higher market value, say 25 per cent, so this does not work if you are thinking of retiring and moving to a smaller house to release some capital for your old age.

This has the advantage for those who want a new house of taking you out of any chain. The builders' lawyers will generally carry out a cursory investigation of your title and will normally ask you to submit the barest minimum of paperwork. A formal Office Copy of your title (if registered), a copy of your title deeds if not, replies to the Seller's

Property Information Forms and the Fixtures Fittings and Contents Form, plus a local search, and that is about it.

You may still need to borrow on the new house, but if not, the deal can go through very quickly. Perhaps as soon as you get a reply to your local search, which can vary from a 24-hour turnaround with some councils to several weeks with others. Five to ten working days however is a comfortable 'norm'.

Mortgages

Many of you will have to borrow money to aid the purchase. Time was when the only serious options were the building societies and 'mortgage famines' were not unknown. If they did not know you, you joined a queue. Sometimes the queues were limited to first-time borrowers. In other cases, perhaps you got to jump the queue if you were an existing member. Perhaps you borrowed from them last time, or perhaps you were saving up for a deposit. Then the banks started to become involved, and then many building societies decided to convert to public company status, and so on, and lack of money to lend has not been a major problem in recent years.

Time was also when the building societies operated prudent, if inflexible, rules. A sole buyer could not borrow more than two and a half times his salary. Couples could not borrow more than three times the higher salary. Other permutations were acceptable in some cases. If the surveyor selected to value the house for the building society felt it was worth less than you were paying, that did not always matter if you were providing a substantial contribution to the house. You are at liberty after all to lose your own money. But not theirs and so if they felt there was a risk, the answer was to insure. They took out, at your expense, a mortgagee protection policy. If the house was sold at a loss by the lender, they recouped the loss from the insurers. Unfortunately, they were their insurers not yours and so - invoking the insurance concept of 'subrogation' - the insurers would then chase the borrowers (if they had any money) for the loss.

In time, back in the 1970s, some institutions started to lend without asking for proof of ability to pay, particularly the secondary lenders. This worked well when prices were continually on the up, but when they fell they often recouped the loss by suing the surveyor or if that failed, the solicitor. Sloppy file-keeping or inadequate procedures cost the legal profession a great deal, but at least the borrower was not chased for the loss!

In those days there were few payment options. A repayment mortgage involved the payment of interest and some capital each year. An endowment mortgage involved paying interest only. The capital came from an endowment policy that had to be paid for each month as well, but the theory was, at the end of the 20- to 25-year period, the insurers would pay more than you needed to pay off the mortgage, and you would make a profit. Or you could rely on your pension insurance policy's lump sum to cover the capital. Unfortunately, your insurance salesman can only guess what the results are in the light of circumstances prevailing when you take out the endowment or mortgage. Unfortunately for many borrowers, a stable economy with low rates of inflation has resulted in an lower performance for these schemes than expected and there will be borrowers with endowment and pension mortgages who will have less than they need when the money becomes available to pay off the capital.

Nowadays there are so many different types of loan on offer that the best that can be recommended is to shop around.

Nowadays there are so many different types of loan on offer that the best that can be recommended is to shop around. You will be expected to meet the costs of a valuation and the lender may or may not accept your nominee surveyor. The valuation is just that. It is not a structural survey and although the law requires a person carrying out a valuation to spot some of the more glaring faults, a large hole in the roof or major cracks suggesting subsidence, for example, there are limits to what the borrower can sue for.

Some lenders use in-house surveyors. That is, surveyors on the payroll. However the norm is for a local firm to supply a report in a more or less standard form, so ascertain what levels of report are available (simple valuation or full structural survey) what they will cost. Note also that surveyors frequently highlight problems for referral to others. If a major structural problem is highlighted, try a civil engineer; these can be relatively rare in any area and can be overworked folk and so do not expect them to rush around at the first sign of a cheque. Wiring, heating, rising damp, etc: with all these problems, the surveyor is likely to recommend you hire an appropriate specialist.

If you hire someone to check on the damp course and timber, try to make sure you keep their survey and their guarantee (one without the other is useless) for when you come to sell and try to select a contractor whose guarantee is backed by insurers. Contractors come and go and after a year or so it is not unknown for guarantees to become simply pretty sheets of paper with no legal or practical value whatsoever.

6 No agents, please!

Why private vendors win

There are a lot of houses to be sold. In Great Britain there are nearly 12½ million owner-occupied houses. On average, spread over a year, close on a million houses change hands.

How, you may ask, can I compete in such a crowded market?

You must find some ways of drawing attention to your house; of marking it out from all others; of making potential buyers curious enough to come and view it. Not to worry.

You have already taken a decision that singles your house out as something different and especially attractive to any buyer. YOU HAVE DECIDED TO JOIN THE ONE-IN-THREE OF ALL VENDORS WHO SELL FOR THEMSELVES.

As soon as you announce the sale, you will signal to the whole wide world (particularly the twenty odd square miles that really matter) that your property is so good it is expected to sell itself. It does not need the wiles of a high-powered salesman to push it onto someone who doesn't really need it, at a higher price than they wanted to pay. It is also attractive to a lot of potential buyers who want to avoid agents because:

(a) They know that an agent's commission is added on to the price, so in effect it is the purchaser who pays it.

(b) An established agency cannot have avoided making enemies along the way. YOU ONLY NEED ONE BUYER, and that buyer might be so embittered by previous experiences with estate agents that never, ever, will that person have anything more to do with agents.

(c) Inexperienced buyers are afraid of smooth-talking salesmen, particularly those who, to hide the fact that they have no special expertise, overlay what they have to say with an inappropriately pompous language which hermetically seals off conceptual orientational realisation, and assails the unfortunate recipient auditory structural system as a load of bull falling from a great height.

(d) Experienced buyers know that they can bargain directly with a private vendor. Quite rightly, they expect to get more sense out of the butcher than the block.

(e) Buyers are sick of collecting particulars from agents who by describing the property in a different way, disguise the fact that every agent in town has the same rubbish for sale. The luckless viewer has wasted journeys. When they come to a private vendor it is delightfully uncomplicated, and they will not get involved as witnesses in disputed commission claims.

A quick look at the houses for sale pages of your local newspaper could easily lead you to believe that private sales are very few and far between. But, a recent survey found that only two thirds of all house sellers used estate agents. That leaves a third who didn't. Over three hundred thousand vendors a year go it alone and win. Just keep your eyes open. Count the private adverts. Count the private for sale boards – are they anywhere near a third of the total? Isn't that proof that a private sale does not have to be advertised again and again, and that a private for sale board does not take root?

Private sales are prompt sales. So, all in all, yours has the edge over the other properties with which you are in competition. You will get more viewers, and therefore sell quickly. That's another privately-sold house off the market; buyers have to jump at an opportunity to buy privately or they miss out.

Don't worry that by working on your own you will miss the one (in twenty) potential buyer who comes from out of town. My experience is that they have always researched the market thoroughly. They have to; they can't afford wasted journeys. They know what they are looking for, where it should be, and about what price it should be going for. They also know the districts in which they are likely to hunt down their quarry, and will be cruising past your house this weekend. When you put your for sale board up they will see it. They know everything about every other house in the district from the agents' particulars. But there is something crucial that they don't know about your house just from the board: the price.

The car will have to stop. They will have to walk up your whitewashed path, stare at your dozzled-up front door, ring the bell and wait for you to come and offer to show them why yours is better than any of the rest, and if any mention is made about yours being higher priced than the others, 'Well, we can talk about that when you have looked round can't we.'

There are two other situations which many think cannot be coped with unless an agent is brought onto the scene – they are wrong!

Just because you live alone and are fearful of having a stranger in the house does not mean to say you can't sell without an agent - you certainly can.

Just because you live alone and are fearful of having a stranger in the house does not mean to say you can't sell without an agent – you certainly can. You can certainly do without those who let it be known that they specialise in helping widows, orphans and the elderly.

When alone, you should follow your usual precaution of having the door on the chain. If you make a telephone appointment get the name, address and telephone number of the caller and check identity by ringing back, also check with the telephone book and/or directory enquiries and then arrange for a near neighbour, clergyman, or social worker to attend. Or if the prospect comes from the board, ask them to wait while your friend can pop round. No prospective viewer will object to waiting a few moments – not if their intentions are honourable.

Even if you got an agency which promised to accompany viewers, that would not mean to say that, having given a false name and address, the conperson, whose face you now know, would not come back to wreak villainy upon you. In any case, estate agents have not been able to protect themselves or property against violence.

Selling a vacant house which is at a distance from your home is really a simple job. Don't fall for being the cat and allowing the mice to play. What you require is someone to hold the particulars and the keys, who was a friend and neighbour of the previous occupant. Get your board up with your own telephone number on and you are in business. Such a key holder will have a friendly and true interest in getting you good money because they will wish to protect the value of their own greatest asset which lies hard by.

7 Selling

Fixtures and fittings: what is included?

More trouble and anguish is caused by the failure of people to decide what they are selling than by any other single cause. Get it clear right at the start.

When you do move, leave more than you said you would. It doesn't need to be much to make the purchasers feel they have done better than they really expected.

As a matter of courtesy, curtain rails and all but the most expensive light fittings should be left. Don't mention them all in the particulars, or some smart alec will say he doesn't want them, so 'how much off the price' for putting you to the trouble of taking them down.

What constitutes a fixture and a fitting, nobody seems to know. So try appealing to common sense; it's quicker and cheaper than consulting a professional.

Custom seems to say that fixtures are permanencies and semi-permanencies that one can't simply pick up and walk away with. Television aerials, for example, are fixtures. You can put the lamp shade under your arm and walk away with it but the light switch is a different matter. It is the bits and pieces other than what are obvious parts of the house (such as the doors) and what are obviously not part of the house (such as a heavy plant pot in the garden that's too heavy to lift) which cause the trouble. Situations where it's not strictly breach of contract to remove an item but would be a breach of good faith to do so should be avoided. All this is not to say that you simply cannot take the doors. Of course you can – but you must make it clear to the purchaser that you so intend because anyone can reasonably assume that a door is a fixture and part of a house. So have a slow walk round every room and look at everything in it. Look, and think about things like the cooker or fixed washing machine that someone else might assume should count as a fitting and be included in the price without being detailed or argued about. In each of the rooms make a decision. Is it to be left or not?

> Custom seems to say that fixtures are permanencies and semi-permanencies that one can't simply pick up and walk away with.

Make a list of the things which someone might assume you are including in the price. Decide which you would sell and at what price. Mark the prices on a separate list from your list of particulars, the drawing up and printing of which will form the content of a later section. This early appraisal of what you are selling is your first step towards your valuation. Most buyers now expect to receive the Fixtures, Fittings & Contents Form published by the Law Society and available through legal stationers.

Valuations are easy: use comparisons

If you go to a rent or land valuation tribunal or arbitration, you will see and hear the professionals at it: people who can hardly squeeze through the door for the spread of letters behind their names.

'It's far too much. One on the east side of it went for much less', says the one in the natty blue suit. 'Ah, but one on the north and another on the west side brought substantially more', drawls the fat one.

The arbitrator listens to their comparisons and decides on something near the middle. In the end, comparisons and compromise are the only sensible way.

You can compare your own house with similar ones, and do it as well and better than anyone else. As a matter of fact, you have started already. Since the day you bought the house you, like other proud owners, have taken an interest in the property for sale in your district. You will of course, have marked and remembered the ones that were offered for sale at more money than you browbeat the previous owners down to, and ignored the ones sold at a lower figure. You did right at the time; it made you feel much better and more successful.

You need to collect information on two points: how much similar properties have actually fetched, and what opposition there is in the market on this very day.

But it's down to brass tacks now; how accurate your valuation is will determine how long it will take you to sell, and whether you get what you ask, or what someone else is prepared to give.

Forget what you were asked to pay when you bought. If you actually paid less than the original asking price for your house, that price was the best that the vendor could get for it. If the vendor could have got more he would have. If you were left thinking you had been done a favour, try to remember how it was done and use that bargaining skill when your prospects arrive, and do them a favour. It's only fair.

You will sell quicker than the opposition if they have decided their price by adding up such things as: so much to pay off the mortgage, deposit for new house, new car, new washing machine and a good holiday – what the vendor wants as opposed to what his property is worth.

Do not let anyone flatter you into wishing for the moon. There are plenty of agencies who, to get a job, will raise your hopes unduly. They know the market. They also know that vendors will always come to their muttons later. In the meantime it swells the number of houses they have on their books. It makes them look big now at the expense of making you look small later on when you have to reduce your price.

Start comparing by collecting details of properties of a similar age and type from your local paper's property column. If an agent to whom you apply for particulars asks for your name and address give it. Don't play about with the 'It's for a friend' routine. The thing here, as in all house buying, selling and conveyancing procedures is: be bold. And that is what we will call the users of this book 'Mr & Mrs Bold.'

When you have found some properties which you think will make useful comparisons, go and do the viewing bit. Ask the vendors how they decided on their price. If the way they shape the reply is persuasive, note it for future use, if not, make a note not to say such silly things yourself when the time comes.

I know it is extremely hard, but do not look for the faults, and therefore justifications for why your house is better and consequently worth more than theirs. Try to see those elements that are better than yours and could justify the vendor's price. For instance, if the house you are viewing is set well into the middle of a large development, give it points for not having to suffer as much early morning traffic noise as a house at the entrance and exit of the same estate. But if yours is at an entrance, do not continue comforting yourself with the vain thought, 'Oh, we soon got used to it, after a while you don't hear them. In any case, we might get someone whose job takes them out before anyone else'. Such musings, when you first moved in and discovered the disadvantage, might have made you feel better about the bargain you had made, but it's for real now.

Don't be shy about viewing other properties just for your own valuation purposes. No doubt others will do the same to you later. In any case, when you have read the section on 'Showing them round', you will realise that no viewer is an absolute waste of time.

Tradition says that purchasers always want something knocked off, so when you have worked out the going rate for a house such as yours, add about two per cent on to that figure to arrive at your asking price, thus leaving yourself a little room for negotiation. We will look at what, when, where and how to bargain later.

When you are fixing your opening price do not let anyone flatter you into asking way over the odds, with the hare-brained notion that you might catch an out-of-town buyer (more about them later too!) or someone who is desperate or doesn't know what he is doing. 'You can always come down later', is a prescription for an idiot. Of course you can always come down … and down … and down again. Making a deal when time has run out and it is you who are desperate is no time to decide on a price. So do so before you announce the sale. Make up your mind what you will take and not what you will be given.

It is silly to miss a perfectly good buyer who won't even come to view during the period you are trying for top price. By the time you come down to a realistic figure your buyer could be happily settled into another house. Your best buyers are those who come first. Don't miss them. Give them credit for having researched the market and done their comparisons too.

If you ask too much your house will become a drug on the market even after being reduced below its real value.

If you ask too much your house will become a drug on the market even after being reduced below its real value. Don't let greed make you miss a buyer. You only need one!

Buyers know that private vendors do not have to pay agents' fees and therefore expect that fact to be reflected in the price asked. So take that into account when you decide what is the lowest price you will take. Vendors of property advertised by agents do not get the asking price. What they do get is what is left after the traditional two per cent put on to knock off has been negotiated away; less the professional creaming off; less the dreaded VAT and advertising costs. Because private vendors' houses sell quicker than agency houses, your advertising costs should be lower than theirs, you pay no VAT or the rest of the list. So you can keep your price down and still make more money than if you let an agent mess about with it.

Now set about making the house itself look attractive.

Window dressing

This is the acquisitive society. We are all at it. But last year's luxuries give way to this year's pressing desires. And we need somewhere to store what, to us, are former favourites to which we are sentimentally attached, but to viewers will look like junk.

As soon as you decide to sell and have given notice of intention to your lender, get rid of the junk as quickly as the dustbin men will take it away. Bottles, jars, containers of all sorts that you never had time to fill with home-made preserves. Magazines and newspapers you intended to read again and never did. Offcuts of material from cotton to chipboard that you were sure would come in useful, together with the bent nails and screws which never did either. The clothes you hoped would come back into fashion. Let the lot go. Make it look as if there is bags of cupboard room. The fewer things there are on the wall-to-wall carpeting, the larger the room looks.

We all imagine that a house or garden which is neat, tidy and well-kept will easily remain so. Viewers seem to think so, too. A mucky house in a tatty garden has to be sold muck cheap. So, tidy it up. It makes the happy home look more spacious and valuable, immediately you have done so.

Modernisation

If, after looking at other properties, you feel that you have been left behind in the race to fit new kitchen units, central heating, bathroom suites and the like, think long and hard before, in a bid to compete, you decide to make such improvements yourself. You will have to add the cost to your asking price. And what if the first person to answer your advertisement would have bought, except that the style of your new bathroom suite brought out an instant attack of the dry heaves? As a matter of fact, you can, in your advertisement, use an unmodernised state to mark yours out from the rest.

'Built 40 years ago and now due for a face-lift, will suit handyman' – there's a disadvantage turned into an advantage for you!

If you have not already been tempted to become a do-it-yourself home improver, the present is not the time to experiment. A pressed-for-time reluctant handyman's botching shows.

There are plenty of enthusiastic improvers who are never so happy as when the house is in the process of transmogrification. Who are you to deny them the pleasure – at a price? Let them do it at their leisure. What is more, there are always one or two hopefuls looking for just such houses as yours, and to hear that the house has 'every modern refinement' is an immediate turn-off for them, even though in the long run such a house will cost them more than a fully modernised one.

Decorations

Viewers are a suspicious lot. Is there any wonder? So, although you are not covering up any cracks and damp patches, a full paint-and-dec job is not recommended. It would be unlikely to deceive anyone, anyway. It's a simple device and people know about it. No matter how old the decorations and fittings, the essential thing is for the house to be clean and give the impression that it could be lived in until such time as a buyer can cover up your 'vile interior decorations'. There is no harm in a bit of judicious touching-up. Odd spots where paint has been chipped off over the years can be improved with a deft stroke of coloured chalk.

Give the whole house a spring-clean. In particular:

1 Clean and polish the windows.

2 Shine up the furniture.

3 Burnish the brasses.

4 Replace or cut shorter the dirty ends of dropcords.

If you are selling an empty house where someone has died, or moved out into an institution, make sure you remove all remaining day-to-day personal effects such as engagement calendars, part-used tubes of toothpaste, and bottles of pills and potions which evidently failed.

The hall

Decide where the negotiations are to take place after viewers have looked round the rest of the house (the hall is a good choice), and give it the full treatment, knowing the viewer will get the first, and final impressions there. If you have the nerve for it, during the negotiations, you can say modestly, 'Sorry about the state of the hall. It's the only place we haven't got round to.'

Central heating

Let air out of the radiators. You don't want the diabolical bangings to start in the middle of a viewing session.

Gates fences and paths

Take an objective look at the outsides. If the gate is hanging off, take it down to the rubbish tip or put it well out of site so that your purchaser can discover it later, and smarty that he is, put it back securely. It won't matter what kind of lazy so-and-so he calls you then – you won't be within earshot. If a fence is dilapidated, tidy it up. A viewer might wonder if you are in dispute with a neighbour about whose responsibility it is. And if there is a sacked estate agent's board hanging around – get rid!

Tidy up the verge, sweep the pavement and gutters. As a matter of fact, you should do this whether you are selling or not. Look after the area and it will look after you. If you have some white paint left over from doing the outside walls, or failing that some white emulsion, add plenty of thinners and give a concrete drive, path or steps the treatment. If you are not sure it will 'take' on your particular brand of concrete, experiment on a small section first. A parked caravan or boat should be moved to some other friendly haven for a while and any oil stains cleaned off. Buyers don't always have sufficient imagination to conjure up a vision of how expansive your uncluttered drive would be. But if they start eyeing it up because they too own a caravan you can come clean and inform them, going on to say, if it is true, that you have never had any complaints from council and neighbours.

Gardens

Tidy up. If the job would be too much, get some weed killer for the beds and then give it a light forking. 'Lovely colourful garden this can be, just haven't had time this year, except to make it ready for planting'. If you can't even do that much, wait until just after Christmas, there is not much to choose between one snow covered garden and another, but in any case, get cracking with the weed-killer on the paths, it is neither time-consuming nor costly. Lop any overhanging shrubs, which, after a shower of rain, would drench a viewer's coat sleeves as he pushes by.

The front door

If necessary replace the front door handle, letterbox and any other adornments. In summer or autumn a colourful hanging basket can work wonders. If there happens to be a hook to hang one on, it would be cheap at the price. If the door sticks, for goodness sake have it adjusted, even if it means your family having to put up with a few draughts for a week or two. It is the first impression that counts, and your viewer's first is formed while standing staring at your front door.

Ventilation

No matter what the season and what the cost in extra heating, open doors and windows every day, making sure the house gets a complete blow-through, particularly if some chain-smoker has just been in to view.

Delightful as the roly-poly dachshund draught excluder might look at the foot of a door, send it walkies. You don't want viewers to think that you live on windy ridge.

House names

If your house has both a number and a name, take the name down. Names are a matter of taste and we all know there is no accounting for that. A Yorkshire person might find 'Beck Side' pleasantly inoffensive – but a southerner …!

What if your house is only identified by the name? It isn't everybody who knows that the name can be changed by telling the local authority (usually buildings department) of one's intention; so you are allowed to drop that into the conversation. However, if the name includes, more or less truthfully, the words 'old' or 'cottage', that is more than all right. They are sure winners at attracting viewers.

Spend only what you must on making your house and its environs look attractive and free from problems.

The message that you should be getting so far is: spend only what you must on making your house and its environs look attractive and free from problems. You should do the same even if you decide to use a property shop. Having done what you can, you are now ready to put a for sale board in your neat garden, or for sale bills in your sparkling windows.

'For Sale' boards

From first to last you need viewers. It is said that one picture is worth a thousand words and one demonstration is worth a thousand pictures. So, unless you have the most compelling reasons against it (they are sometimes prohibited in Conservation Areas - check with your local authority), you must put out a For Sale board. If not a board, then a bill in the window. You will be surprised how many people will see it, even if you live in a cul-de-sac. Postmen, milkmen, newsagents, canvassers and neighbours can all spread the word if you only let them know.

Estate agents admit that they get 30 per cent of their buyers from For Sale boards and went barmy at the government's proposals for only one small board in any garden and no 'sold' boards anywhere. But now that the law has been changed, they are having to settle for spending more of their clients' money on newspaper advertising.

If estate agents are sending hopefuls to other houses in your vicinity, they are bound to see your board or window bill, and if your outsides look OK they won't want to buy the one the agent has for sale without first hearing about and seeing yours. In fact, they might only cruise by the agent's; they know all about that one already from the particulars they collected. Curiosity killed the cat, and your board will attract the curious.

It is worth the expense of getting a professional-looking board. Window bills or For Sale boards can be hired and put up by firms found under 'signs' in the Yellow Pages.

How to put up your own For Sale board

You need:

1 About 8 feet of 3 x 1 inch wood for a post, if it is to be sunk into the ground, less if you screw it to the gate post.

2 4 bricks.

3 A screwdriver.

4 A garden spade.

Do not have anything more on your board than 'FOR SALE Apply within' and your telephone number. 'By appointment only' is rejecting, and wise birds think: 'Hello, you can only go when the bagpipe teacher next door isn't giving lessons'. 'View weekends only' tells the burglar when to call. Let them get out of their cars and ask you for the details or, if you are not indoors, they can have a quiet look around the outside. Why not? You've nothing to be ashamed of, have you? If you have, get it attended to, now!

If you are putting the board in soil, dig a hole about eighteen inches square and about eighteen inches deep. Stand the board in the hole. Place two bricks at the bottom of the hole, one on either side of the post and parallel with one another, cover with about six inches of soil, then place a further two on top of and at right angles to the first two. Fill in and tamp down. You will be surprised at how firm your home-made board will be.

If you have a wooden gatepost, have the post for your board a little shorter, drill a couple of holes about eighteen inches apart in it, and screw the post to the gatepost.

If people come in from a board or a window bill you are halfway there. You haven't wasted an afternoon waiting in, when you could have been watching your favourite football team making a mess of it again. Indeed, you could have been doing something useful like drafting an advertisement to open up the market even further.

Advertising

This is a case of following the crowd. If it works for them it will for you; hopefully your board in the garden will have done the trick and, if not, your very first advertisement might.

Not all advertising has to be paid for; if you can come up with a story about why you are moving that looks like a news item, you could keep all the money in your pocket.

Anyone changing job, emigrating or doing anything adventurous or unusual should certainly contact the local newspaper and radio station to tell them about it. If you have children at school, is there a school magazine? Other parents might want to buy your house, believing that it is the atmosphere seeping out of your walls that makes your children so well-behaved and brilliant. Do you have a parish magazine? Do you belong to any organisation to which you can give advance information of your move by sending an apology for absence, so that it goes into the minutes? You are not supposed to advertise in a radio interview, but what is more natural than, to the presenter's question 'when', you should reply 'when the house is sold, and that will be the biggest wrench because I doubt whether we'll get another with a spring of real ale gushing from the rockery and an open view over the nudist camp' … Keep the list going until you are stopped.

If you are moving away to be near your daughter, who everyone will be glad to hear has just had a baby – tell them. You've met some of the people in the area to which you are moving, and though they can't compare (who could?) with your locals; they seem a splendid bunch.

All these little strokes can be pulled for the sake of a short letter and a postage stamp or a telephone call. At the newspapers, ask for the news desk. At radio stations, ask for a presenter by name if you know one. They all need something to fill their columns and programmes and you really ought to help – where's your public spirit? Another 'free' advertisement is someone else's, so answer private 'wanted' advertisements.

Advertisers who spend millions on media space know that only a proportion of it works; the trouble is they don't know which! Estate agents have a better idea because their advertising is specific and so it is easy to monitor the source of each response. They know where and when is best: follow their example and use the same papers on the same days as they do.

Do not be tempted by reductions for a series of advertisements. If your first attempt does not work, you might want to alter the 'copy' in some way.

The copy – composing your advertisement

There are three formats to choose from:

1 **Display**: one which will be placed among other 'boxed' adverts. The trouble with display is that it can get lost among the others, so ask if you can have a choice of borders. Borders to display adverts can be varied. Look through the paper at the different styles and choose. If you do not see anything outstanding, ask if they will accept a border drawn by you. If they will, get a sheet of Letraset transfers from an artists' shop and make your own. If you fancy white print on black background, that is called 'reversing out'.

   It won't cost anything to ask if you can have your advert placed in one of the better positions. Although we read from left to right we

Still another way of keeping your money where it rightly belongs is by putting postcards in local shop windows. At least it lets the talkative shopkeeper know.

only do so when we have time. Right hand pages and top and bottom right hand corners are said to be best.

If there is a property section, the first page is best and failing that, the last. Ask: if you don't ask, you don't get.

2 **Semi-display (classified)**: your advert appears in the column to which the class of thing you are offering refers – hence classified advertising – in your case the class is property. You will have noticed that a semi-displayed advertisement has lines (rules) separating it from other advertisements and you can choose where you want capital letters and where smalls, and how many spaces between the lines.

3 **Classified**: What you get for your money varies a little between newspapers, but generally it is a capital letter for the first word and the rest in smalls, apart from proper names where good grammar demands a capital. Do not spurn the classified. Anyone who is actively in the market will be searching the whole paper. They won't miss you, neither will the nosey parkers who are usually gossips and will spread the word for you.

Research shows that nine out of ten buyers move less than 10 miles, and only one in a hundred moves more than 100 miles.

Advertising in national newspapers is costly. The first thing to consider is this: research shows that nine out of ten buyers move less than 10 miles, and only one in a hundred moves more than 100 miles.

For every reader of one of the nationals, there are ten for the local paper and the cost of advertising in a national is ten times that of a local, added to which, buyers don't expect to see local properties advertised nationally, unless there is something very special about them.

So stick to the locals, unless your house is special because:

a It is in the upper bracket and has loose boxes, paddocks, fishing rights, private golf course, sound and video recording studio or other necessities for the rich;

b It is in the area to which a large company is relocating staff from all over the globe; or

c Houses in the area are being sold as weekend homes.

In any case, a local buyer is much easier to deal with than the man from Timbuktu.

The wording: what to put on; what to leave out

You need a headline. As we know that people don't move very far and their choice is governed by district and price, these are two essential elements of your advertisement. If nothing else is read, those two items are, so make them your beginning and end. Least said, soonest mended.

Say what is for sale, give the asking price and arrangements for contacting you. Best to give the enquirers an invitation to view over the weekend. If they all come at once, so much the better, it proves what a good house it is, otherwise why are so many people interested? People always want what they think others want.

If you have an answerphone, assume that every call is a response to your advertisement, and put a message on giving viewing particulars. Just because callers are ringing about some totally unrelated subject, it does not mean to say that they or their friends wouldn't be delighted to buy your house now that they know it is for sale.

Don't bother unduly about the name and address of an interested party. The wicked give fake ones anyway. Estate agents dress it up as part of the confidential professional service that they are giving you, when they insist on names and addresses from enquirers. But the real reason is far more mundane: their own need to prove that they introduced the buyer – their commission claim rests on it.

From escorting a lady to view once or twice, I knew that she was insisting on a walk-in pantry. I also knew she adored wisteria, she thought it the epitome of elegance and class. I got a house for sale in exactly the right location for her and not only was there a wisteria but it was in full bloom. I telephoned and said we were giving her the first chance, even before full particulars were ready. One of our representatives was going to view in an hour's time. Could he pick her up on the way? Yes, it was a bungalow; yes, it had a garage. But for the moment that was all we knew, apart from the fact that, in an aside, the owner had said the wisteria was a picture. The lady viewed, found for herself that there was no walk-in pantry, and went on to convince herself that walk-in pantries weren't the be-all and end-all of life. But to get a wisteria like that going from scratch could take at least seven years. SOLD, to the lady who liked wisteria.

However, if you have a fine wisteria or fine anything else, do not put it into your advertisement. There are people who can't stand the sight nor smell of things creeping up the walls, but if they view and are impressed by your electronically operated garage doors, they will make light work of digging the offending plant out. On the other hand, the one buyer you want might not come if he knows about those doors; his cat might have lost a life in one.

Photographs

Sometimes, there is case for using a photo of a detached house if it is individually styled, but as builders have, in recent years, built thousands of detached houses having only minimal variations in their elevations there are few compelling reasons for using one.

As for semi-detached or terraced (mews, town, etc.) houses, I don't know how anyone interested in buying a house in this country can have avoided learning what they look like. Indeed, the mere mention of a development is sufficient bring to mind the type of houses there. So why our eyeballs have to be rattled week after week, with page after page of silly little photos of semis and terraced houses I'll never know, and as for a tiny picture of a block of flats ... who wants to go viewing a barracks? Because that is what many agency photos make them look like.

Instructions to printers

Always make your instructions to printers as clear as you can. Compositors work at speed and they are not mind-readers. Instructions should always be circled and preferably in a different colour.

Words that will conjure up a picture in the reader's mind must be carefully chosen.

Words that will conjure up a picture in the reader's mind must be carefully chosen:

backing onto woodland: burglars lurking

oak beams: charm, cosiness

exceptional opportunity: why hasn't somebody taken it then?

great potential: work

sea view: peace or bank holiday chaos on the roads

overlooking river or lake: damp for the old, too deep for the young

PARTICULARS OF PROPERTY FOR SALE

Mr & Mrs R Bold

offer

FOR SALE PRIVATELY
(no agents)

14 Plevna Place, Blossomtom

£155,000 Freehold

Registered at Her Majesty's Land Registry Title No. EDN999707

- Entrance Hall
- Lounge
- Separate Dining Room
- Kitchen
- Utility Room
- Cloaks with WC
- Good decorations
- Central Heating
- Large Bedroom with en suite shower

- Second Bedroom
- Good third Bedroom
- 2nd and 3rd Bedrooms have washbasins
- Bathroom with WC
- Well insulated loft
- Quality fittings throughout
- Manageable gardens
- Garage and car port off wide street

Gas, electricity and mains water are connected. The Council Tax paid last year amounted to £790.

Vacant possession by arrangement.

There are nursery and playschools within walking distance. A sitter-in club operates in the district. The Orchard shopping centre is just around the corner, as is the regular bus service to town. Ten minutes' car journey to mainline and inter-city trains.

Plevna Place is off Orchard Road which is directly off the A444 at Bericote Cross Roads close to the local park.

Viewing at any reasonable time.

If you wish to confirm, please telephone (01234) 28370

This house is in a very pleasant and respectable neighbourhood and has been very reasonably priced at £155,000 for an EARLY SALE.

No agents   Mr & Mrs Bold, 14 Plevna Place

These particulars are believed to be correct but do not constitute an offer or any part of a contract.

Fig 7.1   Example Particulars

near golf course: can nip over the fence for a few quick swings or collect other peoples' lost golf balls

old: immortal, tried and trusted

Victorian: solid, spacious

prestigious: schoolteachers and many others know the words come from prestidigitation –which means trickery!

cottage or cottage style: if you can use it, do so. It's the biggest crowd-puller there is. But the picture some people conjure up at the thought is so chocolate-boxy, that you are in grave danger of disappointing them, should they come and you have no white palings, no roses round the door and it's simply an old house in a street.

So, don't overdescribe: people will drive by instead of coming in to keep an appointment. You are buying disappointment and will lose confidence.

There is a buyer for everything

If your For Sale board and your first advertisement don't work, immediately remember that the hallmark of true entrepreneurs is that they are never 'counted out'. They try and try again. So alter your advertising copy a little. Go from one section of the paper to another; if you didn't succeed in the classified, try display and so on.

Tomorrow is another day. New buyers come into the market every single day.

Don't advertise more than twice in the same paper in the same week. Be ready to change the wording.

Your predecessor sold the house to you, your old neighbours sold to your new ones. The area isn't littered with empty houses that no one will live in. Of course you will sell your house and you will sell it yourself, keeping your money where it belongs.

Particulars

People have come to expect a set of particulars. If for no other reason, that is why you should have some, but you must not allow interested

> If your For Sale board and your first advertisement don't work, immediately remember that the hallmark of true entrepreneurs is that they are never 'counted out'.

parties to use them as a substitute for viewing. At the risk of boring you, curiosity killed the cat.

Salesmen believe that one demonstration is worth a million words. It is certainly true of houses. Differences can be so subtle, only inspection can prove which is the best buy. Yet people are basically idle, it does not take a lot to put them off. They sit in their armchairs, leafing through a fist-full of agents' particulars, and no matter how well a house has been proposed and worthily recommended, they will blackball it without actually seeing it for themselves. If they got everything they thought they needed to know from the particulars, what need is there to view? How can a house get sold if it is left to buyers to decide, on a whim, which is best for them? They need our encouragement to work at it, which translated into a few words means: view and buy ours.

Try to restrict the distribution of your particulars to those who have been shown round. Give a copy to help them remember you and yours better than all the other run-of-the-mill properties they have seen.

Estate agents can get away with the most appalling rubbish and the silliest descriptions, because people don't take a lot of notice of their 'bijou residence of great charm and delight', knowing it means 'a poky hole with old fashioned fittings', although agents can now be prosecuted if they do misrepresent key information.

Private vendors can stick to plain language. Describe but don't overdo it. Big is as good as six and three quarter metres – or is it kilowatts? Who knows? Who cares, apart from surveyors, who have to make a great performance with their tape measures in an effort to impress the gullible. If your rooms are the wrong size for other people's carpets and you have given the game away in your particulars, they won't view. If they only find out when they come, they'll be delighted to hear that one of their neighbours-to-be is a carpet fitter, who needs a bit of weekend work: he's good and he's cheap!

Photographs

If you think a picture stuck onto your particulars will help prospects to remember your house, get some self-adhesive mini-prints made. All you need to do is send the developed 35mm negative to one of the specialist printers who advertise their services, and for very little you will get 50 prints almost by return of post.

When taking the photograph, stand on a stepladder; it helps to keep the walls in proper perspective. Wait until fog, cars, vans, police, cats and dogs and canvassers are out of the way. Shut the garage doors, draw all but decorative curtains well back and take all of the washing in.

Drafting

If you can type the particulars so well and good, but if your handwriting is clear, that's something different. Failing your being a typist or a handwritist, your local duplicating agency or photocopier will do both the typing and printing on A4 size paper for you. Choose a copier who has a standard border that your particulars can be laid on for copying. Just because it's cheaper for quantities, don't buy more than you need. Twenty should be plenty. In any case, you might want to make some adjustments later.

On our specimen particulars on page 61, we have tried to give the prospects plenty of reading. Not as much as would make them feel they knew it all without viewing, but more information than they are likely to get from an agent.

If your house is registered, this is obviously a good thing to show. Estate agents don't show it, and one can only speculate on the reason. It can't possibly be the cost – it's free! Perhaps they don't understand the matter, or if they do they want to keep the knowledge to themselves believing that a little knowledge is a dangerous thing for clients to have.

But as Huxley says, if a little knowledge is a dangerous thing, where is the man who has enough to be safe? Or as I would have it: a little knowledge in the hands of house buyers is a dangerous thing for the professionals in their search for easy pickings. But no matter who is right, estate agents and solicitors don't seem unduly disturbed at the moment. They know that no matter how many For Sale boards rot away, how many sold-subject-to-contract slips dance on and off the boards, how many mortgage applications fail, how many bridging loans have to be paid or chains collapse – most people get moved, jobs get cobbled together somehow, and if sleep is to be lost, it won't be theirs. They have seen it all before.

Knowing so early on in the proceedings whether the house is registered or not is valuable.

If, because you have a mortgage, or for any other reason you haven't got the deeds to flash under a prospect's nose, put your name and address on a Form 96 and send it to the Land Registry. In reply you will receive an official Land Registry certificate of search, proving the registration and the title number. You can then show it to a prospect, who might be one of the growing band of buyers who know they can buy without the aid of a solicitor. Knowing so early on in the proceedings whether the house is registered or not is valuable. In any case it is something new and different, and gives a stamp of approval to the proceedings: they'll remember YOUR house all right.

Although you would not wish to print it on the particulars, another thing you could usefully do would be to call at the local council office and ask if there is anything special about to happen round your way, such as a new building, a sewage farm, or road widening. It is as well to know about it now. Knowledge is power, and sometimes very profitable. Some kinds of development enhance a house's value. If so, you don't want to sell to some speculator, keep the profit for yourself.

Disclaimers

All estate agents write one at the foot of their particulars, some briefly, and some at great length such as:

Allwind & Waters state for themselves and the vendors of the property described herein that the acceptance of a copy of these particulars is made on the understanding that the applicant has read and understood the content and meaning hereof and that these particulars are intended as a general guide only and do not constitute any sort of contract or offer or part thereof and that no person of either sex in the employ full or part time of Messrs Allwind & Waters has any authority to make any representation warranty or give any guarantee whatever in relation to this property.

Why any honest, hard working qualified and competent persons should subject people with whom they are trying to do business to such an eyesight test I don't know. If staff are incompetent, they should be moved on, and certainly not be let near the tens of thousands of pounds of 'what is most probably our most important and valuable possession.'

Private vendor's disclaimer

Having been rigorously honest and above all painstaking about the things you do put in, you can use the delightfully simple: These particulars are believed to be correct but do not constitute an offer or any part of a contract.

Showing them round

Lonely, elderly and single people fear lest having a board in the garden will attract all sorts of villains. That fear is no reason for paying a thousand pounds or more to an agency.

Though an agent might get the name and address of every enquirer, do you really expect any villain whose dearest wish is to rape, plunder, pillage and set fire to you to give a correct address? Even if an agent accompanies every enquirer, having once seen the house and ingratiated himself, the enquirer can call back unaccompanied and wreak villainy upon you.

If you don't use, or haven't yet got a chain on your door, you must. If you don't, sooner or later you will be done over, selling a house or not, agents or no agents. You can always keep an enquirer on the other side of the door and make an appointment for a time when a friend can come round, or even when you have arranged for other viewers to come.

Ask yourself, could anyone sell me a house I didn't really want? Even if he had graduated from a top business salesmanship school, got a gold medal from the professor for it, had all the patter and ready-thought-out glib answers to all the searching questions, had manoeuvred you into saying 'yes' at every twist and turn in the conversation, including the final yes, so that you could get home in time to watch The Party Political Broadcast – would you really feel bound? Wouldn't you find some reason for, at least, forgetting it?

Buyers have plenty of time to forget it. The cooling-off period allowed in consumer protection legislation is but a fleeting moment compared with the time solicitors take to get contracts signed and exchanged – the point at which, and not before, neither party can back out except at the risk of severe penalties.

The message with regard to selling houses is that if they have been properly prepared, they don't need super-salesmen: they sell themselves.

No matter how many books you have read on selling, no matter how many seminars, courses or lectures you have attended to be talked at, or successful role-plays you have accomplished about selling, the message with regard to selling houses is that if they have been properly prepared, they don't need super-salesmen: **they sell themselves**.

Your task is to allow someone who wants your house to know that it is for sale, and then to let them have it (the house). Put no obstacle in their path. Smooth that path. Prepare yourself, and any other members of your household who might come in contact with viewers to do just this:

1 Let them in.

2 Show them round.

3 Let them know that others are interested.

4 Bargain if you must.

5 Carry out the instructions on what to do when a buyer says 'I will.'

If people knock on the door in response to seeing the board in your garden, and you are not alone in the house, let them in. Only if the most embarrassing scene is being enacted within should you ask them to come back later. From first to last, remember that doubtless this is your most prized possession that you are trying to sell. You must be prepared to work at it and accept some inconvenience.

You only need one buyer and she may well be standing before your very eyes. It might cost you another £50 in advertising before you get another viewer, so a bird on the doorstep can be worth two in the bush.

If people ring up for an appointment to view, remember the walk-in pantry lady, and say as little as possible over the phone.

Do not worry too much about the problem of time-wasters. They might arrive at the same time as a genuine prospect, and the so-called time-waster might just jerk the prospect into action.

When the viewers come in daylight make sure the curtains are drawn well back. Have doors onto landings and passages open to let light in. It all makes a house look more airy and spacious.

For evening viewers, use only the softest of lighting and try to have lamps already switched on. Don't switch lights off as you vacate rooms.

They might think you extravagant, but if they ask to see the electricity bills, they will be convinced that they, being more careful than you, will have less to pay.

The television, radio or CD player should only be playing if your neighbour is giving a bagpipe lesson.

Decide beforehand who is to lead the conducted tour if there should be more than one of you at home when the viewers arrive. Leave the others seated comfortably in the lounge. They must not be smoking, arguing or drinking anything because you don't want to look unfriendly by not offering a portion to the visitors. The television, radio or CD player should only be playing if your neighbour is giving a bagpipe lesson. Otherwise, all that the loungers have to do is politely acknowledge (they must not ignore) the presence of the viewers. Children should be introduced properly.

Those who are light-fingered work to the four As: they will steal anything from anybody, anywhere, any time. So don't leave pocketable things around. Don't actually search viewers as they leave, but just have it at the back of your mind that everybody is not as honest as you are.

You should enter each room first, and then invite the viewer to follow you. If the view is worth seeing, ask them to step to the window. Open cupboard and wardrobe doors to show how spacious they are. Draw attention to thermostats on radiators and situations of power plugs. Do not draw attention to things that are big enough to see such as fireplaces and tiled walls. Demonstrate water pressure at sinks, baths and WCs. Similarly, an electronically-controlled garage door needs to be demonstrated, because it too is not immediately obvious to the unassisted eye.

When you've shown them round, invite their questions and answer as honestly as you can. If you don't know the answer, say so.

If they say, 'Oh dear, I thought there might be a bidet', keep your witty remarks to yourself until after they've gone. And don't let it cast you down. It could be you've got a buyer here and such carping is a tactic in the strategy of bargaining, about which more later.

You can't put anyone off buying their dream home but do avoid any unintended insult. They'll only get their own back later if you give one.

Safety lies in getting as many clues about them as soon as possible. Ask the Royal question, 'Have you come far?' The answer to that or subsequent get-to-know-right-by-guessing-wrong statements will help you get the picture and determine your future chat.

If you are asked how long your house has been up for sale and the truthful answer is: just this week, say so. If it is a while longer say, 'Oh, not long, houses along here never are'. If the viewer is a smarty and bowls you a guess-wrong-to-get-to-know right, such as 'A week?' it's own-up time folks, because such a questioner will treat you with the utmost suspicion from then on if you don't.

Don't introduce negative thoughts by bragging about the money you have spent on eradicating woodworm and the guarantee against its recurrence that you got.

Owner-occupiers are inordinately proud of their houses and when they are conducting prospective purchasers round it shows, so the sensitive viewer will often say anything to avoid giving offence when trying to bring the visit to a comfortable close. Team viewers, such as husband and wife, will naturally wish to discuss together the merits of the house, not in front of the vendor, but after leaving, and the real purchaser can quite easily turn out to be the one who walks round without saying a word, and succeeds in leaving you with the feeling that you have been wasting your time.

Prospects who have made appointments will turn up to view. At the gate, they will realise that yours is not for them, but for courtesy's sake will come to the door.

As soon as a viewer steps over the threshold, most of us get a feeling of whether what we have to offer is what they are looking for.

However, as soon as a viewer steps over the threshold, most of us get a feeling of whether what we have to offer is what they are looking for. If you sense it is not – show them round and show them out. In the cases where you feel that there is a glimmer of hope, keep them there and take your time in showing them as much as possible, with such little tricks as asking them to admire the view. But do not let the conversation stray, for long, from points about the house, keep to such things as the local shops, and the price.

Nevertheless, the safest plan is to treat every viewer as a buyer, but ignore what they say, or fail to say, initially about their intentions. Prefer to wait for further action to develop and until it does, keep on showing viewers round.

How to negotiate

You will have already calculated what is the very best deal you can hope for and what is barely acceptable to you: what are the optional extras you will sell and what are the extras you intend to include in your price. You can then bargain on these points if required to. Being prepared, you won't have to rely on the other party to make up your mind for you.

Do not bargain at all unless you have to. Put it off as long as possible. As you are showing the nicest part of your nature, the more time viewers have to get to know you, the less they will want to offend by offering too little. In any case, there are still a few around who find it embarrassing and ill-mannered to bargain and that is still another reason why your price must be realistic in the first place.

If, initially, you are asked 'Will you take an offer?' answer 'Of course, come in and have a look round and we'll have a talk about it'. Then get off the subject with, 'have you come far?'

The opening from a serious prospect

It usually goes something like: 'Will you take an offer?' Well, you are open to an offer; it all depends what they have in mind. When you are given a figure, no matter what it is, look shocked. If no figure is forthcoming, keep fencing, saying that you have stated your price and hope to get it, but for a quick decision from a good buyer you will talk. By the way, have they sold their house? Will it be cash, or will they require a mortgage, how quickly could they complete?

He who has the most facts wins, so get to know as much as you can about the other party as soon as possible.

There is a lot of guesswork in bargaining. He who has the most facts wins, so get to know as much as you can about the other party as soon as possible. In a bargaining situation, delay is a most useful weapon so use it if you can.

If they won't talk, you must ask questions: the other side then has to reveal some of their hand.

Reluctant bargainers

If you really don't feel up to all the argy-bargy you could advertise 'no offers'. But as your first task is to draw as many viewers as possible and 'no offers' could stop some coming, prefer to wait and reply to offers with, 'I know that people expect to bargain for houses, but I have never been accustomed to it and have therefore made sure that my asking price is the most reasonable that anyone could expect to get it for'. Then hand them a copy of your particulars on which you have already written that little lot, or words to that effect.

Never accept the first offer. The deal will collapse if you do, because the prospect thinks he could have got it for less. Never say no, say maybe.

Hide this book from the gaze of prospects. Because you are selling for yourself, they think you are an amateur and they will be relaxed, an ideal bargaining atmosphere – don't lose it.

Give satisfaction. People get more satisfaction from the things they have to work for.

Bargaining points

Half a loaf is better than none, particularly if your half has the butter on.

Use things you intended to include in the purchase price as bargaining points; i.e. if you had included the carpet and curtains, you can counter with 'all right but I couldn't possibly include the carpets and curtains at that price.'

Making a benchmark

When some people receive their first offer, they are known to say, even though it is hardly true, that they have got as good an offer already, so if, just for the look of the thing, the new man will add £2,500 to his offer, that could tie things up and leave things comfortable all round.

Anglers need patience

If people don't bite first time, don't worry, they might have taken the bait.

The harder you fight in the beginning, the less you give away in the long run.

Keep reminding the bargainer of the bargain he is getting, compared with what is being offered elsewhere.

Use stamp duty bands. If you really want somewhere around, but less than the figure which happens to be the point at which stamp duty becomes payable, make your asking figure a little above it. You can then, with a long face, agree to bring your price down to save him the duty. The purchaser has won, honour is satisfied, big deal!

Never show triumph. Always let them appear to win.

If they send an expert

He is on their side. About the dry rot, lay off the tommy rot, don't try to influence him. If you can overcome your generous instincts don't even offer a cup of tea. Let him report – 'Hard people, they won't give anything away, don't seem to care whether they sell to you or not, maybe got a queue.

The manipulators

This is the one who, when you think it is all agreed and you are waiting for contracts to be signed, comes back time and again for more. Remedy: ask for a final set of demands in writing. Another good reason for knowing about contracts and how solicitors work. Read on – all will be revealed.

Box yourself in

Cut off your retreat. Burn down your bridges: tell the bargainer that you are anxious to move quickly and, to get a quick sale you set your price where you did, in spite of being told that you could get far more. As a matter of fact, agents have never stopped ringing, offering to do just that, but you know what they are – anything to get people signed up. But you have pitched your price with just the odd bit added on, to allow a modest bargain and you can't possibly go lower, what with the mortgage and all that.

If in doubt, say nowt. **Do not leave the bargaining to an agency or a solicitor** but if you find he has got involved don't tell him your rock bottom deal. He wants the job out of the way, he has not got the time for lengthy bargaining sessions.

Forget pride

Derogatory remarks about your pride and joy are intended to cost you money.

Free option

If you agree to let someone know, if and when you decide to reduce your price, make sure that you have got an offer out of them first so that when you do go back, you go with a new price that allows you some elbow room.

Problems

They do not go away – they go into corners and breed.

Our ruin is often caused not by what we say, but what we fail to say and/or get into writing.

Closing an interview

'We are expecting someone else soon. Will you let me know by next Wednesday as I have half made promises elsewhere.'

To sum up

Cups of tea, a guided tour of your holiday snaps, or a privileged look into the eggcup containing your gallstones will not sell your house. Nor will playing the supersalesman. Your job is to get the viewers. Houses sell themselves if you will only:

1 Let viewers look round.

2 Let them bargain if they must.

3 Let them agree to buy.

4 Let them pay a deposit.

5 Let them go home.

6 Be natural – be yourself.

7 Be a listener as well as a talker.

8 Be modest about the house.

9 Don't show off; it's the house that is on view, not you.

What to say when a buyer says 'I will'

'Who is your solicitor?' 'I am acting for myself and you can tell your people to get in touch with me. Will you please pay me a deposit now as a sign of good faith?'

Of course people have to get mortgages. Of course, many have to get their own houses sold and of course, if they are really serious they will have done as much as they can towards sorting these problems out before they meet you. Ask them where they are at in the process and if possible check their answers. Acting for yourself you can then so easily be honest and fair to everybody – but chiefly yourself.

For instance, you can keep a buyer keened up while you are looking for reserves by being ready to say, 'I do hope you will be able to buy it, but as you know, there's many a slip twixt cup and lip, so I will have to keep the board out. But I promise you that you are top of my list. I won't sell to anyone else without getting in touch with you. That's fair, isn't it?'

Even if there are a dozen, they are all top of the list, because you don't really fancy the chances of the previous ones if someone turns up an hour later with the folding money, ready to sign a contract then and there. It can happen and it can be done – see later.

Never say die

If your home is clean, neat, tidy and properly priced, your buyer will come. See the bargain-hunter off. Keep on showing viewers round right up to the minute you get a contract signed.

8 Contracts

What transforms a simple agreement into a contract is that the contract is made upon a 'consideration'.

A contract is an agreement to do something. Contracts for the sale and purchase of property must be in writing. Parties must be identifiable and over 18 years of age. Lunatics and some drunkards are debarred. What transforms a simple agreement into a contract is that the contract is made upon a 'consideration'. Consideration is a matter of inducement for something promised, so it has to be valuable, for example, money.

A vendor's contract says in effect: you Mr Rashley, have induced me to promise you vacant possession of my house by offering to pay me £75,000. And if Mr Rashley puts his signature to this agreement (upon that valuable consideration of £75,000) called a contract (that the vendor, too, has signed), and fails to keep his bargain, then he is bound and can be sued if he does not complete the bargain contracted for.

The Law Society and Oyez publish a property contract called an 'Agreement (Incorporating the Standard Conditions of Sale (Third Edition))'. All the main headings required for a contract for the sale of a freehold or leasehold house situated in England & Wales are there - see example at the end of this chapter. If you are selling, have three copies ready as soon as you put the house on the market.

Solicitors will choose from either the Law Society's contract or draft their own. The conditions are set out in full on the inside of the Agreement. These conditions occupy line after line of fine print (literally as long as an arm). So stand well back and if any of it has been altered, have a closer look, and if you still do not know what is going on, ask for an explanation.

Just remember

Vendor: you want the money.

Purchaser: you want the house.

That's all there is to it!

Contracts for the sale of land (in our case with buildings on) usually include the following:

a **Description of the parties**: Names and addresses of both vendor and purchaser.

b **Description of what is being sold**: A plan of the area should accompany the draft contract. If the property is unregistered there will be, if the conveyances say so, a plan among the deeds. If there isn't a mention of such a plan, then there will be a description. Plans are better than descriptions. If registered, you will receive a copy of the plan with the office copies (something else which you will learn about in a few pages' time).

Included in the description of what is being sold should be a recital of any rights there might be, such as light, water, way, drainage. But they are usually referred to in general terms at this stage, and answered in a little more detail when requisitions (questions) on (about the) title (ownership) are received after exchange of contracts.

c **The price.**

d **The amount of deposit (customarily 10 per cent of the price, but often less)**, and how it is to be paid and by whom it will be held acting as stake-holder (agent/bank manager/solicitor or vendor and purchaser who open a joint bank account for this purpose only). If the other side has a solicitor who will agree to be stake-holder, you can agree.

It is quite normal for a seller to borrow his buyer's deposit for use as his deposit, and so on up the buying chain, if there is one. This applies only by agreement, as set out in Standard Condition 2.2.2. This often means it is the poorest person at the bottom of the chain who has to stump up the deposit, then used by each person up the line.

e **The date for completion**: This is a matter for agreement between the parties. The purchaser should make up the difference between the deposit paid and the purchase price on the completion date, and in exchange the vendor should give full vacant possession. What, you may ask, if either side finds that they can't complete to the exact date? Don't be frightened, and furthermore, don't despair – it isn't a legal problem yet. Whether you are doing the job for yourself or paying a Skinner, the hiccup would have occurred and it would have been yours to cure.

If your opposite number to the contract gives what sounds like a good reason for delay, then you must come to some new understanding, and if your vendor is being silly and says he wants more money, has changed his mind about the house he wanted to buy or move into, or simply changed his mind full stop, then you have to make some decisions. What are your options? If it is postponement, you can calmly accept his new date. But if you decide that the contract should be kept, then you must give the other party written notice to complete. The notice must be reasonable and take into account the circumstances of the particular case. If you are faced by this very unusual circumstance, have a look at the Standard Conditions of Sale.

If you had a problem with your washing machine, you would first look at the instructions and if you were stumped, you would not be afraid to consult a service engineer. So if after giving notice you have not got a sensible new arrangement, then consider going to a solicitor for advice only.

The only (very rare) circumstance in which either or both of the parties to the contract can insist that the contract be completed or come to an end on the very date contracted for, is where a clause has been inserted in the contract saying that time is the essence of the contract. Otherwise, exactly the same rights apply on the date on which the notice to complete expires, which is the number of days (after service of the notice) which is set out in the contract. If time has been made the essence and say, a purchaser says, 'but I can't complete until the day after the date specified for completion', the vendor is at liberty to put the contract at an end and confiscate the deposit. If it is the vendor who cannot or will not complete, and time was the essence, the purchaser can demand the deposit back, put an end to the contract and possibly sue for damages.

f **The capacity in which the vendor sells**: You must choose between 'full' and 'limited' guarantee in the contract. Full title guarantee is for both freehold and leasehold. It implies that vendors:

1 have the right to dispose of the property as they are purporting they have;

2 will at their own cost do all that they can reasonably to give the purchaser the title that they purport to give, which includes doing what they reasonably can to ensure that the purchaser is

entitled to be registered with at least the class of title registered before the disposition;

3 assert that the property is free from all financial charges (e.g. mortgage) and incumbrances and all other rights exercisable by third parties that the vendor knows about and could reasonably be expected to know about; but you do not have to refer to items already on the register or overriding interests of which the purchaser has notice.

The circumstances whereby a vendor could not give full title guarantee include:

1 Where a trustee disposes of property under a will, then he would not sell with full title guarantee.

2 A mortgagee in possession would also not sell with full title guarantee.

3 Executors selling following the death of the former owner.

g **Extras (or 'chattels')**: Items which are not fixtures and fittings, which can pass by delivery, and have been bargained for separately are sometimes included by reference to a separate inventory. If included in the purchase price (stated in the contract) and a separate value has been agreed for them, that price is stated in this clause, particularly if doing so will reduce the stamp duty payable on the transfer or conveyance (more about this later).

h **Covenants**: These are notified to the purchaser in the contract and a full copy is attached to the draft contract. The seller should always mention those he knows of, even if he has no idea who can enforce them, or whether they can be enforced. The buyer must decide what relevance they have. The clause in the contract will say that the purchaser, having been supplied with a copy, is deemed to have full knowledge of them and no requisitions (questions) nor objections shall be raised in respect thereof. Normally this means that the vendor will answer questions about the covenants having been kept, but that he is not getting himself involved in trying to get any of them changed.

i **Freehold or leasehold**: In the latter case the lease should be referred to. Put the lease through the copier and attach to the draft contract. Again provide in the draft contract that there are to be no requisitions or objections, but be prepared to answer sensible questions if you know the answer for sure. If you are buying freehold and Skinner offers limited title guarantee or puts any fancy work on the contract that you do not easily understand, the Registrar will always give limited guarantee in cases of doubt.

j   **The rate of interest to be paid or contract rate** for the period between the completion date in the contract, and the date on which completion actually happens. Fix the rate at a little above your bank's minimum lending rate, or the prevailing building society rate, or just write 'Law Society rate', which is usually a rate above the base rate, currently four per cent above the base rate of Barclays Bank.

k   **Title**: A statement about how the vendor intends to prove that he is the owner. This is done by: (i) registered property: saying that the office copies will be supplied; or (ii) unregistered property: quoting a conveyance or some other good root of title of the property which is at least 15 years old. More about (i) and (ii) later.

l   **Risk**: What happens if the house is destroyed or seriously damaged between the date you exchange contracts and the date your were to complete? If the Law Society's contract is being used, the answer is simple. The buyer can withdraw from the contract and ask for his deposit back. By the way, be very wary of buying under a contract that places the risk on the buyer from date of exchange. In the absence of any contract clause to the contrary, when the parties exchange contracts, in a sense the property becomes the buyer's. It is his property subject only to paying the price and taking a transfer or conveyance. So at common law, if it is destroyed, it is his problem. It may also be the seller's if the buyer cannot raise funds to complete - which may well be the position if money is being borrowed.

Historically, the buyer insured from exchange but insurance is not the whole answer. The reinstatement moneys are not really likely to equal the purchase rice and a bridging loan to complete may not be readily available given the buyer needs the purchase price but the land and the smouldering ruins are likely to be worth considerably less. If you draft your contract using the Law Society's contract, you are unlikely to change the position, but if you are the buyer reading this to see what the vendor is up to, note that if the written contract says 'Condition 5.1 does not apply', it means the risk is yours!

So that's what a basic contract is all about. Further clauses can be added, and in the crusade against the gazumper on the one hand and the gazoffer on the other, suggestions follow in the next chapter for some additional clauses that have already saved thousands from nervous breakdown.

Fig 8.1   *Completed Example of Agreement*

AGREEMENT
(Incorporating the Standard Conditions of Sale (Third Edition))

Agreement date	:	12th July 2001
Seller	:	Mr and Mrs R Bold 14 Plevna Place Blossomtom BX10 1AB
Buyer	:	Mr John Smith 12 Quain Road London SW10 7XX
Property **(freehold/leasehold)**	:	14 Plevna Place Blossomtom BX10 1AB Freehold
Root of title/Title Number	:	EDN999707
Incumbrances on the Property	:	
		N/A
Title Guarantee **(full/limited)**	:	Full
Completion date	:	21st August 2001
Contract rate	:	
Purchase price	:	£155,000
Deposit	:	£15,500
Amount payable for chattels	:	
Balance	:	

The Seller will sell and the Buyer will buy the Property for the Purchase price.

The Agreement continues on the back page.

WARNING	**Signed**
This is a formal document, designed to create legal rights and legal obligations. Take advice before using it.	
	Seller/Buyer

Reproduced by Law Pack Publishing with the permission of the Controller of HMSO

Fig 8.1 Completed Example of Agreement, continued

STANDARD CONDITIONS OF SALE (THIRD EDITION)
(NATIONAL CONDITIONS OF SALE 23rd EDITION, LAW SOCIETY'S CONDITIONS OF SALE 1995)

1. GENERAL

1.1 Definitions

1.1.1 In these conditions:
- (a) "accrued interest" means:
  - (i) if money has been placed on deposit or in a building society share account, the interest actually earned
  - (ii) otherwise, the interest which might reasonably have been earned by depositing the money at interest on seven days' notice of withdrawal with a clearing bank

  less, in either case, any proper charges for handling the money
- (b) "agreement" means the contractual document which incorporates these conditions, with or without amendment
- (c) "banker's draft" means a draft drawn by and on a clearing bank
- (d) "clearing bank" means a bank which is a member of CHAPS Limited
- (e) "completion date", unless defined in the agreement, has the meaning given in condition 6.1.1
- (f) "contract" means the bargain between the seller and the buyer of which these conditions, with or without amendment, form part
- (g) "contract rate", unless defined in the agreement, is the Law Society's interest rate from time to time in force
- (h) "lease" includes sub-lease, tenancy and agreement for a lease or sub-lease
- (i) "notice to complete" means a notice requiring completion of the contract in accordance with condition 6
- (j) "public requirement" means any notice, order or proposal given or made (whether before or after the date of the contract) by a body acting on statutory authority
- (k) "requisition" includes objection
- (l) "solicitor" includes barrister, duly certificated notary public, recognised licensed conveyancer and recognised body under sections 9 or 32 of the Administration of Justice Act 1985
- (m) "transfer" includes conveyance and assignment
- (n) "working day" means any day from Monday to Friday (inclusive) which is not Christmas Day, Good Friday or a statutory Bank Holiday.

1.1.2 When used in these conditions the terms "absolute title" and "office copies" have the special meanings given to them by the Land Registration Act 1925.

1.2 Joint parties

If there is more than one seller or more than one buyer, the obligations which they undertake can be enforced against them all jointly or against each individually.

1.3 Notices and documents

1.3.1 A notice required or authorised by the contract must be in writing.

1.3.2 Giving a notice or delivering a document to a party's solicitor has the same effect as giving or delivering it to that party.

1.3.3 Transmission by fax is a valid means of giving a notice or delivering a document where delivery of the original document is not essential.

1.3.4 Subject to conditions 1.3.5 to 1.3.7, a notice is given and a document delivered when it is received.

1.3.5 If a notice or document is received after 4.00pm on a working day, or on a day which is not a working day, it is to be treated as having been received on the next working day.

1.3.6 Unless the actual time of receipt is proved, a notice or document sent by the following means is to be treated as having been received before 4.00pm on the day shown below:

(a) by first-class post:	two working days after posting
(b) by second-class post:	three working days after posting
(c) through a document exchange:	on the first working day after the day on which it would normally be available for collection by the addressee.

1.3.7 Where a notice or document is sent through a document exchange, then for the purposes of condition 1.3.6 the actual time of receipt is:
- (a) the time when the addressee collects it from the document exchange or, if earlier
- (b) 8.00am on the first working day on which it is available for collection at that time.

1.4 VAT

1.4.1 An obligation to pay money includes an obligation to pay any value added tax chargeable in respect of that payment.

1.4.2 All sums made payable by the contract are exclusive of value added tax.

2. FORMATION

2.1 Date

2.1.1 If the parties intend to make a contract by exchanging duplicate copies by post or through a document exchange, the contract is made when the last copy is posted or deposited at the document exchange.

2.1.2 If the parties' solicitors agree to treat exchange as taking place before duplicate copies are actually exchanged, the contract is made as so agreed.

2.2 Deposit

2.2.1 The buyer is to pay or send a deposit of 10 per cent of the purchase price no later than the date of the contract. Except on a sale by auction, payment is to be made by banker's draft or by a cheque drawn on a solicitors' clearing bank account.

2.2.2 If before completion date the seller agrees to buy another property in England and Wales for his residence, he may use all or any part of the deposit as a deposit in that transaction to be held on terms to the same effect as this condition and condition 2.2.3.

2.2.3 Any deposit or part of a deposit not being used in accordance with condition 2.2.2 is to be held by the seller's solicitor as stakeholder on terms that on completion it is paid to the seller with accrued interest.

2.2.4 If a cheque tendered in payment of all or part of the deposit is dishonoured when first presented, the seller may, within seven working days of being notified that the cheque has been dishonoured, give notice to the buyer that the contract is discharged by the buyer's breach.

2.3 Auctions

2.3.1 On a sale by auction the following conditions apply to the property and, if it is sold in lots, to each lot.

2.3.2 The sale is subject to a reserve price.

2.3.3 The seller, or a person on his behalf, may bid up to the reserve price.

2.3.4 The auctioneer may refuse any bid.

2.3.5 If there is a dispute about a bid, the auctioneer may resolve the dispute or restart the auction at the last undisputed bid.

3. MATTERS AFFECTING THE PROPERTY

3.1 Freedom from Incumbrances

3.1.1 The seller is selling the property free from incumbrances, other than those mentioned in condition 3.1.2.

3.1.2 The incumbrances subject to which the property is sold are:
- (a) those mentioned in the agreement
- (b) those discoverable by inspection of the property before the contract
- (c) those the seller does not and could not know about
- (d) entries made before the date of the contract in any public register except those maintained by HM Land Registry or its Land Charges Department or by Companies House
- (e) public requirements.

3.1.3 After the contract is made, the seller is to give the buyer written details without delay of any new public requirement and of anything in writing which he learns about concerning any incumbrances subject to which the property is sold.

3.1.4 The buyer is to bear the cost of complying with any outstanding public requirement and is to indemnify the seller against any liability resulting from a public requirement.

3.2 Physical state

3.2.1 The buyer accepts the property in the physical state it is in at the date of the contract unless the seller is building or converting it.

3.2.2 A leasehold property is sold subject to any subsisting breach of a condition or tenant's obligation relating to the physical state of the property which renders the lease liable to forfeiture.

3.2.3 A sub-lease is granted subject to any subsisting breach of a condition or tenant's obligation relating to the physical state of the property which renders the seller's own lease liable to forfeiture.

3.3 Leases affecting the property

3.3.1 The following provisions apply if the agreement states that any part of the property is sold subject to a lease.

3.3.2
- (a) The seller having provided the buyer with full details of each lease or copies of the documents embodying the lease terms, the buyer is treated as entering into the contract knowing and fully accepting those terms
- (b) The seller is to inform the buyer without delay if the lease ends or if the seller learns of any application by the tenant in connection with the lease; the seller is then to act as the buyer reasonably directs, and the buyer is to indemnify him against all consequent loss and expense
- (c) The seller is not to agree to any proposal to change the lease terms without the consent of the buyer and is to inform the buyer without delay of any change which may be proposed or agreed
- (d) The buyer is to indemnify the seller against all claims arising from the lease after actual completion; this includes claims which are unenforceable against a buyer for want of registration
- (e) The seller takes no responsibility for what rent is lawfully recoverable, nor for whether or how any legislation affects the lease
- (f) If the let land is not wholly within the property, the seller may apportion the rent.

3.4 Retained land

3.4.1 The following provisions apply where after the transfer the seller will be retaining land near the property.

3.4.2 The buyer will have no right of light or air over the retained land, but otherwise the seller and the buyer will each have the rights over the land of the other which they would have had if they were two separate buyers to whom the seller had made simultaneous transfers of the property and the retained land.

3.4.3 Either party may require that the transfer contain appropriate express terms.

4. TITLE AND TRANSFER

4.1 Timetable

4.1.1 The following are the steps for deducing and investigating the title to the property to be taken within the following time limits:

Step	Time Limit
1. The seller is to send the buyer evidence of title in accordance with condition 4.2	Immediately after making the contract
2. The buyer may raise written requisitions	Six working days after either the date of the contract or the date of delivery of the seller's evidence of title on which the requisitions are raised whichever is the later
3. The seller is to reply in writing to any requisitions raised	Four working days after receiving the requisitions
4. The buyer may make written observations on the seller's replies	Three working days after receiving the replies

The time limit on the buyer's right to raise requisitions applies even where the seller supplies incomplete evidence of his title, but the buyer may, within six working days from delivery of any further evidence, raise further requisitions resulting from that evidence. On the expiry of the relevant time limit the buyer loses his right to raise requisitions or make observations.

4.1.2 The parties are to take the following steps to prepare and agree the transfer of the property within the following time limits:

Step	Time Limit
A. The buyer is to send the seller a draft transfer	At least twelve working days before completion date
B. The seller is to approve or revise that draft and either return it or retain it for use as the actual transfer	Four working days after delivery of the draft transfer
C. If the draft is returned the buyer is to send an engrossment to the seller	At least five working days before completion date

4.1.3 Periods of time under conditions 4.1.1 and 4.1.2 may run concurrently.

4.1.4 If the period between the date of the contract and completion date is less than 15 working days, the time limits in conditions 4.1.1 and 4.1.2 are to be reduced by the same proportion as that period bears to the period of 15 working days. Fractions of a working day are to be rounded down except that the time limit to perform any step is not to be less than one working day.

4.2 Proof of title

4.2.1 The evidence of registered title is office copies of the items required to be furnished by section 110(1) of the Land Registration Act 1925 and the copies, abstracts and evidence referred to in section 110(2).

4.2.2 The evidence of unregistered title is an abstract of the title, or an epitome of title with photocopies of the relevant documents.

4.2.3 Where the title to the property is unregistered, the seller is to produce to the buyer (without cost to the buyer):
- (a) the original of every relevant document, or
- (b) an abstract, epitome or copy with an original marking by a solicitor of examination either against the original or against an examined abstract or against an examined copy.

4.3 Defining the property

4.3.1 The seller need not:
- (a) prove the exact boundaries of the property
- (b) prove who owns fences, ditches, hedges or walls
- (c) separately identify parts of the property with different titles

further than he may be able to do from information in his possession.

4.3.2 The buyer may, if it is reasonable, require the seller to make or obtain, pay for and hand over a statutory declaration about facts relevant to the matters mentioned in condition 4.3.1. The form of the declaration is to be agreed by the buyer, who must not unreasonably withhold his agreement.

4.4 Rents and rentcharges

The fact that a rent or rentcharge, whether payable or receivable by the owner of the property, has been or will on completion be, informally apportioned is not to be regarded as a defect in title.

Fig 8.1 Completed Example of Agreement, continued

4.5 **Transfer**
4.5.1 The buyer does not prejudice his right to raise requisitions, or to require replies to any raised, by taking any steps in relation to the preparation or agreement of the transfer.
4.5.2 If the agreement makes no provision as to title guarantee, then subject to condition 4.5.3 the seller is to transfer the property with full title guarantee.
4.5.3 The transfer is to have effect as if the disposition is expressly made subject to all matters to which the property is sold subject under the terms of the contract.
4.5.4 If after completion the seller will remain bound by any obligation affecting the property, but the law does not imply any covenant by the buyer to indemnify the seller against liability for future breaches of it:
(a) the buyer is to covenant in the transfer to indemnify the seller against liability for any future breach of the obligation and to perform it from then on, and
(b) if required by the seller, the buyer is to execute and deliver to the seller on completion a duplicate transfer prepared by the buyer.
4.5.5 The seller is to arrange at his expense that, in relation to every document of title which the buyer does not receive on completion, the buyer is to have the benefit of:
(a) a written acknowledgement of his right to its production, and
(b) a written undertaking for its safe custody (except while it is held by a mortgagee or by someone in a fiduciary capacity).

5. **PENDING COMPLETION**
5.1 **Responsibility for property**
5.1.1 The seller will transfer the property in the same physical state as it was at the date of the contract (except for fair wear and tear), which means that the seller retains the risk until completion.
5.1.2 If at any time before completion the physical state of the property makes it unusable for its purpose at the date of the contract:
(a) the buyer may rescind the contract
(b) the seller may rescind the contract where the property has become unusable for that purpose as a result of damage against which the seller could not reasonably have insured, or which it is not legally possible for the seller to make good.
5.1.3 The seller is under no obligation to the buyer to insure the property.
5.1.4 Section 47 of the Law of Property Act 1925 does not apply.

5.2 **Occupation by buyer**
5.2.1 If the buyer is not already lawfully in the property, and the seller agrees to let him into occupation, the buyer occupies on the following terms.
5.2.2 The buyer is a licensee and not a tenant. The terms of the licence are that the buyer:
(a) cannot transfer it
(b) may permit members of his household to occupy the property
(c) is to pay or indemnify the seller against all outgoings and other expenses in respect of the property
(d) is to pay the seller a fee calculated at the contract rate on the purchase price (less any deposit paid) for the period of the licence
(e) is entitled to any rents and profits from any part of the property which he does not occupy
(f) is to keep the property in as good a state of repair as it was in when he went into occupation (except for fair wear and tear) and is not to alter it
(g) is to insure the property in a sum which is not less than the purchase price against all risks in respect of which comparable premises are normally insured
(h) is to quit the property when the licence ends.
5.2.3 On the creation of the buyer's licence, condition 5.1 ceases to apply, which means that the buyer then assumes the risk until completion.
5.2.4 The buyer is not in occupation for the purposes of this condition if he merely exercises rights of access given solely to do work agreed by the seller.
5.2.5 The buyer's licence ends on the earliest of: completion date, rescission of the contract or when five working days' notice given by one party to the other takes effect.
5.2.6 If the buyer is in occupation of the property after his licence has come to an end and the contract is subsequently completed he is to pay the seller compensation for his continued occupation calculated at the same rate as the fee mentioned in condition 5.2.2(d).
5.2.7 The buyer's right to raise requisitions is unaffected.

6. **COMPLETION**
6.1 **Date**
6.1.1 Completion date is twenty working days after the date of the contract but time is not of the essence of the contract unless a notice to complete has been served.
6.1.2 If the money due on completion is received after 2.00pm, completion is to be treated, for the purposes only of conditions 6.3 and 7.3, as taking place on the next working day.
6.1.3 Condition 6.1.2 does not apply where the sale is with vacant possession of the property or any part and the seller has not vacated the property or that part by 2.00pm on the date of actual completion.

6.2 **Place**
Completion is to take place in England and Wales, either at the seller's solicitor's office or at some other place which the seller reasonably specifies.

6.3 **Apportionments**
6.3.1 Income and outgoings of the property are to be apportioned between the parties so far as the change of ownership on completion will affect entitlement to receive or liability to pay them.
6.3.2 If the whole property is sold with vacant possession or the seller exercises his option in condition 7.3.4, apportionment is to be made with effect from the date of actual completion; otherwise, it is to be made from completion date.
6.3.3 In apportioning any sum, it is to be assumed that the seller owns the property until the end of the day from which apportionment is made and that the sum accrues from day to day at the rate at which it is payable on that day.
6.3.4 For the purpose of apportioning income and outgoings, it is to be assumed that they accrue at an equal daily rate throughout the year.
6.3.5 When a sum to be apportioned is not known or easily ascertainable at completion, a provisional apportionment is to be made according to the best estimate available. As soon as the amount is known, a final apportionment is to be made and notified to the other party. Any resulting balance is to be paid no more than ten working days later, and if not then paid the balance is to bear interest at the contract rate from then until payment.
6.3.6 Compensation payable under condition 5.2.6 is not to be apportioned.

6.4 **Amount payable**
The amount payable by the buyer on completion is the purchase price (less any deposit already paid to the seller or his agent) adjusted to take account of:
(a) apportionments made under condition 6.3
(b) any compensation to be paid or allowed under condition 7.3.

6.5 **Title deeds**
6.5.1 The seller is not to retain the documents of title after the buyer has tendered the amount payable under condition 6.4.
6.5.2 Condition 6.5.1 does not apply to any documents of title relating to land being retained by the seller after completion.

6.6 **Rent receipts**
The buyer is to assume that whoever gave any receipt for a payment of rent or service charge which the seller produces was the person or the agent of the person then entitled to that rent or service charge.

6.7 **Means of payment**
The buyer is to pay the money due on completion in one or more of the following ways:
(a) legal tender
(b) a banker's draft
(c) a direct credit to a bank account nominated by the seller's solicitor
(d) an unconditional release of a deposit held by a stakeholder.

6.8. **Notice to complete**
6.8.1 At any time on or after completion date, a party who is ready able and willing to complete may give the other a notice to complete.
6.8.2 A party is ready able and willing:
(a) if he could be, but for the default of the other party, and
(b) in the case of the seller, even though a mortgage remains secured on the property, if the amount to be paid on completion enables the property to be transferred freed of all mortgages (except those to which the sale is expressly subject).
6.8.3 The parties are to complete the contract within ten working days of giving a notice to complete, excluding the day on which the notice is given. For this purpose, time is of the essence of the contract.
6.8.4 On receipt of a notice to complete:
(a) if the buyer paid no deposit, he is forthwith to pay a deposit of 10 per cent
(b) if the buyer paid a deposit of less than 10 per cent, he is forthwith to pay a further deposit equal to the balance of that 10 per cent.

7. **REMEDIES**
7.1 **Errors and omissions**
7.1.1 If any plan or statement in the contract, or in the negotiations leading to it, is or was misleading or inaccurate due to an error or omission, the remedies available are as follows.
7.1.2 When there is a material difference between the description or value of the property as represented and as it is, the injured party is entitled to damages.
7.1.3 An error or omission only entitles the injured party to rescind the contract:
(a) where it results from fraud or recklessness, or
(b) where he would be obliged, to his prejudice, to transfer or accept property differing substantially (in quantity, quality or tenure) from what the error or omission had led him to expect.

7.2 **Rescission**
If either party rescinds the contract:
(a) unless the rescission is a result of the buyer's breach of contract the deposit is to be repaid to the buyer with accrued interest
(b) the buyer is to return any documents he received from the seller and is to cancel any registration of the contract.

7.3 **Late completion**
7.3.1 If there is default by either or both of the parties in performing their obligations under the contract and completion is delayed, the party whose total period of default is the greater is to pay compensation to the other party.
7.3.2 Compensation is calculated at the contract rate on the purchase price, or (where the buyer is the paying party) the purchase price less any deposit paid, for the period by which the paying party's default exceeds that of the receiving party, or, if shorter, the period between completion date and actual completion.
7.3.3 Any claim for loss resulting from delayed completion is to be reduced by any compensation paid under this contract.
7.3.4 Where the buyer holds the property as tenant of the seller and completion is delayed, the seller may give notice to the buyer, before the date of actual completion, that he intends to take the net income from the property until completion. If he does so, he cannot claim compensation under condition 7.3.1 as well.

7.4 **After completion**
Completion does not cancel liability to perform any outstanding obligation under this contract.

7.5 **Buyer's failure to comply with notice to complete**
7.5.1 If the buyer fails to complete in accordance with a notice to complete, the following terms apply.
7.5.2 The seller may rescind the contract, and if he does so:
(a) he may
(i) forfeit and keep any deposit and accrued interest
(ii) resell the property
(iii) claim damages
(b) the buyer is to return any documents he received from the seller and is to cancel any registration of the contract.
7.5.3 The seller retains his other rights and remedies.

7.6 **Seller's failure to comply with notice to complete**
7.6.1 If the seller fails to complete in accordance with a notice to complete, the following terms apply.
7.6.2 The buyer may rescind the contract, and if he does so:
(a) the deposit is to be repaid to the buyer with accrued interest
(b) the buyer is to return any documents he received from the seller and is, at the seller's expense, to cancel any registration of the contract.
7.6.3 The buyer retains his other rights and remedies.

8. **LEASEHOLD PROPERTY**
8.1 **Existing leases**
8.1.1 The following provisions apply to a sale of leasehold land.
8.1.2 The seller having provided the buyer with copies of the documents embodying the lease terms, the buyer is treated as entering into the contract knowing and fully accepting those terms.
8.1.3 The seller is to comply with any lease obligations requiring the tenant to insure the property.

8.2 **New leases**
8.2.1 The following provisions apply to a grant of a new lease.
8.2.2 The conditions apply so that:
"seller" means the proposed landlord
"buyer" means the proposed tenant
"purchase price" means the premium to be paid on the grant of a lease.
8.2.3 The lease is to be in the form of the draft attached to the agreement.
8.2.4 If the term of the new lease will exceed 21 years, the seller is to deduce a title which will enable the buyer to register the lease at HM Land Registry with an absolute title.
8.2.5 The buyer is not entitled to transfer the benefit of the contract.
8.2.6 The seller is to engross the lease and a counterpart of it and is to send the counterpart to the buyer at least five working days before completion date.
8.2.7 The buyer is to execute the counterpart and deliver it to the seller on completion.

8.3 **Landlord's consent**
8.3.1 The following provisions apply if a consent to assign or sub-let is required to complete the contract.
8.3.2 (a) The seller is to apply for the consent at his expense, and to use all reasonable efforts to obtain it
(b) The buyer is to provide all information and references reasonably required.
8.3.3 The buyer is not entitled to transfer the benefit of the contract.
8.3.4 Unless he is in breach of his obligation under condition 8.3.2, either party may rescind the contract by notice to the other party if three working days before completion date:
(a) the consent has not been given or
(b) the consent has been given subject to a condition to which the buyer reasonably objects.
In that case, neither party is to be treated as in breach of contract and condition 7.2 applies.

9. **CHATTELS**
9.1 The following provisions apply to any chattels which are to be sold.
9.2 Whether or not a separate price is to be paid for the chattels, the contract takes effect as a contract for sale of goods.
9.3 Ownership of the chattels passes to the buyer on actual completion.

Fig 8.1   *Completed Example of Agreement, continued*

SPECIAL CONDITIONS

1. (a) This Agreement incorporates the Standard Conditions of Sale (Third Edition). Where there is a conflict between those Conditions and this Agreement, this Agreement prevails.

   (b) Terms used or defined in this Agreement have the same meaning when used in the Conditions.

2. The Property is sold subject to the Incumbrances on the Property and the Buyer will raise no requisitions on them.

3. Subject to the terms of this Agreement and to the Standard Conditions of Sale, the Seller is to transfer the property with the title guarantee specified on the front page.

4. The chattels on the Property and set out on any attached list are included in the sale.

5. The Property is sold with vacant possession on completion.

(or) 5. The Property is sold subject to the following leases or tenancies:

Seller's Solicitors   :

Buyer's Solicitors   :

©1995 **OYEZ** The Solicitors' Law Stationery Society Ltd,
Oyez House, 7 Spa Road, London SE16 3QQ

© 1995 **THE LAW SOCIETY**

8.98 F35437
5065046
★ ★ ★ ★ ★
3rd Edition

Standard Conditions of Sale

9 Gazumping and gazoffing

No buyer wants to be gazumped.

Most vendors think they should get more than they have already been offered (and accepted verbally), and fancy a bit of gazumping for themselves.

Vendors hate it when
their subject to
contract buyer goes
off – they are
gazoffed.

Vendors hate it when their subject to contract buyer goes off – they are *gazoffed*.

So this will be an even-handed chapter. In business, few people do their opposite numbers any favours. Why should you expect the housing business to be any different?

You must keep control of events and keep your wits about you, as you do when buying a car or a cardigan. You can't possibly win if you 'leave it all' to solicitors and agents. The lazy and shy buy themselves a lot of worry and aggravation by allowing themselves to be tied up with an unsatisfactory buyer or seller, about whom they do not know enough. They bring in too many cooks, who before spoiling the broth, consume a lot of it.

Weak chains that leave you wide open to a gazumper or a gazoffer are created because people who wouldn't dream of going out to buy anything else without cash or credit card gaily go viewing houses and 'promising' to buy tens of thousands of pounds' worth of bricks and mortar, without a round'un in their pockets. Vendors have already promised 'to buy something from someone who has already promised' – and so on and so forth. The pressure is on from day one of the promise. Mortgages being sought; solicitors making mountains out of molehill 'searches'; buyers have to be found to close one end of the chain and vendors the other. The weeks tick by with everybody making excuses to everybody.

Agencies prefer a purchaser who has a house for sale, as they are a fruitful source of business. Failing that, someone who will enrich them by over £600 by buying a mortgage endowment scheme from their agency. But the slightest hiccup or attack of greed has only to rear its ugly head and it's trouble for all. Big trouble.

It is time for some novel ideas. They won't come from solicitors, estate agents or moneylenders, with whom the market is crowded, all trying to get a slice of your cake. Any time they have for inventive thinking is devoted to that one objective.

The government's conveyancing committee found that over the last 10–15 years, the period of time a sale remains subject to contract has gradually lengthened.

One would have predicted that the time taken would have become shorter. Mortgages are easier to get than they have ever been: a prime reason why purchasers can't sign up is, always was and always will be that they need to be satisfied that the vendor has good title to the property. In those last fifteen years, the areas of the country covered by the Land Registry have increased by nearly 50 per cent. Not much remains unregistered. Everybody in the business knows that anything to do with contracts and conveyancing is simpler, easier and swifter once property is registered than it was before.

Everybody also knows that the longer the time between a buyer saying 'I will', and a contract being signed, the greater the opportunity for gazumping, gazoffing and corruption.

So why don't the parties get signed up? What has happened to cause the delay in getting on contract?

The only coherent reasons that come from the professionals are that some local authorities take weeks and months to return the searches, and: 'We are still pursuing our enquiries on the title.'

Less coherent to the layperson, but equally as daft, is: 'We are waiting for engrossments'. 'Engross' means 'write', and engrossing a contract means entering a few lines into the blanks on a printed form.

By the time you have read a little more, you will recognise these for the threadbare excuses that they, are for not having done little jobs that could have been done in their own offices. For instance, you can see in the section called 'Examples of forms' a copy of an actual search form; judge for yourself how long it would take to fill that in and despatch.

What is new is the proliferation and size of chains in which so-called purchasers haven't yet signed up with their own purchasers, who haven't yet signed up with theirs, even unto the third and fourth 'purchaser'. There are more and longer chains. This is what is new. Why?

How many estate agents per 100,000 houses were there in your town 15 years ago? How many are there today? Four times, five times, six times? And they are all fighting for a share of what remains of the saleable houses, after nearly a third of the vendors have chosen the best purchasers for themselves and given the agencies the cold shoulder. So when an agency gets a house that is really saleable and can choose among potential buyers, it would be daft to choose someone who had nothing to sell! Ergo, a chain is born.

Agents can be very persuasive when they are forging another link in the paper chain. They seem to have a good argument when they say it saves a lot of time and prevents breakdowns in communication, if you take their total package, thus keeping the whole thing under one roof. The promise is false; it can't be kept, because as we have seen, the people who attempt to hold chains together are solicitors, and it is a rigid rule of the Law Society (their union) that a solicitor must not act for both parties to a transaction unless both clients are previously established as such. So if there is to be a master mariner at the tiller to navigate seas littered with the twin icebergs of gazumpers and gazoffers, it can only be yourself.

The cure

Flitsville no longer suits you, and you will be a winner if you can decide to sell first. So be business-like, sit down quietly with everybody who lives in your house and whose life will be affected, and decide what you will do, where you will go, how much you can afford, how you will buy, and how you will go about selling.

If you want to move to within a few miles of where you are now, join the 90 per cent all of house buyers who move less than 15 miles. Look at the local property-for-sale columns. How many houses are advertised in the price bracket you will be able to afford? How many more are skulking in agents' files? If, at the time of your family conference, there are half-a-dozen houses for sale that would suit you (if the vendors knocked a couple of thousand off), be sure that if, when you have sold yours, all those six have been sold or withdrawn, another five or six will have taken their place. Why get yourself into chains, gazumping, gazoffing and generally wasting your time, survey and other fees and everybody else's? You can avoid all this if you sell first. And be sure that when you turn up able to produce an official contract for sale of your own house, and mortgage offer, you will be a sight for sore eyes to any vendor. If they say they can't move out in time, put it to them 'You could move in with relatives, friends, bed and breakfast, or pay for us to go in an hotel for the interim.'

A vendor needs to find out the strength of an interested viewer's capacity to buy. In order of preference they are:

1 First time buyers who have a note from a lender saying that, subject to valuation, more than sufficient moneys to buy your house will be on offer (even try to see their bank book showing that they have the difference between the loan and the purchase price on deposit).

2 An 'own house sold' buyer (see their contract).

3 A 'must sell my own house' buyer.

The excuse, 'We have not completed the searches' sounds awful doesn't it? In reality, searching at this stage consists in sending off two forms with ready-printed questions on them to the local authority, who fill in the answers and return them.

Think! Surely any vendor's Skinner should know how long the local authority is taking to return search forms in that area, so why didn't the agency which brags that it liaises with solicitors, get the process started as soon as soon as they put Flitsville on the market? What are these searches?

How to prepare the 'legal' side of your sale

Not only purchasers need replies to the local authority searches before putting pen to contract. If there is a skeleton or a potential crock of gold in the council's cupboard, don't you think, as a vendor, that it would be a good thing if you knew these things before putting your house on the market? You can easily search to find out if your house is registered. If it is registered, all the nonsense about investigating title is a cover-up for delay and an attempt to justify high fees. So you can prove your title before you start to sell, because once anyone's ownership has been registered at HM Land Registry that Title of ownership is guaranteed by the state. If the house is paid for, you should be in possession of your Land Certificate, to prove your title, with which there can be no argument, to anyone. If you have a mortgage, you send a Form 109 off (with current £4 fee) and get a photocopy from the Registry. You can show this copy to serious prospects. That's the investigation of title seen off.

The last place on earth to have left deeds or Land Certificates is a solicitor's office. I have seen piles of deeds on open wooden shelves, stuffed into old sideboards and, at best, 'fire resistant' metal cupboards. A solicitor likes you to leave valuable documents with him. It is his way of trying to make sure that you will go to him again and again. So well and good if this arrangement suits both parties, but it is nice to be able to change. There is power in holding them thar deeds – so have that power for yourself. Get them into the old homestead – safely filed under the piano lid as did the old gent, to whom I will introduce you later.

So you see, a lot of the talk about why house deals take an age is a cover-up for the unscheduled amount of time a solicitor can be detained at the courts, or called to bail people out; refusal to employ sufficient help, downright disorganisation and the arrogance of those who think that only their time is of any value.

At this stage it is worth checking the Council of Mortgage Lenders Handbook referred to in chapter 1 just to see if you have some problems that need to be addressed. Do you have deeds that refer to covenants but details on which are not available? Did you get married a second time and think it was a wonderful idea to transfer you houses to you and your new husband or wife? These and other situations are problem areas and although you might ignore them, your buyer is unlikely to do so. See what the Handbook says about indemnity insurance.

Not STC but CST ...

(Subject to contract, contract subject to ...)

There will be occasions where the vendor and his purchase very much want to secure the sale but cannot, because something is missing, for example uncertainty on a completion date, absence of a local athority search certificate, some problem in obtaining a satisfactory survey or perhaps a mortgage offer.

These are all problems that can be covered by an adequately drafted contract clause, or at least they can be if neither party has a problem with someone else they are dealing with in a chain. Perhaps the first rule to follow is do not contract to buy a new house if you have not sold your existing house. That can cause an expensive headache. Selling before buying is normally less of a gamble. You can at least park your belongings in store and yourself and your family with relatives. Perhaps this is not to be advised if property prices are moving up by the day! So if you wish to sell or buy and you can live with the uncertainty on the completion date and both sides are in this happy position, perhaps a completion date 3-6 months hence would give all concerned a chance to settle their affairs.

The other problems can be dealt with by making the 'contract subject to' or 'CST' to a satisfactory solution to the problem, in hand. Here the cardinal rule is to define what you need to know before you can safely go ahead, make sure the contract can be terminated if an answer is not forthcoming after 2-3 months (say) and decide how to link this to a completion date.

Suppose for example you want to exchange before you have a satisfactory search. You can make the contract subject to that, but questions need to be addressed. Satisfactory to whom and what would not be satisfactory? Suppose it shows the local authority is taking enforcement proceedings for the removal of an extension erected without planning permission? Would that be satisfactory? Probably not. Suppose it says they are widening a road 150 metres away? Would that be satisfactory? Think what questions are being asked, what the answers might be and what would not be acceptable. Generally where these clauses are used, the parties agree a search is satisfactory if nothing is revealed that would have a material impact on the value of the house. This still leaves room for uncertainty and so if the buyer has a few bottom lines, cover them as well.

Suppose the buyer is willing to exchange if a satisfactory mortgage offer is available? Here too, what is satisfactory? Tie this down. If you are the buyer, perhaps any offer would be satisfactory, so if the seller has a relative who is a loan shark, perhaps the seller could engineer an offer 'you cannot refuse', to quote the movies.

Final comment: when drafting, you may know what you want and may be able to express it, but half the trick with any drafting is asking what you do not want. Make sure you cover it and if in doubt take the advice of a solicitor.

10 The Registers

There are two systems of land conveyancing in England & Wales: the registered system, in which case title to the land is registered at the Land Registry, and the unregistered system, where the title is not registered at all. The unregistered is the older, but not many years will pass before all land is registered and thus conveyancing of property made much simpler for all. By the way, all references to land include everything built on it.

It helps if the layperson conveyancer gets an early grasp of the point that all conveyances are of land whether built on or not.

So, it helps if the layperson conveyancer gets an early grasp of the point that all conveyances are of LAND whether built on or not. Whether it sells for a million, or one pound, the recipe is the same.

Official records of the property with which you are about to deal may be found in the three main categories of registry:

1. **The local council**, who are required to keep a register of notices affecting dangerous structures, public notices about infringements of building regulations, compulsory purchase orders, smoke control zones and other things it wants to make sure do or do not happen to the property. When we come to it, you will see that you quite easily find out about that little lot by the simple expedient of sending off a couple of forms (LLC1 and CON 29) which have printed on them the questions you need to ask.

   When buying, you must always carry out a local search, but it is important to realise that it relates to the land you searched and no other. If the neighbours have planning permission to build something you will be offended by, the search will not tell you this and so if you are that fussed go to the council, ask to see some staff in the planning department and ask what they have on the area that you think might be of importance.

2. **The Land Charges Department** at Plymouth, which keeps a register of various charges (mortgages), interests and notices such as second mortgages and Class F charges (right of spouse to occupy the matrimonial home) which cannot be registered at the Land Registry because the Land is not registered. Pending writs or orders (bankruptcy) and pending actions (bankruptcy) are also kept at Plymouth, and you will need to send off a Form K16 to find out

about any bankruptcy orders, writs etc., whether you are buying on registered land or not.

You normally need to carry out these only searches if the land you are buying is unregistered and try to get from the seller a list of the names of all owners from 1926. You may be able to glean many from the documents they send you, but do ask for more. If the solicitor asks why, you will know he has no great experience of the 'old style' of conveyancing. Although you can accept a title back 15 years or so to a conveyance on sale, you are still stuck with any matters registered since 1926. The government agencies will pay you compensation (if you suffer a loss) for any matters that were registered, but which you had no knowledge. However finding out about these gremlins in advance rather than applying for compensation later if a problem arises is the reason for searching all known owners and it was standard practice in the 'old days' for a buyers solicitor to make this request and carry out these searches.

3. **The Land Registry** is the third place where official records of land transactions are kept. This is the one that did the trick of simplifying the act of transferring the ownership of a house from one owner to another. Where a house is on registered land, all the tiresome business of proving title, and tracing back the covenants and conditions through a series of conveyances is dispensed with, because it was done once and for all when the title was registered. And not only that, when the Land Registry sends you a copy of the register which shows that Feather owns the property, a state guarantee is incorporated in it. When you have a Land Certificate produced by the Land Registry showing you as the owner, that ownership is guaranteed by the state.

Initially, the Land Registry Act covered only London and made registration of title compulsory for any sale which took place after 1898 in that area. No extension of the compulsory system of registration was made until 1925. Since 1925, the system of registration has been gradually extended to cover the whole country. However, though what you are buying is in a compulsory registration area, it doesn't mean to say that the owner's title is already registered. If the owner bought before compulsory registration came in for the area, it will only be registered if it is on a biggish, newish development, or if it was voluntarily registered (pre-1966).

Fig 10.1   Specimen of Land Registry entry

HM Land Registry

Title Number : EDN999707

Edition Date : 16 March 1995

A: Property Register

containing the description of the registered land and the estate comprised in the Title.

EDENSHIRE : BLOSSOMTON

1. (16 March 1967) The **Freehold** land shown edged with red on the plan of the above Title filed at the Registry and being 14 Plevna Place, Blossomton, (ED2 8JD).

2. (16 March 1967) The land in this title has the benefit of the rights granted by but is subject to the rights reserved by the Transfer dated 6 January 1972 referred to in the Charges Register.

B: Proprietorship Register

stating nature of the Title, name and address of the proprietor of the land and any entries affecting the right of disposal

Title Absolute

1. (16 November 1977) **PROPRIETOR:** CLINT SMART and CONSTANCE SMART both of 14 Plevna Place, Blossomton, Edenshire, ED2 8JD.

C: Charges Register

containing charges, incumbrances etc. adversely affecting the land

1. (16 March 1967) A Conveyance of the land in this title dated 27 January 1967 made between (1) Thomas Dick (Vendor) and (2) Charles Harry (Purchaser) contains the following covenants:-

   "The purchaser for the benefit of the remainder of the vendors land hereby covenants with the Vendor to the intent that the burden of this covenant may run with and bind the land hereby conveyed to observe and perform the stipulations and restrictions set out in the schedule hereto.

   THE SCHEDULE before referred to:

   1. No further building shall be erected on the said land without the consent of the Vendor.

   2. Not at any time to carry on or suffer to be carried on the said land any trade or business for the sale of intoxicating liquors and no building erected on the said land shall be used except as a private dwelling house.

Continued overleaf

Reproduced by Law Pack Publishing with the permission of the Controller of HMSO

Fig 10.1   *Specimen of Land Registry entry, continued*

Title Number : EDN999707

C: Charges Register continued

2. (14 February 1972) A Transfer dated 31 January 1972 made between (1) Sunshine Investments Ltd and (2) Brian Feather and Pauline Feather contains restrictive covenants.

    NOTE:- *Copy in certificate.*

3. (16 November 1977) **REGISTERED CHARGE** dated 1 November 1977 to secure the moneys including the further advances therein mentioned.

4. (16 November 1977) **PROPRIETOR:** HEART OF ENGLAND BUILDING SOCIETY of Jury Street, Warwick.

END OF REGISTER

NOTE A: A date at the beginning of an entry is the date on which the entry was made in the Register.
*NOTE B: This certificate was officially examined with the register on **16 March 1995.***

Page 2

Fig 10.1   Specimen of Land Registry entry, continued

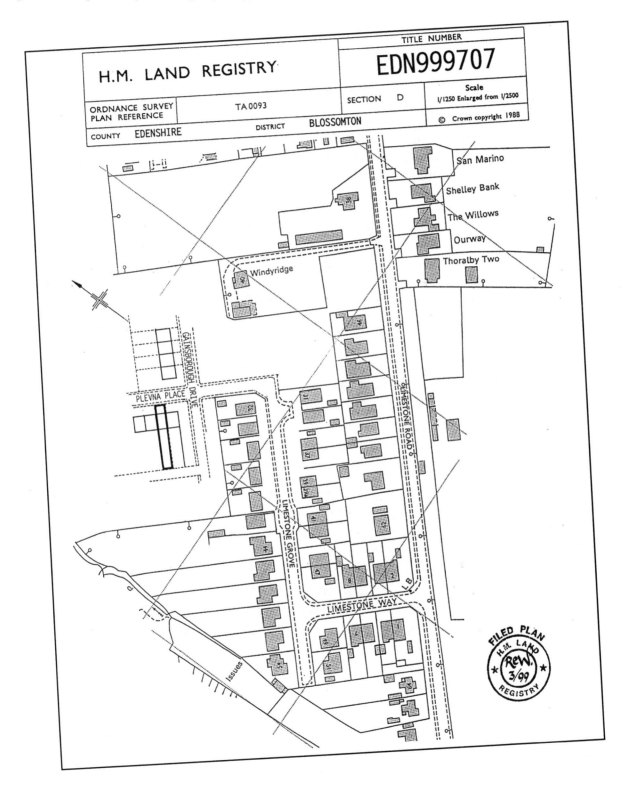

The piecemeal extension of the registration system means that if you are buying in Lambeth, you can be certain that the title will be registered, unless it has been in the same ownership, or constantly transferred by way of gift, since February 1900 (or before); on the other hand, not many properties in Plymouth will be registered because registration only became compulsory in January 1974.

Until 1966, any owner could voluntarily apply to have his ownership registered. But in 1966, registration became limited to compulsory areas, plus those cases where the Registrar can make an exception, e.g. where the title deeds were lost or destroyed during the War, or where there are complex building developments taking place.

If you went to the Land Registry and looked at the actual register, what is produced on the following pages is what you would see. It is also what would be reproduced on the Land Certificate in Mr and Mrs Smart's possession, if they had no mortgage. In view of Charge No. 3 in the Charges Register, the Land Certificate will be held at the Land Registry, and a Charge Certificate issued to and held by the Building Society as proof of their interest.

Though we refer to the Land Registry (singular) it contains a number of registers (plural). These are: The Property Register, Proprietorship Register and Charges Register. The references made to your property in these registers constitutes what used to be known as the 'deeds' to your property and can consist of as few as four pieces of paper having as little as two dozen lines of typing on them.

The registers at the Land Registry are no longer confidential and anyone may inspect and obtain copies of the entries.

The Registrar will at cost supply copies ('Office Copies') of these entries. You are still the registered proprietor, even though you only appear to own financially a tenth of the property, and the lender the other nine tenths. The registers at the Land Registry are no longer confidential and anyone may inspect and obtain copies of the entries. Since 1st April 2000, registered titles disclose the price the registered proprietor paid for his interest in the property. A word of warning: a Land Registry photocopy of the title and of any deeds noted on the title can be produced in court as if they were original deeds; ordinary photocopies do not enjoy this statutory blessing and although this may seem a waste of time and money, a purchaser should always insist on an official Office Copy.

If the vendor contracts to supply an Office Copy or to deduce title in manner stated in section 110 of the Land Registration Act 1925, he is in breach of contract if he fails to do so. One consequence is that if the purchaser does not complete on time, no interest can be demanded for late payment and the powers available to the seller to rescind cannot be exercised till after the breach is remedied.

The key to unlocking the files at the Land Registry is the Title number, which is a reference number. Every registered property has one. The Title number appears at the top of each page of the Office Copies. So that you can see how the Land Registration system works in practice (and what a pleasant surprise awaits you when the simplicity of it all is proved to you on the arrival of the Office Copies), let us take a look at a set which shows the various types of entry which could appear on Mr and Mrs Smart's title to No. 14 Plevna Place, Blossomton, Edenshire. Title number EDN999707.

A swift look through our example will convince you that it is mostly self-explanatory; where it is not immediately clear, hold tight, just a little detective work and clarity is at hand. However, first of all note the number of pages and check you've got them all. Just for fun, the old-style manual register of your property may consist of say five pages and you only get three. Don't panic, it turns out that two are blank, and somewhere on your office copy it will be noted 'pages 4 and 5 are blank. Not photographed'.

Section A: Property Register

This describes the land by reference to the title plan and the postal address, because that is sufficient to identify it. In the case of leasehold property, details of the lease (date, parties, term and ground rent) are given. In this section there is also mention of an entry in the Charges Register – its bark is worse than its bite – more about it later.

Section B: Proprietorship Register

Here we see that in our example the proprietor has Title Absolute and this is the one that you will usually come across. It is the best class of title and applies to 99 per cent of freeholds. The Registrar only gives the description Title Absolute where he is entirely satisfied about the owner's ownership of the property. Title Absolute means that the ownership is guaranteed by the state.

A leasehold property might have title absolute. This is only so in cases where the Registrar can guarantee that the lease was validly granted, because the lessor (grantor of lease) had proved that he owned the freehold or a longer lease of the land. Good leasehold title is shown in those cases where the superior title has not been investigated by the Registrar and is acceptable now only if it satisfies the CML Handbook (paragraph 5.4.2).

Possessory Title: This is very rare indeed. It is the weakest form of title and exists where full evidence is not supplied, perhaps because deeds were lost or because it is based on adverse possession, for example so called 'squatter's title'. Possessory title is acceptable now only if the CML Handbook is satisfied (paragraph 5.4.3).

The Proprietorship Register shows the present owners. Until recently, Land and Charge Certificates also showed the names of previous owners. Office Copies now issued do not show previous owners, as in our example. Likewise, the price paid was shown in some old-style manual registers; all registrations since 1 April 2000 show the price paid.

Look closely at the Office Copy. If no price appears, ask why not. If the property was the subject of a gift, even a partial gift where an owner transfers the house into his or her name jointly with that of spouse or partner, you must appreciate that if the person making the gift is later bankrupted, that gift can be annulled if it took place within five years from the date of the presentation of the bankruptcy petition.

Purchasers in good faith are protected, unless they were aware of the surrounding circumstance; and unless they can prove to the contrary, they will not be regarded as having purchased their home in good faith! They will know of the gift, of course, from the Land Registry entry and they will be at risk.

For this reason, where the buyer can tell the property was the subject of a gift within the preceding five years, it may well be unmarketable unless the seller can satisfy the buyer and his lender that no problems can arise. If these assurances cannot be given - and it is difficult to see how they can be conclusively given - the seller should organise and pay for adequate indemnity insurance.

If you are borrowing to fund the purchase you cannot ignore this. No solicitor who knows of this will sign off a certificate of title for one of the CML lenders if he knows of this, unless insurance is taken out. For those of you with access to the Internet, have a look at section 5.12 of the CML Lender's Handbook for England & Wales at www.cml.org.uk.

Section C: Charges Register

This is where the elementary detective work comes in. So gather round, while I tell you the story behind the sample produced here.

On 16th March 1967, a teetotal farmer call Thomas Dick sold his smallholding together with his house and rhubarb shed to Charles Harry, on condition that Mr. C. Harry wouldn't do any further building and wouldn't convert the house to a pub, or the shed to a disco. The years went by and Mr. C. Harry got it into his head that he would like to build a few houses on the land, so on his accountant's advice he and his Mrs. formed Sunshine Investments and tried to look up Mr. T. Dick, but he couldn't even be dug up, for he had been cremated. They therefore searched out his kith and kin, and found, as is sadly the case in such matters, that kith and kin, reacting against the strong strictures of husband and father, had turned to the bottle with a vengeance once he was out of the way, and, now being on the hard times he had predicted for those who took to the drink, were easily persuaded to remove the restriction on building – for a consideration.

Sunshine Investments, alias Mr. C. Harry, built the houses and sold one to Mr. Feather, who subsequently sold to Mr. Smart, from whom you now wish to purchase. However, before Sunshine Investments were able to do their bit towards solving Mr. Feather's housing problem (their own too) the Blossomton Council planning committee had to be pacified, and they made it a condition that no one actually went to live in the new houses until the new main sewer being built from Here to There had been completed. As the condition has obviously been complied with, the entry is now of no interest to anyone.

Sunshine Investments also got themselves a solicitor, Mr. Newman. He was a young solicitor, and being rather inexperienced in the business, thought that creating the legal framework was all art and no science. Like all young artists, he did not know where to stop. He got out the volumes of Forms and Precedents, got every reference on restrictions, covenants, exceptions and reservations, and tacked them on to every transfer to every purchaser. It mattered not that there were no cesspits, he put in the rules governing cesspits, and preceded the rule with the words: 'if ever there be …'

The Registrar couldn't put all Mr. Newman's blatherings into the Charge Certificate, but they existed, so 'copy in certificate' was inserted as a 'Note'. You will be sent a copy. Sometimes the copy will consist of the last conveyance which was drawn before the land became registered. In any case, it will list the restrictions on the property. And that is the copy that the vendor must attach to the draft contract at 'Incumbrances'.

There is nothing you can do about restrictive covenants. You either accept them or try doing what Sunshine Investments did and buy out the covenantee. Anyway, have a look through them, and if you had intended putting up kennels for dog breeding purposes and find that there is a restriction on using the land for any business purpose, put your thinking cap on. If there is no other property around, you'll be pretty safe, but if the house is on an estate, no doubt all the other houses have similar restrictions entered on their titles. You would only need one neighbour, one light sleeper who never seemed able to go shopping without stepping into a pile of ordure, for your life to be made a misery and your doormat fouled with summonses. That said, there is unlikely to be anything really onerous in the covenants, if indeed there are any at all. But for the general run of people, what are the covenants most likely to turn up? They fall into a pattern and the commonest are:

1 Not to use the house for any trade or business.

2 To keep the fence or fences in repair either by yourself or with the assistance of your neighbour.

3 Not to build another house on the plot or extend the present one without permission from the previous owner.

4 If you build a house on the plot it must be of at least £x in value.

5 Not to do anything to cause a nuisance.

6 The dos and don'ts applicable to all owners on the estate

So, if you find any or all of 1–6 above in either the Charge Certificate or in the copy of covenants, etc. which comes with the Charge Certificate, how do you interpret them for your own purposes? If you are sufficiently irreverent you have no doubt cracked the code for yourself. Irreverence is the key to the door to doing your own conveyance, and a sure shield against being showered with a load of bovinus excrementus which might result in a loss of confidence, which would never do. However:

1 So what? You are buying the house to live in.

2 Probably nothing could be done, as money would have to be spent to enforce it.

3 Put it this way: if the house has a double garden and you were buying with the idea of putting a little bungalow on for your granny, you would ask the vendor to put you in touch with the person who put the restriction on. Ten to one it can't be done, because he will have changed his name to Wraith, and there is but the ghost of a chance of finding his kith and kin who either know or care about the covenant. So you could go ahead and be 99 per cent certain you were safe. There are, of course insurance companies who will indemnify you against that one per cent risk of someone turning up and trying to make trouble.

4 As at (3) above. You might ask Skinner to produce evidence that the house you are buying actually cost that amount to build, but you are unlikely to receive much of a reply unless it is something in the nature of 'there is no builder's receipt in the deeds but the vendor has received no notice of breach of covenant.' In any case, inflation will no doubt have dealt with this little problem.

5 Other people might think that we cause nuisance, but we know that it is they who cause it. They are wrong and we are right, but perverse as always, they think they know best. So we can accept this covenant because firstly, we never cause nuisance and secondly, we have an ordinary common law obligation, like everybody else, not to cause nuisance anyway.

6 If we didn't like the results achieved already by this covenant we would not want to live here anyway. There is an added bonus for the layperson conveyancer because you will know, and have a copy of, this little lot and if any of them start upsetting any of us we will know that as usual they are in the wrong.

Covenants are promises, and the only difference between a covenant and any other kind of promise is that it is contained in a deed. At some point in the history of the buying and selling of the land in question, some owner has said in effect to a buyer, 'I will only sell to you if you will promise this that and the other, and also promise that when you sell, you will have your buyer make the same promises to you, and so on ad infinitum'.

There are two important things to be said about this ruling-from-the-grave covenanting. Firstly, many a covenant is so imprecise that it is difficult to say if it is or ever was enforceable, and secondly, it is difficult to say who could enforce it anyway. In general, it is difficult, if not impossible, to enforce any covenant expressed to be in favour of a person, without reference to land he owns or owned and which is affected by the covenant.

If you come across a 'no building or extension' covenant in the Charges Register of a property you are thinking of buying, and your inspection has shown the covenant to have been broken, what do you do about it? The first thing is to ascertain how long the extension or building has stood there. In addition to the owner's say-so, ask for some independent evidence to be produced. Although not conclusive, if reliable evidence shows the breach occurred more than 12 years earlier, the covenant is generally no longer enforceable. But the breach is still a blot on the landscape, as the CML Handbook (paragraph 5.7) requires indemnity insurance to be obtained if the breach is less than 20 years old. Any person who retains a solicitor to act for him whether as a purchaser or as a bank or building society will or at least should know of this requirement and should demand that the vendor fund insurance against risk; not necessarily the risk that the covenant is enforceable, but the risk that any owner who tries to sell or mortgage within the 20-year period will be faced with a demand that he meets the cost of such an insurance policy.

If you are the vendor, you can put the potential buyer's mind at rest by offering to insure him against risk for the next ten years. If you are the buyer, you can pull a long face and say that but for your partner's silly emotional feeling for the place, you would have cried off immediately and you will now do so unless a few pounds are knocked off the price agreed before you knew about this diabolical covenant.

Vendor

Having read earlier about bargaining, you will know that emotion will overpower reason every time so if you can catch the eye of his partner for a few seconds, test the strength of the emotion – if it is genuine you are home and dry at your original price.

However, purchasers who can manage to pull off the reduction-for-covenant gambit, the next step is to get the insurance – if you feel it is really necessary; and that is the dead hand of the past dealt with.

Entries 3 & 4 refer to the present owner's mortgage. 'Charge' is an abbreviation of 'Legal Charge' and that is the fancy term for mortgage.

In our example, we have not been able to cover all the things that might be entered on a Charges Register. For instance, one of Smart's lenders might not like further mortgages to be entered unless they know about it, so you get 'no disposition of the property may be made without the prior consent of the proprietor of Charge No …'. Don't worry, the lenders will not let go without their money, so their charge (mortgage in this case) will be deleted when you come to register your new ownership. There might be something about Capital Transfer Tax monies having to come out of the proceeds of the sale on the death of Mr. Croakes. It's nothing to do with you, it's Croakes' executors' problem.

Another really irritating one is where there is an entry that the land is subject to covenants set out in a deed dated the umpteenth of Nerth. In the remarks you then read 'deed not lodged with the Registry'. If at first and subsequent registrations, nobody bothered to protect their interests by telling the Registry what the covenants were, it is extremely unlikely that they ever will. But like it or not, because of the CML Handbook (paragraph 5.7), the prudent purchaser will now insist that his vendor funds indemnity insurance for the reasons stated above.

You're not really reading a whodunnit, so you are allowed to see how Mr. Newman's story ends when you come across the real mother and father of Rigmarole in, and referred to in the Property Register, and it starts off about sewers and unmade roads and rights across them. Ten to one you will find that the rigmarole was inserted as a condition of planning permission being granted for the estate to be built. Once the house was completed and its drains connected to the main sewer in the road, and the council had taken over responsibility for the maintenance of the road (it had become a public highway) and the sewer, the rigmarole became of academic interest only, except in so far as all subsequent inspectors of Office Copies have, at least, to give it a quick glance.

It is unlikely that you will come up against a caution. Like many other terms and phrases in the lawyers' armoury, 'caution' has an ominous ring to it, so let us cut it down to size before the few readers to whom it might apply are faced with it. Cautions are, almost without exception, hostile. That is because a caution is used where the owner of the property will not co-operate with a person who requires protection of his or her interests. If you come up against a caution, the vendor should already know about it, and as he wants his sale to you to go

If you come up against a caution, the vendor should already know about it, and as he wants his sale to you to go through, should already have made arrangements for the caution to be removed.

through, should already have made arrangements for the caution to be removed.

The most common caution you are likely to see entered nowadays is one by a wife or partner who wishes to let all who are interested in purchasing know that, though the house was not bought in joint names, it is, in fact, the matrimonial home. Registering the caution makes sure that if the person whose name the house is in tries to sell or mortgage the house, the cautioner will get to know if anything is stirring, and can then take appropriate action.

A prospective purchaser who finds a caution on the register will quite rightly ask the vendor to have it removed by clearing up whatever problem exists between himself and the cautioner. A caution against dealing can be withdrawn at any time without fee, using Form WCT. The vendor will persuade or induce the cautioner to write to the Registrar asking for the removal of the caution (Form WCT) from the Register and the caution will be removed promptly and without involvement of fuss or feathers.

However if the vendor knows the caution to be simply silly and vexatious, he himself can apply for its removal. He must do one or the other or both, and purchasers need proof that he has done so before completion. The Registrar then gives the cautioner notice of the proposed dealing, and informs him that he intends to remove the caution. The onus is then on the cautioner to take action, and if he doesn't make a serious objection within 14 days after notification, the caution is cancelled. The caution has been 'warned off'. When he hears from the Registrar, the cautioner may, if he wishes, put his case to him. The Registrar has a wide discretion, and he can, after hearing both sides, do what he thinks appropriate, i.e remove the caution from the Register; refuse to let the proposed dealing proceed; allow the proposed dealing to proceed, but subject in some way to the cautioner's interest; give a time limit within which the cautioner must institute legal proceedings, or have the caution removed. All the Registrar's discretionary decisions in these instances are subject to appeal in the courts.

Note B at the end of the register tells you when the copy, in our example 16th March 1995, was taken from the actual register. Office Copies come to you from the Registry by first-class post, but even so they are obviously out of date by the time you are proving to yourself how simple it all is by glancing through the entries. On the 17th March the Smarts could have sold the house to Mr. GA Zump, and he could have registered the transfer to him on the 18th March 1995 before you have time to do anything about it. Here you are with a copy of the register which clearly shows Smarts as the owners on the 16th March; how could one possibly stop the ubiquitous Mr Zump? There is a way, and again, it is a form, 94A by number. You will meet it again later and be properly introduced.

11 Introducing conveyancing for laypeople

This chapter is an introduction to conveyancing. Liken it to the picture on the lid of a jigsaw puzzle box. Having studied it, you can then start interlocking the pieces contained in the rest of this Guide.

Having read so far, you are ready to do your own conveyance. While reading what follows, if you have a flow diagram-cum-checklist, keep it by your side.

There is of course, a lot that is slightly technical which you might have to read twice before you think that you have grasped the point. You will certainly, as with any technical instruction, find that understanding comes the quicker when, instead of just the printed page, you have the actual nuts and bolts of the job in front of you. Every time you wire an electric plug it becomes easier – it's the same with conveyancing.

In the days when a solicitor could act for both parties, even if he had never acted for them before, I met an aged gentleman who was selling a house he had lived in for over thirty years. When he was asked who his solicitor was, he said quite simply 'I don't need a solicitor. I own the house, the deeds are under the piano lid, and when I get my money, the buyer can have keys, house and deeds, and I'm off into a Home with the proceeds.' I gave him a receipt for the deeds and took them to Donald Turnbull, solicitor for the purchaser, who, being the wise old bird he was, made no fuss and got on with it. After all, what had he to do? He looked at the last conveyance in the pile, made sure that the purchaser therein named was the aged gentleman, and bingo, aged gent had proved title (it is even simpler and safer nowadays where we have registered title). A month later the old boy was ensconced in the Home, terrorising the Matron with his merciless logic.

So if you have got your house paid for, follow the example of the aged gent, by getting your deeds. Whether your house is paid for or not, get the whole file of your purchase transaction from the solicitor who acted for you years ago (as you are fully entitled to it, having paid his bill) and pop the papers under your piano lid to be ready.

As you take your first, confident step, keep firmly in mind that you are out to achieve three things:

1 Save yourself a lot of money, particularly if you are buying as well.

2 Get the purchase price safely out of the buyer's pocket and into yours.

3 Make certain you are completely shot of the house and have no continuing liabilities, which you do by virtue of Clause 3 in the 'Special Conditions of Sale'.

No. 1): to save all that lovely money, read on. No. 2) only requires that you are numerate and can count the money in banknotes or recognise a telegraphic transfer for the same sum. You may have jibbed just a tiny bit at No. 3). Don't. Just think of the hassle, worry and money you're about to save yourself. In any case, even if you pay Skinner & Deskbound, you will no doubt have to do most of the running about for yourself, and also fill in the kind of forms that solicitors send to their clients nowadays.

Selling a registered house

Whether you intend to travel 50 yards or 50 miles, your journey begins with a single step. You may not know whether you can walk 50 yards let alone 50 miles, but you have not much to lose by risking one stride, and emboldened by the success of that one stride, you will not lack confidence for the next two. So let me give you, the layman conveyancer, the confidence to take that first stride by explaining step-by-step how to complete the simplest of all housing transactions, that of selling a second-hand, freehold, registered house in England or Wales, which is free of mortgage.

Step No. 1 is to get out your Land Certificate and copy the title number on to Land Registry Form 109, Application for Office Copies and add your name and address. Look in 'Example of Forms' at the back of this Guide for details. A few days later, you will then receive a set of copies of everything carried by the Land Register about your house. This does not extend however to individual documents noted on the register, such as a transfer where the title says 'Copy in certificate' or where the copy is filed with another certificate. Your buyer will ask for these and they can be ordered using form 110.

While waiting for the Office Copies to come from the Land Registry, spend a few minutes making up three copies of the contract. Keep one copy for your file and put the other two, with the Office Copies, when you receive them, into an envelope, addressed to the purchaser or his Skinner, with a covering letter saying that you are acting for yourself in the sale of your house. Stund, of Skinner & Stund, will probably shudder with horror, but will write back acknowledging receipt, and, as though such a thing had never been heard of before, will ask you to confirm that you are indeed acting for yourself. In return for your confirmation, he will send you a letter giving the game away that he knew all the time that people are doing their own conveyancing nowadays. He will then say he must make it clear that he will 'take no responsibility for you in law or otherwise'.

There is no kind of business in the land that isn't regulated by general and particular laws which protect those with whom they deal. Nobody can write themselves out of the law, and nobody should know that better than Stund. What 'or otherwise' means I just don't know – you try asking. I've never managed to get a sensible excuse, let alone an explanation. Though you might feel like writing in retaliation, don't bother; it is best to take no notice. You have already landed a left and a right where it hurts most, in the pride and in the pocket.

You may now receive from Skinner printed 'Enquiries before Contract' or 'Pre-contract Enquiries' or even his own endless list of typed questions; they are all known colloquially in the trade as 'preliminary enquiries' and they may be referred too as such by Skinner, whatever they are actually called. They comprise questions for you to answer! Or you may be asked for the 'Seller's Property Information Form'; the idea is the same: to supply routine information to the buyer, but here the seller has to obtain the form and volunteer the answers.

It is up to each solicitor to decide whether to send you enquiries or ask for you to volunteer answers by means of the 'Seller's Property Information Form'. However, these are different from an examination paper, because you only have to answer the questions to which you are absolutely certain you know the answers. If you don't know the answers, or are not certain about them, you calmly ask the examiner to check up for himself by replying 'not as far as I am aware, but please make own enquiries', or simply put 'I don't know'. At first reading, the form may appear quite fearsome. But really it is quite straightforward, if you keep it firmly fixed in your head that you don't intend giving any hostages to fortune, and you intend cleaving to the old established precept of caveat emptor, which is Latin for let the buyer beware. Buyers please take note.

> **There is no kind of business in the land that isn't regulated by general and particular laws which protect those with whom they deal.**

In the parcel under the piano lid, you might find the form your solicitor received from your vendor's solicitor when you bought. From that, you will see how little a solicitor is satisfied with, when he is protecting his paying customers in the parlous procedures entailed in the biggest business operation of his client's life. 'To the best of my knowledge, no, but please rely on your own searches'. 'I don't know'. 'There may be, but never brought to my attention'. These are the kind of woolly replies to give and expect to woolly questions. Remember also that if you answer any question 'to the best of my knowledge' or more cryptically, 'not to my knowledge', the law expects you to have made reasonable stab at finding out the answer. If you cannot be bothered and use these phrases to avoid the the trouble of checking out the answer, do not be surprised if you get a writ (now called a claim form) for any loss your buyer thinks he suffered because of your insouciant indifference to his question.

Remember, conveyancing is an administrative business transaction, and only becomes judicial when such things as fraud raise their ugly heads.

Remember, conveyancing is an administrative business transaction, and only becomes judicial when such things as fraud raise their ugly heads. In any case, you are not replying to the Solicitor General, or the Lord Chancellor, or, in most cases, a solicitor even, but to a clerk in a solicitor's office.

However, Skinner could pick on some answer you have given and ask you to be more specific. If so, and you honestly don't know the answer, just stick at it, saying you have nothing to add. If he seems to be giving you the run-around, consider the possibility that he knows the proposed purchaser has gone off. If you do suspect this, check up with the purchaser direct. **Though solicitors consider it unethical for one solicitor to speak with another solicitor's client, there is no law, rule or ethic on earth that prevents the two principals (in this case vendor and purchaser) discussing matters between themselves.**

When your replies to the 'Enquiries before Contract' or 'Sellers Property Information Form' have been accepted and your contract approved, it will be signed by Feather and sent back to you. You now collect the deposit and in exchange, hand over your copy of the contract which you now sign. Do not be surprised if the solicitor tells his client you should not be paid the deposit, in case you pinch it. The solicitor may suggest he be allowed to act as 'stakeholder' rather than you. All this expression means is that whoever has the money must hand it to the seller if the sale completes. If it does not, it stays in limbo unless the contract is rescinded. In this case the seller gets it if the buyer is in default, but it is returned to the buyer if the seller is in default. If you have this problem you will have to deal with it as best you can, but remember if you are buying a house at the same time and are using the Standard Conditions of Sale, you can still require your buyer to allow the money to be released to the solicitor who is acting for the person selling your new property to you. Remind youR buyer's solicitor of this; that might persuade him to review the position. He, after all, will know that if you are paid money without quibble and do pinch it his insurers will probably have to refund it.

If you have arranged for someone else to act as stakeholder, repair to his office and exchange the contract you have signed for the one signed by the purchaser, and see to it that the balance of the deposit is handed to the stakeholder. Contracts have now been exchanged. Your sale is now tied up. If the buyer backs out, you have to decide whether to be merciful or merciless. That is to say, you give him back all, part or none of his deposit, depending on the circumstances.

After exchange of contracts, Skinner may send a questionnaire entitled 'Requisitions on Title'. Treat it with Olympian calm. Requisition means question. Title means ownership. So, he is asking you questions to find out if you are the owner, when all the time you know and he knows you are the owner, because it says so on the Land Registry Proprietorship Register, and your title (ownership) is thus guaranteed by the state. In reality it is very unlikely you will be asked much about the title. They keep changing the form, so you may get questions raising problems which have already been solved, like 'where completion will take place', and 'have you got receipts for rates and such like bills paid?'. In the main, the questions are to do with practicalities: what's the position on rates, do you have the deeds, how do we get the keys, where do we send the money and so on. I know it's difficult, but try to be courteous, remembering all the while that even if you were paying a solicitor, all these problems would still be yours to solve, because he would only be acting as a post box.

Skinner, on behalf of your purchaser Feather, now sends you a Land Registry Form TR1, in draft state, for your approval. This is the form which authorises the Land Registry to transfer the house out of your ownership into Feather's. If the draft is in order, and it can scarcely be otherwise, as it only calls for names and addresses to be filled in, the money and the property, accept it and write acknowledging the fact. Sign the Form TR1 at the first signed 'as a deed line' in the presence of a witness, who also signs, and then hold on to it (see section called 'Examples of forms' for details). There is nothing to do now but while away the time before completion date by dreaming about what you will spend the money on.

If your buyer is supposed to sign it because it contains an indemnity covenant, make sure the buyer signs it before you do. Indemnity covenants? Go back to chapter 10, 'Section C: Charges register' for a refresher. The law on covenants is a bit of a tangle. If you sign a transfer that contains them, the person who sold you the house (or others depending on the circumstances) can sue you if your buyer breaks any of the covenants. Covenants on land are an area (law not geography) where lawyers in Victorian days got themselves into a bit of a tangle. First, they decided positive covenants involve spending money: to keep a fence in good order or to contribute to maintaining a fence, drains or a road. They decided negative or 'restrictive' covenants do not involve spending money: covenants not to run a bawdy house or burn bricks, for example. Then they decided that if X covenants with Y to that do not involve spending money, anyone who can prove they have or acquired the right to enforce restrictive covenants can sue Y's successors. .

This is not the case with positive covenants. So you need your buyer to promise to indemnify you if he breaks them and you are sued. The only remedy your vendor may have in these cases is to sue you, if he can find you. If you can get the money back from your buyer, fine. If not, tough! The Standard Conditions of Sale require your buyer to add an indemnity clause to the transfer, but do not be surprised if the point is overlooked and it never appears in your transfer. As the person at risk, it is for you to make sure it is not left out when you are sent the draft transfer for approval.

If your house has a leasehold title, the landlord can continue to pester you for the rent and service charge if your buyer does not pay it, unless the lease was granted after 1st January 1996. You do not need an indemnity covenant in this instance since the law implies one.

Remember also the covenants you give in the transfer. Your promise to sell with full title guarantee, for example, places certain duties on you. If the house has a leasehold title you promise you have complied with all the covenants. Solicitors normally make a point of adding a clause to the effect that these covenants should not be construed as your promise the premises have been repaired and decorated in strict conformity with the lease.

Sometimes purchasers will ask you to let them have the keys before completion. If Feather needs to get the money from the sale of his own house to Dither, in order to buy yours, it can be difficult for him. But if Dither gets knocked down by a bus on his way to complete, and you have let Feather into possession of your house, it will be a great deal more difficult for you.

Sellers of a vacant property will no doubt be asked to accept an undertaking from Feather that if you let him have the key solely for the purpose of decorating and repair, he will not go into possession. Now it might seem a bit dog-in-the-manger to refuse, and Skinner might try to assure you that it is the usual thing, and the undertaking he has drafted for Feather to sign gives you ample protection. If you feel under pressure, write to Skinner and ask for his personal indemnity underwriting the Feathers' undertaking. You never know, he might give it. But if he can't trust his own client, how can you?

A CHAPS payment is the layperson conveyancer's best friend, but a solicitor is unlikely to make such a payment and trust you to hand over the deeds. A personal completion utilising a bank draft is more likely.

If the buyer is all tied up at his end and cannot attend the completion personally, leave the keys with a neighbour you can trust. A further qualification to being trustworthy that the neighbour requires is to be on the telephone, because the keys must not be handed over until you have rung up saying all is well. On completion day toddle along to the appointed venue. You will have with you your Land Certificate, the completed Form TR1 and the keys (if not with the neighbour). If the deposit is being held by a stakeholder, Skinner will, in addition to handing you the balance of the purchase price, give you a letter authorising the release of the deposit. You give Skinner the Land Certificate, Form TR1 and the keys. And that is your sale completed. That is conveyancing in a nutshell. Now to the detail.

> **A CHAPS payment is the layperson conveyancer's best friend, but a solicitor is unlikely to make such a payment and trust you to hand over the deeds.**

12 Conveyancing: the sale and purchase of a registered house

The previous chapter on selling a registered house confined itself to the work a vendor of such a house is faced with. The reason for limiting its scope was so that you could judge for yourself the simplicity of the operation. Indeed, anyone who is good at making a precis will have already noted that a very simple transaction indeed could be carried out, and it goes like this:

A purchaser goes to a house that is for sale and says, 'I will give you £75,000 for it if you can prove to me that you are the owner'. The vendor says, 'Come back in a couple of hours with the money'. The purchaser returns with the money and confirms that the vendor is ready to leave and the house is vacant. The vendor has his Land Certificate and a signed Form of Transfer in one hand and the keys in the other. The purchaser swaps his £75,000, for those three items. The deal is done.

The purchaser sends the Land Certificate and the Transfer to the Land Registry and is now the registered proprietor.

Because people tend not to take other people's word for things nowadays, it takes a bit longer than this, but basically what appears above is the beginning and end of a sale and purchase of registered land. It contains everything that has to be done to transfer ownership.

The instructions that follow are for the purchase and sale of a freehold dwelling in England or Wales, which is already registered.

The procedures for buying from a council are completely different; leases and gifts are special cases.

The instructions should also be read with reference to chapter 9, regarding contracts. For the purpose of illustration, we will assume that you are a first time buyer and need to take a mortgage, or that you are the vendor of a £75,000 house. There is some repetition of what has gone earlier – unfortunately, it cannot be avoided so please look on it as part of the teaching and learning process.

Vendor: As soon as you seriously put your house up for sale, send off an Application for Office Copies Form 109 and Form 110 if necessary (see 'Examples of forms' section). Fill in your name and address and

Title number, which you have got from your Land Certificate, your lender or the solicitor who acted for you when you bought (he cannot charge you for this service, by rights he should have performed it earlier), and- with a cheque for £4 for each copy required- send it to the appropriate Land Registry, the address of which you will find in the Appendix of this Guide. Notify your lender/s that you will be redeeming your mortgage/s.

Purchaser: Until you are sure you can find the money for the purchase, sign nothing, apart from the lender's application form. Any letters you send to anyone must have written somewhere about them 'Subject to Contract' and it is safest to keep on doing that right up to the point where you do sign the contract.

I take it for granted that you will keep your wits about you, and have at some time completed a licence or passport application form, and have, therefore, clerical expertise. That little caution given, I will not labour the points that are usually made ad infinitum and ad nauseam elsewhere, about how careful one must be. It would be all right if such labourings genuinely helped people either towards a better understanding, or to being able to cope for themselves and ease their worries, but when, after scaring the living daylights out of you, the only advice given is: go to a professional to deal with a contract for you, survey for you, buy for you, sell for you, it's just a waste of reading time. You can always leave things to others – at a price – and people had to when they were illiterate.

One cardinal rule, and it goes for all business transactions is: never let go of both ends. Have the house, or have the money. The cynic would say, preferably have both, but never be in the position where you have neither.

Before committing yourself to anything, re-read the section on contracts because the vendor whose heart you warmed with those magic words, 'I would like to buy your house', has been on the phone to Skinner and gleefully said that he has found a buyer and Skinner says 'Leave it all to me'. What, at this point, Feather has left to him is the sending of a draft contract and that is what in the fullness of time you can expect to receive, but he might also write to you as he did to our vendor in the previous chapter, saying that he won't be responsible for you in law or otherwise. If he does, join in the fun by ringing up Feather and ask what Skinner is covering up – what is wrong with the house, is it down for road widening, is there a deed missing, has he got the scrolls or hasn't he? – plus any further nonsense you can think up. Then forget about it.

Vendor: Send off to the purchaser's solicitor two copies of your draft contract and the Office Copies which you should have received by now.

Purchaser: Receive draft contract and possibly Office Copies. If you do not get a Land Registry office copy and file plan, demand it. The Standard Conditions of Sale make it the duty of the seller to prove his title in this way, admittedly only after the contract, but it is customary for the seller to supply these before contracts are exchanged. Do not be fobbed off with a photocopy made in the office of your seller's solicitors. This may be useful as a starter but do not leave the matter there. The Land Registry frequently update the format of these so why be fobbed off with something that might well be out of date?

Peruse the Office Copies in the light of the knowledge you gained from chapter 11, 'The Registers'.

Put the draft contract on one side for a while. Content yourself with asking the vendor's solicitors if they are sending you the Seller's Property Information Forms and if not, send them two copies of the Enquiries before Contract or preliminary enquiries. Before you do, have a quick look at these, and if the questions they contain don't cover everything you would like to ask about, and hopefully get a sensible answer to, put those extra questions in writing. For instance, buyers of new houses should ask: 'Is the design, construction and layout of the sewers such as will meet the criteria required for their adoption by the water and any other authority?'

Buyers of new houses should ask, 'Is the design, construction and layout of the sewers such as will meet the criteria required for their adoption by the water authority?'

Vendors now have to deal with preliminary enquiries (see page 109), if you have not sent the Seller's Property Information Forms already and purchasers can look over their shoulders. Indeed, anyone who has not coped with these enquiries before, will do well to have his seconds ready in his corner, for this form will be the one that will (at first) make you wish you had never bothered, that is, until you have really started pencilling in some replies in the copy which is intended for you to keep. As you read on and pencil away, the colour will come back to your cheeks, and you will realise how childish it was to be frightened.

Most of the questions are easy, daft, or both, but we will have a quick run down Enquiries before Contract, first noting that in some of the forms the column headed 'Replies' already has displayed in bold type at the beginning or end 'These replies on behalf of the vendor are believed to be correct but the accuracy is not guaranteed and they do not obviate the need to make appropriate searches, enquiries and inspections'.

The law assumes you have made all proper enquiries, so do not place too much reliance on this disclaimer. Also, the law on misrepresentation still applies, as should the good old British principle: 'my word is my bond'. The following are common questions which appear in one form or another.

a   One relating to boundaries and whether you know of any disputes about them. If you know the answers, give them; if you are not sure, use the formula 'I know of none' and give the same answer to the question on notices, particularly in so far as it refers to your predecessors in the house.

b   One asking for copies of any Housebuilding Council guarantee, Insurance Policies covering defective title, or road maintenance agreements, if you have any, comply, if not, you can't; so just reply 'none in my possession'.

c   Questions about whether services such as gas, electricity, water and drains are connected, and if any of them come to you through someone else's property: the first part is easy, the second is easier when you know how. Answer: 'Please rely on your own survey'. Deal with the question about access and roads in a similar fashion. About rights of way: if you know of any say so, if not, say 'I'm not aware'.

d   There will normally be a question that could frighten you out of your wits and send you scurrying off for legal help. Don't let either happen. It asks 'Please give full details of all overriding interests affecting the property as defined by the Land Registration Act 1925. s.70(1)?' This question refers to other people's rights over the property. If you don't know of any, answer 'I am not aware of any, but the property is sold subject to any that there may be'. Having answered that question, you've broken its back.

It's down-hill all the way now and you can answer the remaining questions with variations on our old friend 'I don't know of any, but please rely on your own survey'. Even with the question about Rateable Value, though you have the latest Council Tax bill sitting in front of you, it is safest, and perfectly acceptable to reply 'I think £x, but please check with local authority.'

Even though you have specified the fitted wardrobes, shelving and such like in a final clause of your contract, this doesn't stop the question cropping up again. You will find this kind of duplicate questioning happening all the time. You just have to put up with it and give it the short shrift it deserves. You are asked how long will it be after the exchange of contracts, before the vendor (he means you) is able to give vacant possession. The usual period is one month, but of course you may make it longer, shorter or tag on to whatever date you give 'or before'. So give a date which you think is suitable to the purchaser and also make it clear where and how you insist on having the money: 'Vacant Possession will be given on completion which will take place at (state venue) on the umpteenth of Nerth. A CHAPS payment will be required for the balance of the purchase price.' A cheque or a banker's draft could bounce.

You will also be asked when possession of the property will be given. You answer, 'When I receive the balance of the money by CHAPS payment on completion'. No solicitor would agree to completion not taking place in his office; he would be negligent if he sent off his client to an alternative venue, money and the mortgage money by CHAPS, without having the deeds. If you are also buying a house, you may wish to add a suggested completion date to tie in with your purchase, but see later for more on this subject.

When the preliminary enquiries have been completed to your satisfaction, send them off. They may come back with supplementary questions, and some of them may appear to be intended to annoy you. Don't let annoyance creep in, just press on, courteously pointing out that you can only sell what you have got, but you are not a qualified surveyor, and if he wants to be absolutely certain where such things as the drains run, he is welcome to have a sniff around provided he does no damage.

It takes some believing, but this is the right way to deal with the Property Information Forms, and Skinner's acceptance of your answers will be your proof.

Purchaser: Receive the Property Information Forms form, duly completed and glean from them what you can. Though we made fun of the question about overriding interests on behalf of our vendor, do be careful that as a purchaser the laugh is not on you, because under Section 70(1)(g) of the Land Registration Act, 1925, it is now possible for someone, apart from the registered proprietor, to claim rights of occupation (and the courts will not shift them), even though they have not registered that right anywhere. It is wise to ask if there is anyone over the age of 17 living with the seller who is not also an owner of the house. If the answer is yes, it is wise to get them to sign the contract to provide a written assurance on their part they claim no interest in the house and will vacate on or before the date the sale is to be completed. If you do not do this, they may still be there when you move in and with a better claim to the house than you! In matrimonial situations, the spouse's right of occupation is registerable both for registered and unregistered titles.

So at the risk of repetition: throughout this Guide you will find endless warnings about making sure, before you sign a contract, that the vendor can give you vacant possession on completion, and NEVER EVER complete the purchase of a house before you have seen with your own eyes that the house is completely vacated, and that if there has been any kind of dispute about ownership and/or occupation, that the locks have been changed. If you think you may gain further enlightenment by asking supplementary questions, ask them, but remember they were stock questions, so you can't expect better than stock answers. Best of all is to make a trip to the property and, using the form as a check list, go through the items with the vendor.

At the risk of repetition: never ever complete the purchase of a house before you have seen with your own eyes that the house is completely vacated.

And it is at points like this, that layperson conveyancers like us come out on top because we leave our desks and look at the problems – not the papers about them!

Have a look at boundaries, walls and fences with your own eyes. The general run of houses, in town and suburban areas have clearly defined garden walls, hedges and fences; but in rural areas it isn't always so. However, first check what is within the boundaries against the plan in the Office Copies. A 'T' mark against a boundary indicates that the owner of the land on which the 'T' is situated is responsible for the upkeep of that boundary, wall or fence. Otherwise, strong (but not conclusive) evidence is that the owner of the land on which the fence posts are situated (which hold up the fence) is responsible for that fence. If there is more within the fences than the plan shows, it is possible that your vendor has pinched it. Ask him about it. Ask the neighbour. If there is a problem, it isn't much trouble to move a fence, but what about a garage? Always check that a garage is within the boundary shown on your plan. Indications that there may be a dispute about boundaries, or whose responsibility it is to maintain a particular fence, could be evidenced by its broken-down appearance. If you have any reason to suspect that there is any kind of dispute, go hot foot to the neighbour and ask his point of view on the matter particularly if it is about a shared drive.

Disputes between owner-occupiers of suburban properties about who owns what and who can go where, are the most frustrating, intractable, time-consuming and above all ruinously costly to resolve at law.

Disputes between owner-occupiers of suburban properties about who owns what and who can go where, are the most frustrating, intractable, time-consuming and above all ruinously costly to resolve at law. If you come across a hint of such a dispute, my advice is, run a mile. Hard lines on the vendor who hasn't had the courage or foresight to come to terms with his neighbour; his best hope is that his prospective purchaser has not read this book and the business is being conducted at arms length by Skinner, Write & Reams, so that Feather is blocked from the knowledge by a heap of paper and only finds the pig after moving into the poke.

If, in order to get to the house or garage, you have to traverse an unmade road, or anything which looks as if it may not be a public right of way (the council will tell you if it is, in reply to your enquiry form – see later) there should be a note on the Office Copy, saying you have a right of way over the track or common drive or whatever. On the other hand, does anyone else have a right of way over the land which is shown, on the plan, to be that which you are contemplating buying, and if so, who will be responsible for the shared access way's upkeep?

If the copy of the deed plan which came as part of the Register has produced no satisfactory answer about the approach to the property, ask the vendor or the solicitor what is proposed. Usually, it will be that the vendor makes a statutory declaration that he has used the way for 20 years or more and this is usually thought to be acceptable. It is evidence that the access has been in use for so long and the law will adopt a convenient fiction to the effect that a right of way does actually exist. However if there is any hint that the land is common land, under no circumstances let the matter rest there. The right to drive over common land cannot be acquired by long use; it is a criminal offence to drive on common land without some other lawful justification. If you hope to drive over the common to Shangri-La make sure you have a proper written right granted by the owner of the common to an earlier owner of the house you plan to buy. The same thing goes for such things as fences. If you come across the one case in a thousand where rights of way etc. are diabolically complicated, but nevertheless the house is virtually unique, the house of your dreams and a bargain to boot, what do you do? You make a common-sense appraisal of whether to drop the matter, or try going forward with the purchase by telling Feather's lawyer to have a look in his books to see if he can find a remedy that you can take.

It would be a surprise if you found a house that had electricity which was not connected to the mains. The owner would probably be so proud of his generator and his independence of 'those wicked power workers' that he would show it off without being asked. If the gas supply was bottled you could hardly miss the evidence. Nevertheless, check both.

If you have any doubt about the water supply, have a swift look for the lid of the cast iron box which houses the stop-tap and is usually to be found just outside the boundary to the front garden. If you are buying out in the sticks and think that the water supply may be coming to you across someone else's land, write to the local water authority and ask them. If the answer you receive is in the affirmative, then you have a further point to investigate, 'what will happen if the water supply is stopped, for any reason, by this neighbour?' If the vendor or his solicitor had anything about these matters, there should be such a letter in existence from a previous purchase. Even if there is, it will still be worth while writing and quoting the letter and asking if things remain the same.

Drains can be a bit of a stinker. All your life you have simply pulled the string or pushed the plug, and what has to go has gone, and you never had to give a second thought as to where it was going or how it could possibly get there. The thought that it would answer back and refuse to go was too awful to contemplate. Buyers in built-up areas can be pretty sure it goes into the main drain, where it goes after that we don't worry our heads.

A house which is not connected with the main sewer will almost certainly drain into a cesspit/cesspool or a septic tank. In the case of the latter, the owner will need to have it emptied every four or five years, depending on the size of the family (the former do not have to be emptied). This is no problem. Everything functions as if there were a mains drainage, but when the tank is cleared by hydraulics into a tanker, there is a bill to pay. When the water companies started to send their bills separately from the Council tax accounts, they divided the bill between water and sewerage charges. At which the septic tank owners said 'Oh, no!' to the sewerage charge, and won their point. All of which little excursion into recent history is to tip you off that the water company's bill, unless it shows a specific charge for sewerage, will tell you that you do not have connection to the main sewer.

The Property Information Forms tell you that no building requiring permission has been carried out in the past four years.

More difficult to establish is whether you drain through anyone else's land, or vice versa. The cases where this is likely is where a house has been built in the garden of another house. It could become really important if you wanted to build an extension or garage.

So have a look round at the manholes, you might learn something, but as manholes have sometimes been covered over, this inspection may not be sufficient. If you intend spending a lot of money on your extension or garage, get your builder in to have a poke around – if there is bad news he will delight in giving it to you. If necessary, look in the Yellow Pages for a firm that specialises in sniffing around the drains and get a quote.

You are told that no building requiring planning permission has been carried out in the past four years. Does that square with what you find on inspection? For our purposes, just about everything needs planning permission, but often the permission comes from the law: The Town & Country Planning (General Permitted Development) Order 1995. Telephone the planning department where the house is located to see what they can send you regarding these provisions. It is worth the effort. Houses can be enlarged without permission subject to certain conditions. Roofs can be added or enlarged. Porches can be added. Sheds, garages and swimming pools can be added. Parking spaces can be laid. Satellite antennae can be installed. In all these cases, if the works come within the very detailed limitations laid down by the law, no further planning permission is required. Overstep the mark, and it is! But they still have to get, and be built in accordance with, building regulation approval, which is a different thing from planning approval. If your vendor gives a categorical answer no, or even (if he has lived in the house for less than four years) the time honoured 'not as far as I am aware', you may think that sufficient. A solicitor would, unless someone like his client, alerted him otherwise.

Vendor: Receive any supplementary questions and answer them as best you can.

Purchaser: Receive answers to supplementary questions and decide whether to settle for what you are being offered. If you are satisfied, you can now involve yourself in the expense of sending off a few forms with their appropriate fees.

If you are borrowing money, carry out a Land Charges Department bankruptcy search using form K16 that is sent to the Land Charges Department at Plymouth. The search is against you and your partner if buying in joint names. All you do is write in your names as required in the form and pay £2 per name. It is required by your lender, so first ask if they plan to do their own. If so, you will be charged, so save your money. Otherwise, do it about eight working days before the date for completion. Your lender will wish to see the answer.

Enquiries of Local Authority CON 29, together with Search of Local Land Charges LLC1, can be posted to the local council, just as Skinner & Deskbound would do. Ask about the fee; it varies.

However, I suggest that you take them to the council offices, and do a real search around for yourself while you are there. Ask if you can have a look at the development map and the planning applications approved and pending. Don't attempt to use the jargon. Keep it simple. You will get two surprises. Firstly, how much help you get if you start the service by smiling, and saying to the official, 'I wonder if you can help me?' and secondly, the amount of information you can so easily pick up that you won't if you simply rely on the forms. Care is needed, though. Some local authorities give less information on a personal search than they would in reply to a professional one (in some cases, it is the really important information, such as planning records, that is withheld).

The town development map is divided up and each division is coloured. Some are even coloured and hatched. How a division is categorised tells you what the council intends for it. If the area is coloured, say a dirty brown with black dots, it could mean that the area is intended for obnoxious industries. If anyone owns a house in that area and he wants planning permission to convert it to a bone and bladder boiling factory, he might get it. A nicely coloured pink area might mean an area primarily intended for residential use, and if you send off your forms of local search, those are the kind of answers you will receive. That is to say, you would learn: it is an area intended for say, obnoxious industries, green belt, inner ring road or residential – and that is all.

If you want to know if anyone is even thinking about doing something nasty at the bottom of the garden, ask.

If you want to know if anyone is even thinking about doing something nasty at the bottom of the garden, ask. Particularly if you are buying property bordered by a peaceful plot of land containing succulent fruit and veg; even better, where beyond the prospective patch there are open fields. What a lovely view! What a set up for anger and frustration, if you simply send off the forms in the usual manner and wait for what the gods send.

In a few months you could be looking at a brick wall and someone else's line full of washing where you thought you had a view over the undulating countryside. As soon as you saw the builders coming, you would be off to your legal advisers asking what you could do about it and why you had not been told what to expect. You will now find that in addition to facing a brick wall, you are banging your head on one and paying legal fees for the privilege of doing it. That's when it will be borne in on you that in spite of all your GCSEs, 'A' levels, degrees and diplomas, you are a twit. You bought land (with a house on it) in an area designated residential and you are now surprised when a house builder gets busy with the bricks and mortar creating residences in the area. My dear reader, this isn't a question for a lawyer, it's plain common sense and a problem of understanding the English language!

What can you do to save yourself from twittery? When you go to the local council offices, ask to see the list of planning permissions granted in the area over the last ten years or so (the spread of years is important – people often sit on development permission for years, but councils give the permission subject to time limits which vary – ask). Then be really cute and ask for the list of planning applications pending!

When you leave the forms, the official will tell you when to expect the LLC1 and CON 29 to be returned to you, bearing the council's stamp, which gives a warranty against negligent replies on their part. When they do arrive, have a look through for anything unusual. So unusual is it for anything unusual to appear, the authorities have duplicated replies ready. Even so, duplicated or not, you want the job doing properly, otherwise you wouldn't be doing it yourself, so you will scrutinize each answer. If you find anything you don't understand call the local official and ask.

If in spite of all the form filling and chatting up of the officials, you still suspect there might be something nasty in the pipe-line, have a chat with the Citizens Advice Bureau and the local newspaper to see if they know anything to the area's advantage or disadvantage.

Local Authority fees tend to vary from council to council and may change frequently, so you need to ring them.

There is very little to fill in on the two forms you take to the Council Offices. CON 29 form is in two parts. You require Part I answering and it will cost you a fee to have that done for you. Local Authority fees tend to vary from council to council and may change frequently, so you need to ring them.

You will learn from the replies you receive about such things as whether the road fronting the property is maintained at the public expense, whether the council are about to grab any land within 200 metres of your boundary in order to lay new roads, and whether they or the appropriate Secretary of State intends constructing a road, underpass, overpass, forward pass, flyover or elevated road within 200 metres of the property. The form does not ask about 201 metres plus, that is why layperson conveyancers come off best, because they have a chat with the officials. They do not have sleepless nights every time they read in the newspapers about some poor soul waking up to find the council ready with some diabolical scheme that will either knock the house down or tens of thousands of pounds off its value.

Part II of CON 29 won't get answered by the council unless you specifically asked them to do so. Have a look down the 13 questions and see if you think any of them might have a bearing on the house you are interested in buying. It will cost you extra for each of the questions in Part II that you tick, as an indication to the officials that you require that particular question answering. The kind of things you can learn from ticking a question range from 'Has the council authorised the service of a building preservation notice' to 'Has the council or the Secretary of State authorised the making of an order for the compulsory acquisition of the property?'

The requisition for a Search of the local land charges register form LLC1 is even easier to complete. It has to be sent in duplicate and it comes to you with a copy, all you have to do is insert a carbon, tick that you require all the register searching, put the address of your intended purchase and your own name and address in, enclose the fee and that is it.

There are further searches you should carry out using a letter or appropriate forms. First, telephone the local water company, ask whom to speak to about water and drainage enquiries and then talk to them to see what a search costs. Then write with a cheque. Until recently this information came from answers to CON 29 but no longer. The water company will answer the questions and send along a plan showing what is connected and what can be found in the area, so if your house is not connected to their sewers, you will be able to see if there are sewers in the area and you will be able to ask the cost of connection.

Environmental issues are now all the rage. The CON 29 may give meaningful answers to environmental questions, but many solicitors now carry out online environmental searches or 'envirosearches'. For a fee, these will tell you what is happening in your area - if it appears - in any of a wide variety of paper records. Is your house in a flood plane? Was it built on infill land? What is the risk of subsidence? Have their been environmentally unfriendly activities in the area? etc.

Two specialist searches that may be necessary are coal mining searches and commons searches. You now get coal mining information on your envirosearch (so far as it exists) and commons searches should be made only where it seems relevant to do so. If you are buying a house in an inner London borough there is probably no need for this, but if you are buying in the country there probably is. Even if the area seems to have been residential for some time, open land near by could be common land and there have been cases of houses being registered (incorrectly) as common land so it can be worth checking. This is particularly so if you are buying an idyllic house with a private access across 'Greenfield Common', or similar. Go back to page 121 to see the danger you could be in if the road crosses a common and the house has no reliable paper rights of access.

You the purchaser can now turn your attention to the draft contract. It has to be read through and a decision made as to whether the terms are acceptable or not. It is not a take-it-or-leave-it situation; that is why it is a draft contract. If there is anything about which you are not clear, speak to the vendor, his solicitor, or both, and get one or the other to explain (not explain away with excuses such as 'it's usual') until you understand. If there is anything with which you cannot agree, strike it out. Here are nine points you should watch out for when perusing the draft contract:

1 Compare the information given in the preliminary enquiries with what the solicitor has written concerning the items, referred to as 'chattels' in the Agreement, which the vendor said he was including in the price agreed?

2 Is the amount of deposit stated correctly? If you are using the 'Standard Conditions', you can use the deposit from your sale as the whole or part of a deposit for your purchase, providing it is held by a solicitor as stakeholder. If you aren't using the 'Standard Conditions', put a clause in the contract allowing you to use your purchase deposit.

3 Check to whom and under what conditions the deposit is to be paid. You should insist that whosoever receives the deposit does so as stakeholder, because a stakeholder cannot part with the money unless he has been satisfied that completion has taken place. You may have paid a holding deposit to an estate agent, or even the whole amount of the deposit, if so the clause about the deposit should take care of that situation.

4 There should be a clause stating the capacity in which the vendor sells, called 'Title Guarantee Full/Limited'. If such a clause does not appear in the draft contract, ask for one to be inserted. If the vendor owns in his or her own right insist they sell with full title guarantee. If they do not - executors of an estate for example, they will wish to sell with limited title guarantee. Be especially careful if the vendor is not going to sign but has appointed an agent under a power of attorney to sign. If he sells by power of attorney, you are entitled to a copy of the power; if as executor or administrator, probate or letters of administration with Will annexed out of the Principal Registry or district Probate Registry is sufficient proof of a person's death. In the rare case of a lender selling after a borrower's default, you will be pleased to hear that you do not concern yourself with whether the 'mortgagee (one who lent) in possession' is properly exercising his rights under the mortgage. Ninety-nine per cent of vendors are giving Full Title Guarantee and if yours isn't, ask their solicitor to give you the real evidence that they might have the right to sell.

It is not unusual, however, for a vendor to place some limit on his responsibilities. His solicitor will generally name the bits he does not want his client to subscribe to. You will have no idea what this means unless you look at the legislation which is The Law of Property (Miscellaneous Provisions) Act 1994. A decent local library should hold Halsbury's Statutes of England and you can look it up there. However if you are on the internet or have a friend who is willing to do this for you, print off a copy from www.legislation.hmso.gov.uk/acts.htm.

If there is anything in the contract you feel should be amended, mark it in red ink and send it back to the vendor.

5 Here is a nice easy one for you. Check that the address and/or description of the property to be sold is correct. If the property being sold is part of an existing registered title, then you should also be provided with a plan, for more detailed inspection.

6 If you were told that you are buying a freehold, check that it says so in the description.

7   If your vendor agreed to include items such as carpets in the sale price, they should be in the contract, but if the price you are paying is just over the level at which stamp duty becomes payable, fix a price for the item ($£x$) and ask that the clause has added to it 'and $£x$ of the purchase price shall be apportioned to these items'. On the other hand, take account of how this will affect your mortgage. Building Societies don't lend on furnishings. So, say their maximum advance is 90 per cent and you are buying at $£50,000$, your top mortgage is $£45,000$; so if there is $£2,000$ worth of carpets etc. included in the purchase price, the highest the building society surveyor can value the house at is $£48,000$ and the maximum advance is $£43,200$, so your deposit now becomes $£6,800$ instead of the number you first thought of. Bear in mind, however, that it is highly unlikely that a solicitor, acting for a vendor, would allow unrealistic apportionments to be made, since this would be a fraud on the revenue. Therefore, I leave to your honesty and ingenuity the rest of the sums on which your decision rests.

8   Look at the rate of interest (contract rate) in the contract. This is usually 4 per cent above bank base rate. If it specifies the Law Society's rate, that is 4 per cent over the base rate of Barclays Bank. You will be expected to pay interest at that rate if you delay completion beyond the date which eventually gets inserted in the contract. The most likely reason for you getting caught with having to pay this type of interest will be if your purchase monies are dependent on the sale monies from your present house, and you can't make your purchaser complete simultaneously. If the rate is the same as in your sale contract, and you have your purchaser tied to 4 per cent above bank base rate also, then you have a source from which to collect any penalty money. Unfortunately, the period for which this interest is payable is limited. After the time allowed in each contract, the deposit is forfeited by the seller.

9   Covenants Clause: with the draft contract, Skinner should send you a copy of all the covenants. There is not much you can do about them, but you certainly want to know everything there is to know, because you buy property warts and all, and once you are the owner, you will be responsible for seeing that the covenants (if any) are adhered to.

You can also ask to be assured that the previous owners have kept to the covenants. For instance, if there is a covenant that only a certain type of house should be built on the plot, and plans should have been approved and agreed by some previous owner, ask to see the approvals. If there is anything in the contract you feel should be amended, mark it in red ink and send it back to the vendor.

Remember, if there is a suspicion that there has been a breach of covenant within the last 20 years, no Council of Mortgage Lenders (CML) member will lend money on the house unless someone pays for restrictive covenant indemnity insurance and since it is your vendor's blemish, not yours, make sure it is a term of the agreement that he pays and get an offer before you contract.

Purchaser: When agreement has been reached on the draft contract, you can put it to one side and give your attention to the replies you will have received to your enquiries of the district council.

Enquiries of Local Authority form usually comes back with a printed list of answers. In 999 cases out of 1,000, it will confirm that the road is made up, taken over and maintained at public expense: that there are no road widening proposals, and no proposals to build a new road within 200 metres of the property. If you had been afraid lest the council had an army of workmen at the ready, itching to get on with demolishing a garage or extension which had previously been built infringing building regulations and planning permission, the replies will either confirm your suspicions or put your mind at rest.

If it turns out that the road is about to be made up, you will want to know what the cost is likely to be and how much the vendor is prepared to knock off the price to meet it. If the property is about to be pulled down for slum clearance or the infringement of building regulations, your course of action is obvious.

Having called at the council office, you will have put flesh on the bones of the more-or-less standard answers on the form. You will have found out if there is to be a motorway within 201 metres or whether there is any development scheme in the offing that could affect the property, being either a whole shopping precinct, or an application to convert the quaint little antique shop on the corner to a fish and chip shop. In the unlikely event of you getting a reply which you do not understand, either call in on the council or give them a ring.

Form LLC1 will drop through your letterbox at the same time. The council will either certify that 'the search requested reveals no subsisting registrations' or 'the search reveals the registrations described in the schedules hereto…'. If there are any schedules

> If there is any verbiage that you don't understand in the replies to your searches and you think it could affect you, ring up the local council and ask.

attached, they are likely to refer to smoke control and planning controls that have long since been dealt with. The search might show that an improvement grant was agreed. That does not mean to say the grant was taken up, but you will want to know from the vendor if it was, and if so, whether any part of it has to be repaid on a sale taking place. If there is any verbiage that you don't understand in the replies to your searches and you think it could affect you, ring up the council and ask – council officials are invariably helpful to the learner conveyancer.

You are now almost in a position to send off your signed part of the contract, either in the form it was originally drafted or as amended by agreement.

It is about this time you should be thinking of insurance and so re-read the information on 'risk' at page 79. The first question is should the insurance come into force when you exchange or when you complete? Then how much do you insure for? It should be for the reinstatement value of the house and all necessary expenses and it should be inflation-linked. This sum may well be less than the price you are paying, but then the land is not going anywhere is it? Only the buildings are at risk. If you are borrowing, the lender's valuer will probably have stated the minimum level of required insurance. Otherwise you are on your own!

In its offer of a mortgage, the lender may nominate an insurance company. Unless you have some root and branch objections to the nominees, get your insurance with them then write and let the lender know. Check that the offer of a mortgage which you have received is a firm one. In addition, if your purchase is dependent on receiving the monies from your own sale, you will realise that ideally the contracts should be signed simultaneously, but this is difficult to imagine because it entails getting all the parties together at the same time in the same place, and if everyone is taking the same precaution then all would need to be ambidextrous. The only sensible solution therefore, if your purchase is dependent on your own sale, is to make absolutely certain that you have received your sale contract signed by your purchaser and that any conditional clauses can and will be met, before you sign up to buy, and that if necessary you can find overnight accommodation.

So here is your checklist on the eve of exchange of contracts:

1 Draft contract has been agreed and one of your copies has been returned unsigned to vendor.

2 Satisfactory replies have been received in the Seller's Property Information Forms or Enquiries before Contract.

3 You are satisfied with the replies you received to the forms you sent to the council, what you learned on your fact-finding tour and to your water company and envirosearch.

4 If the Office Copies revealed anything such as a caution or a Matrimonial Home charge, the vendor has obtained cancellation of the registration of such a charge or notice.

5 You have got a firm offer of a mortgage.

6 If it applies, you have your own sale tied up. If a deposit cheque bounces, the contract is automatically washed out.

7 You have checked that everyone over the age of 18 who lives in the house is prepared to move, whether their names appear on the register or not, by getting them to sign a statement to this effect in the contract.

So here goes! Insert the agreed date for completion into the contract. This is usually one month hence, so if you feel there is still a lot of reading left in this chapter also remember there is one month to do it in. There is no reason why it shouldn't be earlier than the usual month if it will save either party paying money on bridging loans. Sign the contract and send it off to Skinner, together with the balance of the agreed deposit, which will need to be sent early enough to clear - the usual period is four working days. Alternatively, you can send it in the form of a bank draft or electronic transfer. Finally, don't forget to put the date of signing at the top of the contract.

Two words of warning. Skinner needs to know whether he can exchange with you or whether you have other plans, e.g. are you waiting for something like a search certificate, amended mortgage offer, or for your own buyer to reach the stage where he or she can exchange with you; so unless Skinner has your carte blanche to exchange on receipt tell him to hold it to your order till you are ready to release contract - that is, allow him to exchange with you. Also, if there is a chain with you in the middle, you may well find you cannot exchange at all since no-one will trust you to honour your word. You can show them your tattoo 'Death before Dishonour', but it will cut no ice. What happens, for example, is the buyer at the bottom of the chain tells the next one up that he is ready and that contracts can be exchanged before, say, 4.30 that day. If the recipient is ready, he tells the next person up the line and so on. The system works because the authority given is irrevocable and is backed by the professional ethics that solicitors adhere to. All of whom should also be insured against error. You do not enjoy this sainted status and will be seen as the 'Weakest Link'. The answer is get Skinner to act as your agent, so it is his word people act on, not yours. What he does for you is purely a private matter between the two of you.

Vendor: we have not forgotten you! The astute reader will have realised by now how little a vendor has to know or do in order to be his own conveyancer. However, you must rouse yourself, at this point, to receive the signed contract from the purchaser. Check that the contract he has signed is identical to the one you have agreed to and have a word with the stakeholder to make sure the deposit will be paid.

> **Lenders need a solicitor to say whether you are getting a good title to the property, and to handle the signing of the mortgage deed and the crucial finale of handing over the money.**

Even if your purchaser is getting a 100 per cent mortgage, I think you should still insist on a deposit. After all, if he is such a good risk that the lender doesn't require him to have a stake in the house, he should have no difficulty in raising a bank loan for 5 per cent of the purchase price. If you don't get a deposit, your contract is shaky. As pointed out before, there is a difference between having rights and asserting them. You really cannot get blood out of a stone and possession really is nine points of the law. Sign your copy of the contract and send it to the purchaser.

Contracts are now said to be exchanged. The deal is now binding and neither side can back out without penalty. If you have a mortgage on the property write to your lender saying that contracts have been exchanged. Ask them how much will be required to pay off your mortgage on the completion date. Also ask for the daily rate that will be charged in the unlikely event of completion being delayed.

Purchaser: receive vendor's part of the contract and check details. Pay particular attention that both parties have signed if it is owned jointly. While all this has been going on, you have been dealing with the solicitor for the lender. Every building society has what it calls a roll of solicitors who act for it in the completion of mortgage advances. Lenders need a solicitor to say whether you are getting a good title to the property, and to handle the signing of the mortgage deed and the crucial finale of handing over the money.

Most solicitors are on the rolls of most mortgage lenders, although CML members are suspicious of sole practitioners. So when a purchaser gets a mortgage, what do you know, the solicitor acting for him in his purchase may also get instructions to act for the lender. It makes sense by saving too many solicitors trailing round too many other solicitors' offices to complete a sale.

The solicitor acting for the lender will write, asking you to produce a number of documents. As the information contained in the papers they request could in the future be quite useful to the layperson conveyancer, photocopy them, because lenders usually keep the lot.

This is what they require:

- Enquiries before Contract and vendor's solicitor's replies or completed Seller's Property Information Forms.
- Local Authority search forms and replies.
- Vendor's part of the original contract.
- Land Registry Office Copies.
- Copy of transfer.
- Replies to Requisitions on Title.

You will have noticed one new item in the above list. It need not cause you any trouble. It is the transfer, the very form which does the trick of getting your vendor's name off the Land Register and putting yours on. The transfer form is TR1, and you will remember meeting it on the very first page of this chapter, and now you come face to face with it, you will find that, though of supreme importance, it is the easiest of the lot (example provided in 'Examples of forms' section at the end of this Guide).

Buyers on new estates will require Form TP1. The draft is usually provided by the developer, because he wants to put in a swathe of conditions that were not in the conveyance of the land to him.

After exchange of contracts, you are expected to send a draft of the transfer form to the vendor's solicitor. At '1. Stamp Duty': when the transfer attracts Inland Revenue Duty the stamps will be impressed here before the transfer is lodged for registration. If no duty, or duty at a reduced rate is payable, complete one of the two certificates below '1.' as appropriate: put 'x' in the first box only if property is exempt from stamp duty, e.g. a gift. There are eleven different categories, so check with an Inland Revenue Stamp Duty enquiry office which yours is. Put an 'x' in the second box if the price of the house is priced £60,000 or below. Fill in the Title number, which by now you will almost have memorised, the address of the property you are buying, leave a blank for the completion date, put in the price you have dragged the vendor down to, exclusive of cost of any extras, then put in the name and present address of the vendor and finish the labour by inserting your own name and new address. If you are married or buying jointly with someone else, decide what is to happen when one of you dies (no. 11). So if you are buying jointly, put both your names. If two names are not those of spouses, the house can still be owned so that the survivor takes all (joint tenants), or so that a share goes into the deceased partner's estate (tenants in common), normally a half. In either case, the Registrar has to be informed and we will deal with how later – for the moment if you want the ownership to be in joint names simply put the two names on the form.

Finally, complete the certificate of value which the revenue man requires –he doesn't trust the property owning classes. If you can manage to buy a house for £60,000 or less you have no stamp duty to pay. Agree to pay the vendor an extra £1 if he will leave the cat-flap and with a purchase price of £60,001 you will have to pay 1 per cent stamp duty (£600). Being a free born Englishman the revenue man expects you to get up to every trick in the book in order to side-skip paying your money over to him. Unless you sign otherwise, he suspects you of trying to buy the house in bits: £5,000 for the billiard room, £5,000 each for each of the bathrooms and £2,000 each for each of the bedrooms and so on, all done in separate transactions. So the revenue insist that you certify that the 'transfer hereby effected does not form part of a larger transaction or series of transactions in respect of which the amount or value or aggregate amount or value of the consideration exceeds £...'. If the purchase price is £60,000 or less, that is the figure you put in. You enter the next higher figure, either at which tax starts to be payable (£60,000) or at which stamp duty increases - at £250,000 it increases to 3 per cent and over £500,000 it increases to 4 per cent.

Vendor: receive the draft transfer and check it. Also check the amount being paid and the spelling of all names.

Purchaser: Your conveyancing doesn't have to be done overnight. If, from reading the instructions so far it seems to you that there are a lot of fiddling little things to do, bear in mind three things.

In the first place they are mainly practical and not legal. Secondly, even after contracts are exchanged, you should have approximately one month to do it all in. Lastly, but fruitiest of the lot, a number of people's hopes are riding on your buying the house and it is surprising how helpful others can be when they need to be.

During the next few pages references to yourself, your lender's solicitor, the vendor's solicitor, his lender's solicitor and where you are selling at the same time, your purchaser's solicitor and his lender's solicitor, not to mention the lender's solicitor for your own sale if you are changing lenders, could lead you to think that for completion day you might have to put up a marquee (light refreshments to be served) in the garden or, if wet, book St. Pancras Town Hall. NOT SO. Solicitors are capable of wearing many hats at the same time and you'll no doubt finish up with only one if you're a first time buyer, or two if you are involved in a chain.

Send off two Requisitions on Title forms. This form asks questions about the date for completion and what money will be required: a completion statement. It also asks the vendor to produce receipts for outgoings and is mainly referring to rates.

If the Seller's Property Information Form or Enquiries before Contract were completed again now, it asks, would the replies be as they were hitherto. A question concerns mortgages. It starts strongly with 'all subsisting mortgages must be discharged on or before completion' but then weakens and goes on to ask what form of undertaking to hand over receipts is proposed. So if on the Charges Register of the Office Copies you received, there was a charge (mortgage) to a finance company, write in the space provided for additional questions: 'Form DS1 to be provided by mortgagee with charge certificate duly sealed and signed.'

The vendor or his solicitor must twiddle his thumbs till the mortgagee condescends to type sign and post it on. They will not issue a DS1 before completion to a solicitor and certainly not to someone representing himself. Plus, some do not do this, taking advantage of the recent Electronic Notification system.

The best a purchaser will get is a solicitor's undertaking to pay off the mortgage and send DS1 on as soon as he has it. If the vendor is acting for himself, no purchaser should accept such an undertaking since it is not backed by The Law Society; but probably in this case the lender has its own solicitor to act on the redemption of the mortgage, so the purchaser can simply ask for information on what is due and then pay it himself out of the purchase price asking the lender's solicitor to supply the undertaking.

He can even do this if the lender is not paying anyone to represent its interest, but trying to get anyone in their offices these days who can be relied on for anything more than reading out blurb on a computer over the telephone can be a bit difficult. The whole point about big money lending institutions is that ideally everyone else does the work for them and without charging; in recent years the dumbest kid on the block, who will still happily do this is, and pay insurers to pick up the tab if anything goes wrong, is the less than street-wise solicitor. He or she rests secure in the vanity they are professionals, and a man or women of note in their community, while everyone else gets on with reality.

A note of warning here to purchasers acting for themselves: most mortgage lenders are CML members and they expect their borrowers to get legal advice on their responsibilities and liabilities as a borrower. Before you contract to buy the house then make sure the people you are borrowing from are not going to insist you get advice or need to sign before a solicitor even as a mute witness. The trouble with borrowing other people's money is that they can lay down rules like this. After all, they do not lend money for your convenience, whatever their marketing department might say.

The vendor's solicitor should provide any information and documents you will require in order to register your ownership, but he might, just for fun, retain papers or information you are going to need. But not to worry, because in sending you the Standard Conditions of Sale, he has bound himself to provide all the documents you will need.

Also, use the space at the end of the form into which you can feed any additional questions that your lender may ask in response to the documents you will have sent them. Their response will also almost certainly include:

1   The printed mortgage form for you to sign in front of a witness. Have a scan through the mortgage form (legal charge) but don't invite a headache. It is a take-it-or-leave-it situation – no variations are allowed. Nowadays, most lenders insist that mortgage documents are executed in front of a solicitor. As you are not planning to use a solicitor, arrange one of two things with such a lender, either to sign on completion in front of their solicitor or for them to waive the point. It isn't a legal requirement, being neither oath nor statutory declaration.

2 An account made up of the fees you have to pay their solicitor, Land Registry fees, pre-completion search fees, stamp duties, etc. The total will be deducted from the money produced on completion day.

3 A sheet of requisitions (questions) about your purchase. Lenders don't have a standard form. You will find that the questions are more or less the same as you asked the vendor's solicitor in your enquiries before contract.

Copy off the answers you were given and if there are any you haven't already got the answers to, get on to the vendor's solicitor right away and get the answers back to the lender as quickly as possible, in case they raise supplementaries, as you can do without being harassed by their questions right up to completion day.

This form will also ask you if you intend to live in the house and to confirm that the whole of the difference between the mortgage advance and the purchase money is being found out of your own resources and without recourse to any other form of borrowing. The lender might also enclose a list of any further documents they require on completion. If they don't, ask them to let you have such a list as soon as possible.

4 If applicable, NHBC Form 12 and the NHBC agreement itself.

Vendor: receive Requisitions on Title. If your purchaser's solicitor is asking for things you simply do not have, say so. Remember, when you bought you no doubt paid a highly trained solicitor to check out that you were getting a good title, so if he was satisfied on your behalf, your purchaser's solicitor should be happy with what his brother in the law did.

Make up a completion statement as requested, by showing purchase price minus deposit paid. Don't worry about the Council Tax because it is levied on the occupier; simply let the Local Authority know the date you are moving out and if you have managed to overpay Tax they will reimburse you. The purchaser cannot be required to pay for water if you have paid in advance; so ask your water company for an apportioned rebate up to completion date.

Purchaser: receive replies to Requisitions on Title Form and completion statement. If you are buying without a mortgage, you can skip the next bit until we come to Form 94A. About this time you should be in possession of the list of documents your lender will require on completion. They will always require a minimum of:

1 Vendor's Land Certificate (or Charge Certificate if the house is mortgaged).

2 Vendor's lender's solicitor's undertaking to send you a Land Registry form DS1 discharging vendor's mortgage.

3 Transfer Form TR1 signed by the vendor. Form TP1 if buying from a builder, TR2 for a re-possession.

These three forms you will, of course, receive from Skinner on completion. The rest of the documents your lender will ask you to produce are:

4 Mortgage form (Legal Charge) signed by you.

5 LA451 Particulars Delivered form sometimes referred to as PD form supplied by Inland Revenue Stamp Offices (see chapter 13 for completion instructions).

The only bits of jargon you will come on will be firstly 'Description of Instrument', and the answer is transfer, and the second is 'Estate or interest transferred', the answer to which is 'fee simple'.

6 The reply you received to the Form K16, the bankruptcy form (see page 124).

7 Form 94A Application by purchaser for official search. Again, a name-and-address job, plus enter the title number and date of issue of Office Copy. If you are borrowing money, give the name of the lender and tell the Land Registry it is for a mortgage, so complete box C on the form. If you are not, search in your name and tell the Land Registry you are purchasing and fill in box P. If you search in your own name as the purchaser, your lender cannot rely on the reply and will not accept it. An important form this, which was mentioned in chapter 11, 'The Registers' so we won't labour it again. Suffice to say that you are enquiring of the Registry whether anyone has registered any dealings in the land since the date the Office Copies were made for you.

There is a fee for this service, currently £4. Don't send this form off until about ten days before the date agreed for completion, for, as you will see it gives you protection (priority expires box) for 30 working days, 6 weeks, in other words, in which to complete and register your deal. Though this is a lender's requirement, you should use this form even if you are not taking a mortgage. If you are buying from a landlord who has other properties registered under the same Title number or a builder who is developing an area of land, use Form 94B, Search of Part. The Registry needs to know which part, and it is up to the vendor to provide you with sufficient identification, (plans, plot no. etc.) to satisfy the Registrar.

8 Form AP1 Application to Change the Register.

9 Form DS1. This is the form that tells the Land Registry to cancel the registration of the vendor's lender's mortagage. Only the vendor can supply this and then not for a week or more after completion. Or not at all if Electronic Notification applies. What the lender will actually want is a cast-iron guarantee the mortgage will be paid off. Normally, a vendor's solicitor's undertaking will suffice, but very recent case law has suggested the purchaser's solicitor could be negligent in accepting an undertaking, so do not be surprised if completion procedures start to change following the publication of this edition. If the discharge is accompanied by other transactions, the form will be lodged under cover of Form AP1. If stand alone, it is to be accompanied by Form DS2 (printed on the back of DS1).

The solicitor for the building society will expect you to produce his fees.

You might not be absolutely certain exactly which forms and documents will be 'lodged with this form' as Panel 3 (DS2) requires. Don't worry, you can safely rely on the lender and Skinner to help you out on completion day, because you are not the only party to this deal and matters have gone so far by now, that in 999 cases out of 1,000 your vendor is just as anxious to see the colour of your money as you are to see that of the person who is buying your present abode. So you have them. And as US President Richard Nixon once said, 'When you have them by the balls, their hearts and minds are sure to follow'!

Vendor: Sign the transfer form and get your partner to sign beside you if the house is in joint names. You will need to sign this in front of an independent, adult witness who should afterwards add his or her name, address and occupation in the spaces provided. If you have no mortgage to pay off, choose your spot for completion. If you have a mortgage, then as the Charge Certificate and the rest of the papers will have to be sent to the your lender's solicitor (if it has one) you will have to use his office. If the lender does not have a solicitor, you are going to have to ask your lender to send the deeds to a solicitor on its panel to act in this capacity, and they might be willing to conduct a completion meeting on site but do not bank on it. They would rather have the money by CHAPS transfer. The lender's solicitor doesn't have much to do, but nevertheless charges the lenders and they in turn charge you by adding the fees on to the outstanding balance of your account with them. His job is to collect and give a receipt for the money and hand over the Charge Certificate to you. Why this bit of a job cannot be done by building societies' local managers I cannot understand. The answer is probably money. Better to shuffle the work and the risk to someone whose bill can be added to your loan (and paid by you) and who can be sued if they get it wrong.

Let your purchaser know the venue and exact time. Also inform him that you will require the balance of the purchase price in the form of a CHAPS payment, which has the advantage over a cheque in that it cannot be stopped and it will not bounce.

In case you are wondering how you would cope with paying off your mortgage in order to lay your hands on the deeds for handing over on completion of a sale, this is how it is done:

Get to know the exact amount of money required on the due date (called a redemption figure). At the same time ask if your lender will give you and the purchaser's solicitor 'the usual' undertaking to send the deeds on to your purchaser's solicitor after completion, in return for a CHAPS payment made payable to your lender, which you will have arranged to be made as part of the purchase monies on completion of your sale, to pay off your mortgage with. You are released from the mortgage, and hey presto, the deeds are sent on to your purchaser's solicitor in a short time. The purchaser's solicitor can also give you the balance of the purchase price in the form of a second CHAPS payment; do not be surprised if a fee for this second payment is debited from the sale price, because the purchaser's solicitor may tell his client that since you have no solicitor who could accept one payment and distribute it, why should his client pay for two? Don't give them the keys of your property until you see the colour of their money.

In practice, do not be too surprised to find no-one trusts you or wishes to meet with you at completion, or can say at what time they can complete. So for a more likely scenario, see 'Planning for completion' below.

About three months after completion you can send off a Form 109 to the Land Registry for one set of 'Registry Entries' and within a fortnight you will receive a set of Office Copies showing yourself as the proprietor.

Purchaser: Receive the completion statement and the request about how the money is to be split. If you don't receive them seven days before completion, gee the other side up – you will soon have plenty of problems coping with crockery and curtain runners, without having uninvited last minute jobs to do on the financial side.

You have no doubt bought and sold motor cars in the past. Collecting the money on one, paying out on another; paying off the HP on one and obtaining HP on another, are all very fiddly; all on the surface very complicated. Housing transactions are much the same, the big difference being that when the money from the sale of one car is being used to purchase another, both cars can be at the scene of completion. Unless you are moving next door or across the street, this is not possible with housing transactions. So look at the purchase at this stage as being of the title deeds (the Land or Charge Certificate and the transfer Form) which represent the house. Anyway, approach the financial side of completion of your purchase as you did swapping cars and you won't go far wrong.

Planning for completion

You now have an interesting dilemma. How to complete? Since you are not a solicitor and since a solicitor will represent everyone or nearly everyone else in the chain, you have a problem. There was a time when you demanded your buyer to come to your property to complete, or if you had a mortgage you would go to the offices of the lender or it's solicitors. Here you would swap deeds, cash (or its equivalent) and the keys. This was common 30 years ago but not now.

The idea that you ask a solicitor to come to your house to complete will cause great merriment. The likelihood is that the solicitor will re-tell the story at dinner parties to the amusement of all and in time the story will no longer be recognisable. You will have become an urban legend, but for all that, you will receive no visitors at completion. What with electronic cash transfers (often the slowest and most annoying part of the whole process), computerised access to Land Registry records, the ability to search using a computer or the telephone, movement of letters and draft documents by post, fax, and e-mail attachments, people do not expect to pay a solicitor to wander around the countryside for completions and so none will. Not that it was ever practicable if there is a long chain that stretched around the country but, here and there, localised completion meetings were once common place.

Every case is different, so try to cobble together a completion plan, but the more people there are in the chain the less likely it is that you will be a welcome visitor to the offices of your lender's or your buyer's solicitor, so be prepared to have to pay someone to complete for you. If you are able to make this call, do not be surprised to find out that no-one will be able to tell you exactly when they can complete. It can take a long time for money to wander around the country from bank to bank.

Also take your passport with you, in case an objection is raised to handing you a bank draft. In fact, all the solicitors you deal with may insist you identify yourself, as a safeguard against fraud and in the belief that they are required to obtain evidence of identity to comply with their obligations under the money laundering legislation. Your lender's solicitor is given guidance on what to ask for. For those of you on the Internet, have a look in section 3 of The CML Lender's Handbook for England and Wales on www.cml.org.uk.

> **Do not part with the deeds until the bank of the buyer's solicitor has irrevocable instructions to send the money to you.**

Vendor: What are the possibilities?

You are not buying and have no mortgage to pay off. Lucky you. Your buyer's solicitor is not going to call on you and you will not be given any cash until they have all that they think they need. Your best solution is to ask if they will accept from you the deeds and the signed transfer to be held to your order until you are paid. They will not be handing you a box of bank notes or a bank draft and will want to send the money to you by CHAPS transfer to an account nominated by you. You should ask that they undertake not to part with the deeds until their bank has irrevocable instructions to send the money to you.

You are not buying but have a mortgage to pay off, so ask your lender to nominate a solicitor to represent their interests and ask him or her to do the same for you as explained in the previous paragraph.

Life becomes fun if you are selling and buying. Your old house is in Devon, the new house is in Essex, your old lender is in Kent and the new lender is in Leeds, and the solicitor who represents your seller is in none of these places. Much the same can be said of your seller, and your buyer. Also there are road works on the M4, and cones (but no sign of work or workman) on the M25 so flying visits are out. Clearly you are going to have to find a solicitor in the chain to act as your agent.

Do not ask your original lender's solicitors. They have absolutely no interest whatsoever in seeing the matter is completed on the day of your choosing. Next week is as good as this week. Your lender will not be that fussed whether the deal goes through on the day or a week late. After all, the longer it takes the more interest you pay them. Try to persuade someone more closely connected with the transaction, such as the solicitor who represents the people you are borrowing money from, for the new house. They do have an interest in completing the loan since that is what their clients do for a living. Lend money. Or try the solicitor who represents the person buying your house or the solicitor who represents the person you are buying from. They too have clients who will expect 'their man' or 'their women' to get the job done.

Assuming you come up with a workable plan, what next?

You are wearing two hats. You are a vendor, and also a purchaser, and the solicitor who is going to do the deed for you, will need the relevant deeds, documents, search certificates and so forth. The best thing to do is to ask what they want. Then if they miss something, it becomes their primary problem. It will also be their task to ensure the correct moneys come and go, to supply any undertakings required and to see you get the residue (if any) due to you.

As the vendor, all you will normally be asked for is the transfer in form TR1 of your house and your Land or Charge Certificate. Your purchaser's solicitors will have typed it, and chances are they will have told you how to sign it.

If anyone is still there do not complete, no matter what fanciful explanations or excuses are tried on you.

You may not have the deeds. The bank or building society that has the mortgage over your house have these, and they will have been passed to their solicitors. The solicitors who will be carrying the sale through for you will supply the undertaking the purchaser's solicitors will demand, namely that the mortgage will be paid off and that form DS1 (the Land Registry's formal release) will be sent on to the purchaser's solicitors when received.

Purchaser: The likely problems and the possibilities are much the same. However, first things first. Arrange with the vendor or his agent for the keys to be available to you or your representative (you can't be in two places at once), for a swift inspection to make sure that everything that was to be left behind is still there, and everyone who was to move out has gone. Make sure you are truly getting vacant possession on completion and if anyone is still there, do not complete, no matter what fanciful explanations or excuses are tried on you. Such a case is one in a million but who wants to be a statistic? This final inspection is made to avoid the greatest calamity of all that can possibly befall a purchaser of a house intended for his own immediate occupation. So whether employing a solicitor or doing your own conveyancing, make sure that no person is left in the house, and also make sure the fixtures and fittings and any extras you are paying for have not been taken.

Now for the possibilities:

You are paying cash and do not need a mortgage. Your seller's solicitor can say where completion is to take place and may just be willing to have you call at their office to complete.

Make sure you have all the identification the solicitor believes they are obliged to see - the Money laundering legislation, remember! - and ask how they wish to receive the money. Do not be surprised if a bank draft is not welcome but if that is how you wish to pay, insist on this if the contract allows it. Have a quick look at the sale contract to see if condition 6.7 of the printed Standard Conditions was altered in the sale agreement you signed. If it was not, you can pay by any of the means listed - cash, banker's draft, direct debit to a nominated bank account or by releases of deposit.

When you get to the meeting, check the papers. First compare the Land or Charge Certificate with the office copy of the title you were given, before exchange of contracts. Make sure the transfer has been properly signed by the vendor and witnessed, and make sure anything else you need (which depends on circumstances) is available. For example, undertakings to pay off an existing mortgage on the house and to send you form DS1 when this has arrived in their office.

When all of this is in order, hand over the bank draft in exchange. On the other hand, perhaps you were properly required to pay by CHAPS transfer and so the money may be sitting in their bank account while you are sitting in their chair! Anyway take up what you want and ask them to telephone the estate agents to release the keys. Then leave!

You are buying and do need a mortgage. In this case, the people you are borrowing money from will have their own solicitor (although you pay normally) and it may be that they have agreed to complete for you (and their own clients). In this case, they will want from you the various papers listed at pages 139-40 as relevant to the transaction.

The probability is that they will have asked you for all these papers before the day of completion and it is extremely unlikely that they will wish to see you at completion, except to the extent necessary to carry out their money laundering checks. In this case, they will be taking up the deeds, checking the transfer and demanding the necessary undertakings for paying off any existing mortgage on the house. They will probably leave it to you to worry about ensuring the keys are released, but you never know. They might just telephone when the transaction was completed.

Whichever option applied, the job is done. You've got yourself a new house!

Cash Buyers

For you, there is still work to do. Your transfer will need to be stamped and registered. If you are borrowing on the house the lender's solicitor will insist on attending to these formalities. Otherwise, it is down to you. There are two deadlines you should comply with:

Stamping

Stamp duty is payable if the cash price stated in the transfer is above £60,000. You get one month to have the transfer stamped. Failing which you will be fined £100. Actually, the duty is increased by £100 but it is the same difference, and at least there is no criminal record! The Inland Revenue claim they pocket this money in the interests of fairness but they would say that wouldn't they? The procedure is very simple. Send the transfer, a completed form LA451, and a cheque for the duty to the Inland Revenue. Not just any office mind. You can attend to this in person if you are willing to travel to Bush House in the Strand (London), failing which the papers must be posted to an Inland Revenue office. Telephone Bush House to see which one is closest to your home for the correct name and address. Under no circumstances whatsoever should you post these papers to your local tax office! It will confuse them, considerably.

Registration

There is no deadline for registering the transfer at the Land Registry but you should aim to see that your application is with the Land

Registry the day before the last day of the priority period noted in your search. Double check Form 94D to find that date. Form 94D is the Land Registry's response to your 94A or 94B search certificate. The reason for getting your application in before 'the search expires' is to make sure you get there before anyone else - a creditor waiting in the wings, for example. Searches can no longer be extended but they can be renewed. However, renewal does not afford the same protection so try to get it right first time. If you slip up, generally it does not matter but it might, and if it does, it could prove to be an expensive mistake. Do not worry about sending in an incomplete application if that is the only way to keep within the priority period. The Land Registry is used to this.

Your application is usually made using form AP1. Complete the form and send along the transfer form TR1, the Land or Charge Certificate, a cheque for the fees, and if your vendor had a mortgage you will also send along form DS1. This might not be available for days, if not weeks after completion, so if necessary just send it along later. It may even be that there is no DS1 if your Vendor's lender is using the recently adopted 'Electronic Notification of Discharge' scheme. If this applies, they tell the Land Registry their mortgage can be cleared from the record rather than issue a DS1 that an applicant can send along. The registration fees change from time to time, so telephone the relevant Land Registry, ask for enquiries and ask for the figure.

Builders

If you bought from a builder, the preceding observations are essentially correct, save that the builder's solicitors will have supplied the transfer and plan using transfer form TP1 and the Land Registry application form is called FR1 for 'First registration'. Plus, the documents you send along with the application are listed by you using form DL and you will also need to tell the Land Registry what the builder's deposit number is.

His Land Certificate will be placed on deposit with the Land Registry and they will issue a filing number called a Deposit Number. Your builder vendor will tell you what that number is. Have a look at the standard forms sent to you when you first received the legal papers. It should be there somewhere. If you do not have it, telephone the relevant Land Registry 2-3 days before completion and ask enquiries if the Land Certificate is on deposit. Tell them the title number and they will tell you the answer. If it is not on deposit, refuse to complete unless you are given an undertaking by the solicitors to place it on deposit forthwith. If the Land Registry does not have it they will not register your transfer and you will not have what you bought - the legal title to your house.

In this chapter and the ones on Contract, Mortgages and Registered Land I have covered the typical and some not very typical situations that can arise. The same situations can and do arise with unregistered properties, so they will be covered again in the next chapter. If necessary, refer to that. If you come across anything else that does not yield to common sense, telephone the Land Registry enquiries department. From a buyer saying 'I will', to completion taking place, occupies one or two calendar months, so you need not feel rushed.

Pundits never tire of telling us that buying our first house is the biggest investment of our lives. If you are young, and have a lifetime of buying and selling in front of you, your biggest investment has been in the time spent reading and putting into practice these few pages. Tell everybody!

13 Conveyancing: the sale and purchase of an unregistered house

In chapter 12, I describe all that has to be done to transfer ownership of registered property in England and Wales.

What about unregistered? It is supposed to be more difficult, or so we are told. Judge for yourself.

This is a brief summary to start you off, but do read the whole chapter!

Overview

First, look at your deeds and extract all the conveyances you can find. Find one which is at least 125 years old and that is your 'root of title'. All this means is you contract to prove you and your predecessors have owned the house for at least 15 years. Perhaps you bought more than 15 years ago? If so your conveyance is your root of title. If not go back in strict date order and pick the one which is at least 15 years old. Copy these to your buyer.

Also send along any Land Charges Department name searches you find with the deeds and look at the conveyance to you to see if there is any reference to covenants in an earlier document. If there is, find your copy of that deed and make sure your buyer gets a copy, even if it dates from before the conveyance you select as your 'root deed'. You may have the original deed, or you may find you have a copy as part of an 'Abstract of Title'. This is a type-written summary of the material contents of the deeds that made up the title at the time the Abstract was typed.

The conveyance or transfer to the buyer is, by custom, typed up by the buyer and it is normally dealt with after exchange of contracts. The buyer can type up another conveyance with the new names and sale price (see the specimen following) or he can use a Land Registry form TR1, provided the property is adequately described. Look for example at the description in the specimen conveyance.

Fig 13.1   Specimen Conveyance

Specimen Conveyance

This Conveyance is made the   day of   19

BETWEEN the Vendors Xavier Lax and Susan Lax his wife both of 14, Plevna Place, Blossomton and the Purchasers Bernard Strong and Ivy Strong his wife both of 127, Lowfield Road, Blossomton.

WHEREAS the Vendor is the estate owner in fee simple in possession of the property hereby conveyed free from encumbrances except as hereinafter mentioned and has agrees with the purchasers for the sale to them of the property for the sum of £20,000 (twenty thousand pounds)

THIS DEED WITNESSETH

1. That in consideration of the sum of twenty thousand pounds now paid by the purchaser to the vendor (the receipt of which the vendor hereby acknowledges) the vendor as beneficial owner hereby conveys to the purchaser ALL THAT land and property known as 14, Plevna Place, Blossomton as shown and outlined in red on the plan attached to a conveyance between Henry Feather and the vendor and dated the first of April 1971 and subject to the covenants therein contained TO HOLD the same unto the purchasers in fee simple as joint tenants in law and equity/tenants in common (decide)

2. With the object of giving the vendor a full and sufficient indemnity but not further the purchasers hereby covenant with the vendors to observe fulfil and perform the above-mentioned covenants and indemnify the vendor against all actions and claims in respect thereof

3. IT IS HEREBY CERTIFIED that the transaction hereby effected does not form part of a larger transaction or series of transactions in respect of which the amount or value or aggregate amount or value of the consideration exceeds £30,000

IN WITNESS OF WHEREOF the parties have hereunto set their hands and seals the day and year first above written

SIGNED SEALED AND DELIVERED by (vendor)
in the presence of   (witness)

SIGNED SEALED AND DELIVERED by (purchaser)
in the presence of   (witness)

This is the main difference between buying and selling registered land and buying and selling unregistered land. The title searches are a little different but see below. As for stamping and registration everything I said in the previous chapter applies bit in this case the Land registry application form is called FR1 not AP1 and it must be accompanied by a list of the documents your are submitting called Land Registry form DL.

Looking more closely at the deeds

Conveyances and transfers are deeds and a deed is an instrument in writing, signed, sealed and delivered; such an instrument of transfer of property, from one person to another, is called a conveyance. If you were the cautious buyer of a second-hand lawn mower, and asked the seller to prove it was his to sell, he would produce the receipt. It is the same with an unregistered house. The first part of any conveyance shows this clearly as you can see from our specimen conveyance on page 150.

It is interesting to play detective with a pile of conveyances, but the important ones are the last one and the one before that which is more than 15 years old.

Like the lawn mower buyer, the purchaser of a house needs to be convinced that what the vendor is offering is his to sell. This is usually done by producing a copy of the conveyance which the vendor obtained when he bought. It will be something like our specimen. A copy of the covenants referred to will come with the draft contract. If the date on the conveyance, showing the present vendor as the purchaser, is more than 15 years old he has proved title, because when X Lax moved, his solicitor proved to Strong's solicitor that everything was in order.

It seems to be assumed that if, within 15 years of a person taking possession of a property, no one comes along kicking up a fuss about the ownership, then everything must be in order. But what if the house has changed hands 11 times during the past 15 years? Simple enough, if every transaction was a straightforward sale and purchase; you need to see 11 conveyances, linked in the progression A to B; B to C; C to D;… K to Lax. When you are purchasing an unregistered property that has changed hands a number of times in the past 15 years, apart from wondering why it was so unloved, comfort yourself with this thought about the title: all the purchasers in the chain are likely to have employed highly trained solicitors either to check the title or to supervise their clerks' checking of it. No doubt lenders' solicitors will have satisfied themselves about it, too. If you are taking a mortgage, the lenders' solicitor will be giving things the once over at your expense (plus VAT) and you might feel justified in relying on him. If you have any queries please ask him or her. Ask nicely; you can only be refused.

It is interesting to play detective with a pile of conveyances, but the important ones are the last one and the one before that which is more than 15 years old. Add a clause to the draft contract saying that copies will be provided which cover the previous 15 years, and ask for them to be forwarded as soon as possible.

I have never met anyone who paid for a house, and was subsequently in trouble because one of William the Conquerer's hangers-on hadn't the right to sell. It's the last conveyance that counts and you've met the vendor. You need to check that the person named in the last link of the chain as the purchaser is the same as the one named in your contract; that the address of the house you are buying corresponds; that the plan is the same as the one sent with the draft contract, and that after the words TO HOLD it says 'in fee simple' because these two words define the property as freehold, as opposed to leasehold; if it were leasehold, it would refer to the lease in the section beginning, ALL THAT.

A mortgage also constitutes a good root of title, because presumably people don't lend money on security without first checking that the borrower owns the property.

If your vendor hasn't owned the property for 15 years or more, you will have to apply all the above checks to the conveyances which take you back over the period required.

As we have said, a conveyance forms what is known as 'good root of title'. It is the most usual because it indicates that an investigation of the title was carried out at the time of its making, and in 99 cases out of a 100 proof of ownership of the average house will be by production of a conveyance, or a series of linked conveyances.

Sometimes, another document is required to forge a link. Obviously, a deceased person cannot pass on ownership by making a conveyance. In such a case a devise (see glossary) is a good root and the document which forms the link between the deceased owner and the next is a copy of the grant of probate, or letters of administration, issued by the High Court out of the District Probate Registry, which shows who was appointed to administer the deceased's estate.

When the personal representatives ('executors' if there is a will, 'administrators' if not) have finished administering the deceased's estate, they will wish to transfer the property to a beneficiary. They do this by means of a document called an Assent. It is necessary to appreciate that since 1st April 2000, the beneficiary must register his title and so if you are offered a title with an Assent granted after this date, insist the property be registered before you contract to buy it.

A purchaser need not worry overmuch lest a solicitor fails to tip up all these documents, because in sending you the Law Society's Standard Conditions of Sale contract, he has bound himself to do so. A vendor will expect to find all title documents in his deeds parcel, for the same reason.

If the above last four paragraphs apply to your case (and they normally do) please read them again. After all, you did not fully grasp that two plus two equalled four, the first time you heard about it. At the moment, you are dealing with a hypothetical case. Once you have a set of forms and documents on the table before you, it will be that much easier to shuffle them about with the aid of these paragraphs.

In case of difficulty, and if the vendor's solicitor hasn't already sent one, ask for an 'epitome of title', which is a list of the deeds that take you back to the root of title or the deed which created the covenants, or both.

In the rest of this chapter, the information will be divided between that for a purchaser and that for a vendor. But don't eschew the other side's information; it's good to know what the other chap is up to, and in any case, you may well be changing roles in a few years' time.

Vendor: Your first step is to get hold of the deeds. If your house is paid for and you haven't already got the deeds at home, go to wherever they are and get them. If the property is still mortgaged, write to the head office of your lender and ask if they will send the title deeds to their branch office nearest your home, as you are selling the property, acting for yourself, and will need to make copies of the relevant documents. Bear in mind that the title deeds are yours. They are only deposited with the lender as security for the money he has lent you.

The bundle, though referred to as 'the deeds' is made up of all sorts of papers that are and are not deeds. There will be copies of old Land Charges Department search certificates, receipted mortgages and, of course, conveyances, and it is the latter with which you concern yourself at this stage. They are typed on stout paper, folded and marked on the outside front:

DATED 8th June 1920

Mr. V.A. CATER

to

Mr. N. SCONCE

Conveyance

of all that messuage or dwelling house known as and situate at

14 Plevna Place, in the County of Eden

Skinner, Standing & Still

Solicitors

Blossomton

When you look at your deeds, bear in mind the three things your purchaser needs to know about the property at this point: (i) that you own it; (ii) what, if anything, goes with it – rights of way etc.; and (iii) what can and cannot be done with it.

If you bought 15 years or more ago your luck is in. Photocopy the conveyance to yourself, make a copy of the plan if there is one, and copy out the covenants and conditions if they are not 'recited' in your conveyance. But if, during the past 15 years, the house has changed hands a few times you will need to copy each of the conveyances covering the period that takes you back to the root of title, as given at paragraph 4.2.2 of your Agreement.

But what if the house is built on on a plot of land sold off from a larger area of land? In that case, you can only expect to find a written summary of previous deeds on which the builder's solicitor (clerk) will have endorsed something like 'examined against originals at the offices of Messrs Skinner & Stonehart solicitors of that parish'. Copy it.

You will also have to photocopy more than the conveyance to yourself (even if you've been the owner for more than 15 years), if the mention of restrictive covenants in your conveyance confines itself to saying that the benefits, easements and covenants are those 'contained, mentioned or referred to in a conveyance dated … between So and So and Thingumy'. You root out the conveyance to Thingumy and hopefully the list is set out there of what you HOLD/SUBJECT NEVERTHELESS to. This is the set of capital letters which usually heralds the covenants, restrictions etc. in a conveyance. Photocopy the whole conveyance. Sometimes it will be easy: a straightforward conveyance to you without a covenant in sight. Sometimes you have to beaver away at the pile.

Hopefully, you will get all that is required at the first go. Even if you only think you have, that is what matters at this stage, because you send the lot on to your purchaser's solicitor. And if what you have sent is accepted, you move to the next step. On the other hand, if you have made some mistakes or omissions, Skinner will let you know that you've missed a link in the chain, so off you go to the originals again, this time knowing precisely what you are looking for.

If you are not sure of your purchaser and think the sale might go off, either take two copies of everything (because a solicitor might be on holiday when you request a return) or take one copy and, at this stage: (a) rely on paragraph 4.2.2 of your contract or (b) if there is an epitome of title, copy that and add on short notes regarding transactions since the last one mentioned on it. In your covering letter to Skinner itemise what you are sending, as a reminder for yourself and to avoid disputes later.

But for the present, concern yourself with preparing your draft contract. From the conveyance to you, get the date to answer the question beginning 'root of title/title no.'. If the conveyance to you is less than 15 years old, you have to rummage around to find one that is more, and put the parties and date of that in. Completion date is usually left blank at this stage, but there is nothing to stop you putting a date in if you wish – the purchaser can always ask for an amendment. If you are using the Standard Conditions of Sale, 3rd edition, and you wish to include anything in the purchase price that you think needs specifying, there is provision for the cost of chattels and a list of itemised chattels on a separate pre-printed form.

Although it need not be done until after contracts have been exchanged, enclose with the draft contract as much of the photocopies of the deeds as you think will prove that you are the owner.

Send two unsigned contracts to Skinner, send along the Fixtures Fittings and Contents Form and ask Skinner if he will accept a completed Property Information Form or whether he prefers to send you his own preliminary enquiries (see page 109) and send along your Epitome of Title. This is a form that lists the documents of title. Copies must also be sent along. The list is in columns and contains certain information: date, document name, type, whether you are sending a copy or the original, whether a copy or an original will be handed over on completion, etc. It is not just a list; it is an explanation. Years ago, before the days of photocopies, the practice was for the vendor's solicitors to type out a resume or abstract of the more important clauses in all the required documents. These are called 'Abstracts of Title'. No solicitor is going to do this now, but if the property has not changed hands for years or if a very old document is referred to and has to be produced to the purchaser's solicitors, you might be shown an abstract for the relevant title or copy.

If your house is mortgaged, you will have to obtain copy documents from your lender or its solicitors. Ask for a copy of all deeds, all searches, all planning permissions and other consents issued by anyone, and the NHBC papers.

When you have Skinner's answer on enquiries versus the Property Information Form, act accordingly. As for your answers on either, he will no doubt be fully satisfied with your information, but if he isn't, he will write for more information. In that case, reply as best you can.

Do not part with any original deeds at this stage.

Purchaser: You have viewed the house a couple of times and if you need a mortgage, you have got at least half a promise of one. You have bargained the price down with Feather, told him you are acting for yourself and given him your name and address. Receive the draft contract from your vendor's solicitor who may well not be as helpful as the vendor (above) and you may only receive the draft contract with a copy. Don't worry, he will give evidence of title later on. If you don't like the look of anything in the contract, give the vendor's solicitor a ring and agree the alterations you require and write them into the draft. The kind of things you are looking for are basically the same as for the purchaser of registered property.

The covenants are included in a conveyance, not necessarily the one to your vendor. His may only give the date and the parties to the conveyance in which the covenants were set out in full. Skinner must either set them out in full in the contract, or supply you with a copy of them and refer to the conveyance from which they came, and if he doesn't, insist, because if you are a surgeon and there is a restrictive covenant against surging in or around the premises, you will not wish to waste further time and money on surveys and such like.

Land Registry: Send off search Form 96. Give the address and either cut a piece out of a local street map or sketch a little plan of the surrounding streets (it needn't be to scale) to help with identification, if you think the postal address might not be sufficient. When you get the form back it will reveal if there is a caution against first registration, and whether the land is registered or not (don't take the vendor's word on this – he might not know what he is talking about). If it is registered, you will be given the Title number, and your task is much simpler from now on – you take your instructions from the previous chapter. After you first find out why your vendor did not know this! If in reply to Form 96 they give you anything you don't understand, ring the enquiries department.

Usually the sending of Form K15 is delayed until three weeks before completion, because a certificate of search gives you protection for 30 working days against anyone putting nasty things on the register.

Land Charges Form K15 Application for an Official Search. Search against the names of all owners since 1926. If you cannot extract this information from the copy deeds you have been sent, ask your vendor for a list. He may not have them but ask just in case.

Your lender will require to know if you have been bankrupt. So together with your search Form K15 you can send an application for an Official Search (Bankruptcy Only) K16, provided that completion is not more than a fortnight ahead – lenders need up-to-date information. Put in the name/s of the intending borrower/s, enclose a cheque to the tune of £2 for each of the names to be searched on the K15 and K16 forms, and send them off to the address at Plymouth given on the back of the forms.

It is not strictly necessary to search between the dates they acquired the property and sold it (or died) since you can always search from 1926 to the year of your search. It is a good idea to include the name of the vendor at this time on your form K15, just in case a nasty turns up, but remember you do need a clear certificate that covers the vendor's name on date you are actually completing the purchase. The priority period, i.e. when the search expires, will appear on the reply.

For instance, your vendors may not be as lovey-dovey as they appeared when they showed you round 'Shangri-La', and if the house was bought in one name, the partner might have registered a Class F charge to protect matrimonial interests. You need to know about any Class F charge as soon as possible, and certainly before you get too involved. If they have come to some arrangement about sharing the proceeds of the sale, so well and good. However, as soon as you receive your protection period certificate from Plymouth get the cautioner to sign an application to cancel the charge. See chapter 'Matrimonial Homes'. A lender's solicitor will expect you to produce the certificate on completion.

Couples do some barmy things when love turns, at best to indifference, at worst to hate. They often do all they can to make things difficult for the other side. If you had been buying a registered title, the Office Copies would have wised you up on this problem. It is so that you don't get caught in the crossfire that I say: K15 to Land Charges Dept. as soon as possible and certainly before you sign the contract.

It is all very well having a contract that is enforceable, but who wants the bother and expense of enforcement? And what if you came up against someone who thought that they and their case were something special, and it would be unjust for the law to be applied to them?

Such a situation has all the makings of a House of Lords case. Having rights and asserting them are two vastly different things. Possession really is nine points of the law! And another thing – always change the locks when you move in, particularly if the house has been standing vacant for any length of time.

'Enquiries of Local Authority' Form CON 29' together with 'Search of Local Land Charges LLC1': councils require you to provide two copies of each.

Take them to the council as recommended earlier. CON 29 is in two parts. If you want both parts answering it costs more. You must tick any of the questions in part 2 to which you need an answer. The kind of questions in part 2 are such as relate to public footpaths, existing and contemplated, building preservation orders and so on, also questions about registration of houses in multiple occupation. If you tick any of them, look up the fee given on the form and add it to the standard fee.

The LLC1 form is printed in duplicate, one copy for the council to retain, and one to be returned to you with the answers. Use a carbon to complete. The local land charges register is divided into 12 parts, and the first question which faces you on the form is which parts you require searching. Strike out 'Part(s)...of' and you will get the lot. It's much simpler, and costs very little more than picking and choosing. Like a lot of things the prices keep moving up, but mercifully the charges are, in this instance, printed on the back of the form. The reference in the fees section of the form to 'each parcel' means plots, so it does not concern the buyer of a single house.

'Seller's Property Information Form': two copies will normally be volunteered by the vendor's solicitor. If your vendor is a company (has 'Ltd' after its name) you need to be extremely careful that the company is not in the process of being wound up. If you are buying such a house that is not registered, you should make a company search at Companies House, Crown Way, Cardiff CF4 3UZ, tel. 02920 380950, www.companies-house.gov.uk/info/ (check fee), either by calling there, or if it is too far away, by asking your CAB to give you the address of a land agent or credit reference agency who might help. The trouble here (and a solicitor is just as subject to it as you are) is that it takes time for a note of a winding-up petition to be put on a company's file. Nevertheless, any sale made after winding-up proceedings have commenced is only a purported sale and is null and void.

Keep asking for explanations and never be fobbed off with 'it doesn't really mean what it says' or 'it's usual, but doesn't apply in this case'.

As the case where you are likely to come across a company as a vendor is with a newly-built house, and it will be on an estate where the Registrar has already agreed to register the property, the chance of your having to cope with this problem is extremely remote. It could occur in the case of a shop and house, because many small shopkeepers have been persuaded to trade as limited liability companies in the last few decades. In such cases, caution is the order of the day.

Vendor: Cope with any amendments to the contract, but don't be bullied into giving undertakings, or adding anything to the contract you don't fully understand. Keep asking for explanations and never be fobbed off with 'it doesn't really mean what it says' or 'it's usual, but doesn't apply in this case'. If it doesn't mean what it says or doesn't apply, it may as well be struck out. On the other hand, if you are asked to take something out and you are told, 'Oh! you don't need that' you can riposte, 'Well, if you know it is doing no harm, you won't object to it remaining'.

Purchaser: Receive the Seller's Property Information Form from Skinner and glean from his answers what you can. Remember that the vendor might not want to buy these forms and send you the answers, in which case it is for you to buy some forms called Enquiries before Contract (or similar). (see page 109). It does not really matter what they are called, since they generally cover about the same issues. If you are not satisfied, or suspect that he knows more than he is telling you, send him a few supplementaries in the form of a letter, but remember he was answering stock questions first time round, so it should occasion little surprise that all you got in return were stock answers. There is a time limit on post contract requisitions - Condition 4.1.1 of the Standard Conditions, so it is vital to get the title approved before contacts are exchanged, by the solicitor acting for your lender. On the other hand no one will thank the vendor's solicitor if he refuses to answer sensible questions that might lead to a satisfactory completion.

Using the Seller's Property Information Form as a guide, carry out your inspection of the property and its environs, paying particular attention to the area of land within the fences, any facilities such as drives which are shared, and the neighbours' attitudes towards them.

If on inspection, it turns out that the road leading to the house is badly potholed, it could be an indication that it is not maintained by the council because it is not adopted by them, so pay attention to Enquiries of Local Council. If it is a private road, after the description of the property in the contract it should say 'together with a right of way over the road coloured sky blue pink on the said plan.' On the other hand it might say the words 'and the road has been taken over.' Not to worry: of such redundancies are roots of title made up.

CON 29 and LLC1 will come back from the council with their printed answers. Check them through. If replies on either form cause any head-scratching, ask the person who wrote the replies what they mean. Council officials will always explain meanings, what they are not empowered to do is advise what should be done about them. But you never know. A remark such as 'my goodness, I wonder what other people do in such a circumstance', might just elicit a useful hint of how to deal with a problem that is not simply of a technical nature.

Remember also to carry out your water and drainage searches and check out environmental issues. Consider also whether you need to carry out a common search. See the chapter 12 for details of what needs to be done and why.

By now, the Land Registry should also have returned your search of index map Form 96, showing the house to be unregistered, but if there is any kind of entry it is your vendor's problem. Let him know, or to be more accurate, remind him, because he will almost certainly already be aware of the entry.

The reply to your K15 will come to you in the form of a Certificate of Result of Search. Whereas the Land Registry keeps a register of land and the name(s) of the owner(s) of each registered parcel of land, the Land Charges Department keeps a register of interests, which third persons can have in an unregistered house, and which can be registered against the names of **people**. So if your vendor is called Tom Jones, the computer will throw up all the Tom Joneses known to it and you will have to decide which entries belong to your vendor. Luckily, it also gives the addresses where the ubiquitous Joneses lived when the various charges were registered against them. If none of the entries applies to your vendor, he or his solicitor must write on the Certificate of Result of Search words to the effect that it is certified that none of the entries applies to him.

Obviously, a bankruptcy charge would alert you to the fact that all is not well. More likely than not your reply will show 'no entries'. If there is one, it is likely to be one of the following: C (i) is a second (puisne) mortgage. D (ii) is a splatter of covenants which no doubt you already know of. F is a matrimonial home entry. One of the spouses, not being a joint owner, is protecting rights.

What do you do with any of these in the unlikely event of one or all showing up? In the case of C (i) second mortgage, as the reply you get will say no more than that the entry exists you write, quoting the date and reference number, to the Land Charges Registry, asking for a copy of the details. You will have to take appropriate steps to ensure it will be paid off on completion. Get an undertaking form the vendor's solicitor, or if the vendor is acting for himself, you may be at your lender's solicitors' office at completion. Get the vendor to authorise him to pay off the second charge. He will take up sufficient funds on completion to pay off both debts. Matrimonial Homes Class F we have already dealt with.

You will no doubt already know the contents of a D (ii) entry. The vendor or his solicitor should have put a copy with the draft contract. If he hasn't, ask him to bring the job to the top of the pile of 'things to be done today'.

By now, you have sufficient knowledge to give you confidence to go forward, or back out of the deal.

So let us have a little re-cap of what a purchaser of an unregistered freehold house in England or Wales will have done up to this point.

He will have:

1 Received the draft contract in duplicate with map.

2 Called at the local council and deposited LLC1 for information about the council's interests in the property.

3 Sent or taken Form CON 29 to the council asking questions about roads, drains and restrictions on use.

4 Sent Form 96 to Land Registry to find out if registered, and if not, any cautions against first registration.

5 Received Seller's Property Information Form from vendor's solicitor, with what they know about any boundary disputes, rights of way, planning consents and such like, or sent his own questions, the Enquiries before Contract, to the vendor's solicitor.

6 Carried out a Land Charge search using form K15 against the name of the vendor and all known owners since 1926.

7 Dealt with drainage and environmental issues.

It looks a pretty big list of forms, but you should be able to cope, particularly as nowadays solicitors seem to think nothing of taking two calendar months to get to the stage you are now at – I've seen houses built quicker. If you can deal with this increasingly bureaucratic world, and are in a position mentally and financially to buy a house, the forms should not cause you any difficulty, which with the application of a little logic and common sense, you can't solve for yourself.

Having received satisfactory replies, or your vendor being able to satisfy you on any points raised, you are now ready to exchange contracts, provided you have received a satisfactory mortgage offer from your lender.

Our vendor, doing his own conveyance, has been told to send off copies of the previous conveyances with his draft contract. It seems a sensible way to do things, but sometimes solicitors acting for vendors will only send you the draft contract and won't let you have a copy conveyance or an epitome of title (see page 153) until contracts have been exchanged. This is rather unusual in this day and age so persevere and insist on a proper epitome of title with all relevant copy documents.

If you bought less than 15 years ago, the only link in the title chain before the conveyance to you might be an abstract, and a solicitor will have endorsed it 'Examined against the originals at the office.

Note that in the contract, the covenants will be either set out in full or reference made to their first appearance in the deeds and you should expect a copy of them (written out in full) before you sign the contract. And remember that if the covenants predate your vendor's ownership, there is nothing you can do about them.

However, by now, all things having gone well, you can agree a completion date with the vendor. Enter it into the final copy (engrossed) contract, sign but do not date it, and send to the vendor's solicitor, together with the smallest deposit you have been able to get away with.

For the purchaser, this is also the time to decide if the house needs to be insured before contracts are exchanged or whether insurance can be left to between contract and completion. That is after you have exchanged but before you complete. See further at page 79.

Vendor: Receive the contract signed by the purchaser, check that the deposit is with a stakeholder or in a joint bank account. Enter the completion date on your copy, sign it, enter the date of your signing and send it off to the purchaser. You have got his part of the contract and he has got yours. Contracts are now said to be 'exchanged'.

If you have not already sent copies of the deeds and documents which prove your title, let Skinner have them now.

If you bought less than 15 years ago, the only link in the title chain before the conveyance to you might be an abstract, and a solicitor will have endorsed it 'Examined against the originals at the office.' This type of endorsed abstract is intended to be used as if it were a set of deeds when you come to sell, and any solicitor would accept it from a brother solicitor.

If in response Skinner sends some obscure requisitions (questions), answer fully, but be ready with the masterpieces:

Question: Who now holds the 1876 indenture?

Answer: I don't know.

Question: Was the plot conveyed in 1975 part of the one conveyed in 1920?

Answer: I suppose so, but form your own view.

If he persists in asking what this or that means give him 'it means what it says'. Eventually, they give up what they should never have started.

Purchaser: Receive vendor's signed and dated part of the contract. Contracts are now said to be 'exchanged' and the property is at the buyer's risk. So check that the contract is in the same terms as the one you signed, and if you have not already done so, immediately arrange for the property to be fully insured with the same company as your lender will eventually use.

If you did not receive copies of the deeds (conveyances, etc.) you should expect them now. Check the conveyances, watching for the points at pages 142 and 143.

An abstract should show, in summary, an unbroken chain of ownership leading to your vendor. It might compress on to three or four pages the meat of a dozen conveyances, mortgage deeds, deeds of gift, probates and wills. In an abstract, the full names and addresses of parties are not repeated over and over again. When an identical description of a property appeared in a subsequent deed it is referred to as 'all the before abstracted premises'. Exceptions and reservations are similarly treated, and wills are not set out in full, but only the date of the will and names of the executors are put in.

Abstracts of title are written in lawyer's speed hand, which consists of abbreviations which are based on omitting vowels. However, Absd does not mean absurd but abstracted. Here are a few more abominations to be going on with:

thereabouts:thrbts, vendor:vndr, property:ppty, hereditaments:hrdmts, indenture:indr, Solicitors:slrs, mortgage:mtge.

You soon get a grsp of it, but be crfl not to let it creep into your gnrl vcblry or it might be thought you need new dntrs.

Requisitions on Title form should now be dispatched.

Vendor: Receive the Purchaser's Requisitions on Title. You only have to prove title going back to the conveyance you agreed to deduce title from, your 'root of title'. Remember that when you and previous owners bought, highly trained solicitors checked out the title so there can't be much if anything wrong with it. That is the theory! However, do your best and give the answers required in relation to providing a completion statement. This is an account showing the precise amount you will require to be paid when you hand the keys over and sign the conveyance. It is sufficient to let your local authority know the date when you are moving out and they will split the Council Tax and anything you have paid in advance will come back to you. Water companies are not always so obliging, so check with them and if necessary, show in your completion statement how much you need in order to reimburse you for the water rate paid in advance. So make up the bill and send it off with your replies.

Purchaser: In reply to your Requisitions on Title, you receive a list of the documents that will be handed over to you (or your lender) on completion and you are informed who will give a statutory acknowledgement and undertaking for the production and safe custody of any document of title not handed over. The form also asks for receipts for last payments of outgoings. Some purchasers' solicitors get all hot and bothered about whether the previous owner is doing a moonlight flit leaving the Council Tax unpaid. Council Taxes are a personal debt on the occupier, so if they are outstanding for a period before you became the occupier, that debt does not belong to you – the council must look to your predecessor for payment. There is a space for further questions.

If you have raised some questions on the title and feel you haven't altogether got satisfactory answers, bear in mind two things. Firstly, if the conveyance to your vendor looks all right and the person described in there as the purchaser is now your vendor, then it should be all right because a wizard of the law checked out that his predecessors were all that they had cracked themselves up to be. Secondly, if you are taking a mortgage, the lender's solicitor will make sure that you are getting good title, and will keep on asking questions which you pass on to Skinner until the lender is satisfied. After all, if you default in your payments and they have to sell the house to settle your account, they will only have as good a title (proof of ownership) as you got at this point.

You now prepare a draft of the 'instrument of transfer' you intend to use. As your purchase is subject to compulsory registration use TR1 (TR2 for repossession). If you are buying in joint names and you wish survivor to take all put 'x' in the first box at 11. In layman's language, the clause now reads : If between now and the next time the house is sold, one of us dies the remaining partner/spouse is entitled to the whole of the sale price, on the strength of the survivor's signature alone. For Consideration put 'x' in the first box and the agreed price. The space for Title number you leave blank, because one has not yet been allocated by the Registry.

If you are buying a new house on a development, the builder's solicitor should provide the 'instrument' Form TP1, because only part of the vendor's land is being transferred.

Vendor: Receive and check the draft. Look for any deductions or additions that have been made to the one you got when you bought. If there are any with which you disagree, amend in red ink and bounce it back. Heed previous warnings about 'Oh, it's usual' and 'It doesn't mean what it says'. Make sure that indemnity covenants have been correctly entered. If needed, see page 112. When you are satisfied send it back marked 'approved'. But do not sign it. You do that when you get the money.

Purchaser: When your draft instrument of transfer comes back, look for the red ink. It is extremely rare to find any, but if you do and you understand and accept, so well and good. If you don't accept, argue about it. If you don't understand, ask for an explanation, as you are perfectly entitled to one. When you are satisfied send it to Skinner so that he can have the vendor sign it ready for completion day. (You only need to sign it and have your signature witnessed if you are giving a covenant.)

From now on, your job is basically the same as that handed out to the purchaser of a registered house. What differences there are only arise if you are taking a mortgage, and in relation to what your lender's solicitor will want you to produce just before or on completion.

The lender's solicitor will, no doubt have written to you asking for the following: (even if he hasn't written, get them off to him as soon as you can and ask him if there is anything further required because of the time limit there might be for asking questions on title).

1   Local authority search forms and replies.

2   The results of your enquiries concerning water drainage and environmental issues.

3   The Seller's Property Information Forms or your own Enquiries before Contract.

4   Contract.

5   Copy title deeds and the replies to your Requisitions on Title received from vendor's solicitor.

6   Transfer Form TR1 to yourself (one of your copies).

7   Replies to your Land Charges searches in Form K15 plus copies of any specific entries you ordered from the Land Charges Registry.

8   Reply to your bankruptcy search (against you) in Form K16.

9   Letter from the water company regarding sewers and water mains.

10 Any indemnity policies, old or new. That is policies copied to you by the vendor and any policy you have taken out.

11 Any indemnity insurance obtained by you, etc.

12 Form LA 451 (below).

13 Form Stamps 61 (below).

14 Form FR1 (below).

It is customary for the lender's solicitors to do virtually nothing so normally you will be required to supply forms he or she would have completed (items 12-14 above) had he acted for you as the buyer and not for your lender at your expense.

As most lenders don't return these documents, it is useful to keep copies for your use in future transactions.

The lender's solicitor will respond by sending you the mortgage deed, an account of fees and stamp duties, a sheet of requisitions on title and a list of the documents required to be handed over on completion. Deal with them as the purchaser of a registered property was instructed on pages 133 to 134.

Stamps L(A)451 (from any Inland Revenue Stamps Office): Description of Instrument is answered with Land Registry Form TR1, as the case may be; the transferor is the vendor and you are the transferee. If you are buying any kind of building, the postal address is sufficient; 6 is answered with 'fee simple' for a freehold property where you are to be absolute owner/s. 7: put the same figure as in 9. in TR1. 7. tells you what (a) to (f) are looking for and your answers will usually be 'none' as will be the case with 8 and 9. Sign 10.

Stamps 61 Listing: The only document you present and describe is your 'instrument of transfer'.

Vendor: Receive the supplementary requisitions on title, and root about in the conveyances for answers, not forgetting the time honoured 'I cannot say', 'I presume so', and other such masterpieces. If you have paid for the house, all you are waiting for now is the money and you will have notified your purchaser of a suitable place for him to pay it over. If you still have a mortgage, completion will take place at your lender's solicitor's office whither the actual deeds will have been sent. On your Form of Requisition you told him to whom you wanted the CHAPS payment sending to. If you need the completion monies splitting between yourself, mortgage redemption monies, or even between you, the redemption monies and the vendor of the house you are now buying, say so.

You will also be asked when possession of the property will be given. You answer, 'When I receive the balance of the money by CHAPS payment transfer on completion'. A solicitor acting for a purchaser would be negligent if he sent his client's money off by CHAPS to a private individual, without having the title deeds; expect completion at Skinner's office. If you are also buying a house you may wish to add a suggested completion date to tie in with your purchase, but see later for more on this subject.

Purchaser: Pass on the vendor's replies to your lender.

You are now geared up for completion. The problems and pitfalls and the completion procedures are essentially the same as those applicable to buying and selling registered land and reference should be made to chapter 12.

Form FR1: First Registration Application. No. 5: enter the value fee. Check the rate with the Land Registry.

A registration fee is normally payable for registering a Legal Charge (mortgage), but when it is done at the same time as a first registration or a transfer for monetary consideration, an abatement of fees applies, i.e. there is no fee to pay for registering the charge. Make sure that no one charges you for registering both your purchase (dealing for value) and for registering a legal charge.

Cash buyers will, in the fullness of time, receive a Land Certificate. Make sure you put a note of the Title number in one or two safe places and put the certificate under the piano lid ready for the next time.

I do hope you will have noticed that throughout this book the few dire warnings given have been about parting with your money for nothing, or making untested assumptions about what other people who are involved in your house buying and selling will do, won't do, will charge and won't charge.

So maybe a final caution will be acceptable. Your goal is to get the job done – your means are the best and easiest you can find. Your goal is not to do as 'good a job' as solicitors do by aping their style and means. No matter how expert you try to make yourself look, no solicitor I have ever met will recommend you for an honourary law degree. Neither should any layperson conveyancer go lording it over those poor souls who do employ solicitors.

They are, no doubt, already smarting from being smacked in the face by the solicitors' final account.

There are those who are capable but haven't, as yet, tried, and you will get more respect if you tell them what, at the end of the transaction you honestly feel about it as I did years ago saying, 'I don't know what all the fuss was about, it will be a cakewalk next time!'

14 Matrimonial homes

Hitherto, care has been taken not to offend half the population by giving the impression that only the male sex is capable of understanding and coping with a property deal. Hence the use of the all-purpose 'person', or 'spouse', and sometimes leaving the reader to decide whether Skinner is Mr, Mrs. Miss or Ms. But in this chapter taking the risk of giving unintended offence, such general terms will be abandoned. It will be assumed that we are dealing with property where the ownership is vested solely in the husband's name, and a claim to have the house treated as the matrimonial home is being made by the wife. This is done for two reasons: firstly because clarity demands it, and secondly because it corresponds to the situation in the real world. However, any husband who needs to protect his interests in a house that was 'put in the wife's name' will not find it too difficult to transpose the term 'husband' for 'wife', and vice versa as necessary.

A wife might not be certain whether the house was in fact purchased jointly by her and her husband. If there is a mortgage, it's easy – ask the building society. In other cases, ask the solicitor who acted. If you suspect that the solicitor might be afraid of breaching confidence (or is biased in favour of your husband), make the enquiry in writing, because if it is in joint names then as you paid half the solicitors costs, you have a right to any information in his file. For him to refuse you the information is naughty and he knows it. A wife who knows or learns that the house was bought in joint names is fully protected. The house cannot be sold or mortgaged without her consent, nor can she be evicted without a court order – such a wife need read no further except out of curiosity and academic interest.

Reference here to 'the Act' will be to the Family Law Act 1996. The purpose of the Act (and earlier legislation) was to protect the right of a spouse (normally a wife) to occupy the matrimonial home if owned by the other spouse. Once a wife registers her right in the appropriate register, all intending purchasers and lenders of money on mortgage will have notice of her rights and they continue negotiations at their peril, until they have the written assurance in the correct form that the wife will agree to withdraw her charge from the register.

But before sending off forms in all directions, the wife needs to establish whether her husband is the freeholder or holds the property on lease. 'Lease', by the way, includes tenancy. In the case of a leaseholder, unless the lease was for more than 21 years when it was granted, it is incapable of registration at the Land Registry, and is a short tenancy. Even so, a wife cannot be evicted without a court order.

Another simple point, but worth making, just in case, is that before a wife can protect her interest in and right to occupy the house, her husband must have a right of occupation. Wives' rights of occupation arise on the latest of the following events:

1 the date when the husband acquired the house;

2 the date of the marriage; or

3 1st January 1968.

So how does one go about registering a wife's right to occupy? As you have already suspected, it is a matter of form-filling again. It is something you can do, easily and cheaply, for yourself. Where you do not know whether the house is registered or not, send off Form 96 to the Land Registry for your area with 'This search is being made solely for the purposes of the Family Law Act 1996' written across the top, and no charge will be made.

You will get a reply within a day or two telling you whether it is registered or not; if it is registered you will be given the Title number. You then send off Form MH1. There is no fee. The Registrar will inform your husband of the registration.

In the case of an unregistered house, the required form is K2, which is sent to the Land Charges Department, Plumer House, Tailyour Road, Crownhill, Plymouth, PL6 5HY, no matter where the house is situated. The fee in this case is £2 and you will be informed within a day or two that a Class F Land Charge has been registered in your name. Again, your husband will not know unless you tell him.

Where you suspect that dealings are imminent, and the time taken in to-ing and fro-ing outlined above might be too long for safety, I suggest you assume both that it is, and that it isn't registered. Send a Form 96 (no fee) as recommended above, and pin it to a Form MH1. In the box for the title number write 'please supply Title number for purpose of Matrimonial Homes Act 1983. URGENT'. At the same time send off a Form K2 with its £2 fee to Plymouth. That's belt and braces for you!

Once you've got a charge on a Register (or both as in the previous paragraph), basically it stays there until death or divorce you do part, and it is known as a charge, and constitutes a caution against dealing. Nevertheless, a judge can make what is known as a 'continuation order' of the wife's right of occupation, which can now continue even though the marriage is at an end. But note, though the judge has said so, it does not mean that the whole world has notice. The charge did die with the marriage, so get a copy of the judge's order from the court office quickly and attach it to a Form MH2 in the case of a registered house, or K8 if the house is unregistered. There is no charge for a Form MH2, but the K8 requires a £1 fee and goes to Plymouth. If for any reason you hadn't got a charge on to one of the Registers before the court hearing, then you must get a Form MH1 or K2 off as swiftly as possible, as explained before.

Judges don't always make continuation orders – the reverse may happen – he may order that the right of occupation is at an end. In this case, a copy of the order with a letter form MH4 is sufficient if the property is registered. No fee is required to have the Charge removed at the appropriate Land Registry.

In the case of unregistered land, you need to send the evidence, a covering letter, and a Form K13 together with a fee of £1 to the Land Charges Department, Plymouth, to have the Class F Charge removed from the register.

A wife may apply to have the registration removed at any time, by sending form MH4 to the Land Registry, or in the case of an unregistered house, Form K13 to the Land Charges Department.

Once a wife's right of occupation is registered, it does no more than ensure that the house is not sold or mortgaged except with her consent or a court order.

Once a wife's right of occupation is registered, it does no more than ensure that the house is not sold or mortgaged except with her consent or a court order. When a wife is in occupation she can achieve the same end for some time, by simply refusing to show viewers or building society and finance company surveyors round the property. No lender will want to lend, and no purchaser will want to negotiate for a property that has such an uncooperative person living in it.

A wife can only protect her right of occupation in respect of one house; so if her husband owns more than one, she will register her right for the one she prefers.

A registration of right to occupy says nothing about how the proceeds will be divided if and when the house is sold. It is essential that the parties try to find a solution between themselves on this point. Recourse to the courts should be the very last resort. Costs can be ruinous, and you might eventually have to pay them yourself, even though you were granted Legal Aid. A person who lodges a caution without reasonable cause is liable in damages to anyone injured as a result.

Earlier in this book, purchasers were advised to treat these entries with grave suspicion, so you will realise that the sooner cautions are removed the better. When an armistice is being arranged, consider putting in a condition that the house be put in joint names (transfer of ownership by way of gift), a little job that you can easily do for yourself.

For a more detailed account, readers with access to the internet should access the Land Registry's Home Page www.landreg.gov.uk, where two explanatory leaflets can be found - Explanatory leaflet 4 for members of the public and Practice leaflet 10 for legal practitioners. All the Land Registry forms mentioned in this article can also be printed off and completed before printing. This does not apply to the Land Charges Department's K forms but these can be purchase from The Stationary office. As can the Land Registry MH forms. Readers who do not have access to a computer can obtain the two leaflets from the Citizens Advice Bureau.

15 Tricks of the trade for layperson conveyancing

Having read this Guide, you can assume you know at least as much about conveyancing, particularly your own, as any solicitor or clerk who might be acting for the other side. Because most Skinners are gentlefolk, they will, in the hope of future non-conveyancing business from you, be helpful and treat you kindly. However, if they seek to put you in the wrong, refer back to the Guide, thank them for their interest and tell them you are working out of the Bradshaw, for sadly, there are people who having heard that conveyancing is only a form filling job, get a few forms and have a go, and building society managers and solicitors do right to give them short shrift.

Conveyancing is not like fitting a bath panel. You just can't get a pack of forms and hope to 'figure it out on the job'. So please, when recommending layperson conveyancing, make sure the aspirant conveyancer has a guide to work from. Reading someone else's guide and then trying to muddle through will get you wound up into Skinner's wringer.

- If you bought a property before the date when compulsory registration was extended to the area you live in, you are under no obligation to register it now. It will have to be registered by whoever purchases it from you.

- A leaseholder paying an annual rent for the privilege of standing on someone else's land with a lease which has a long time to run (say over fifty years) can ask the freeholder to sell. Offer about a twelve year purchase: for example, rent £20 per annum times twelve equals £240.

- You must be careful not to get into disputes with your neighbour, particularly about a few inches of a boundary. If your neighbour insists on making trouble, let it be he who traipses off to a solicitor. Let it be he whom the solicitor warns about high costs in such a case. But at least Skinner can get something out of it by sending you one of his bullying letters threatening you with virtual destruction and certain damnation if you don't let Mr & Mrs Angel have all their own way. Treat the letter with a pinch of salt, unless you happen to know that your neighbour is extremely rich. In such a case telephone your CAB for advice.

- While there are no registers from which you can learn who owns vacant land or derelict property, you can ask around. Local parsons and old established doctors are likely sources of information. Alternatively, you could complete an Index Map Search, Form 96, to find out if the property is a registered title. If it is, you can then find out further details by applying for Office Copies, using Form 109.

- People with property do well to make a will. The trouble is that will makers often give more thought to who gets what, than what will remain to go to whom. Appointing banks and other professionals to be executors can turn out to be very costly. Typically 3per cent is charged on the first £100,000 of an estate, 2 per cent on the next £150,000 and 1per cent on the remainder. Now, if the main asset is a house worth £100,000 that means to say the trustee takes £3,000 – for what? For telling Hand & Glove to be the estate agents and Skinner, Standing & Still to do a conveyance. The beneficiary will get what's left after the estate agent's and solicitor's charges have been added to the £3,000 – all plus the dreaded VAT – ouch! It pays to make a new will every time you move house.

- Quarter days are 25th of March, 24th of June, 29th of September, and 25th of December. A lease may select some other date such as the 1st of April, July, October and January.

- You will have fewer questions from Skinner & Probe when you do your sale conveyance if you have already bought out the owner of any Rent Charge there might be on your property. You are entitled to redeem a rent charge/chief rent/ground rent for approximately ten times the amount of the annual charge. Get yourself an application form from: Department of the Regions, Environment and Transport, 2 Marsham Street, London SW1P 3EB.

- Some conveyances do not contain a plan showing the boundaries and rely only on words. Sometimes you get both words and plans and sometimes one clashes with the other. Words are the stronger unless the conveyance says otherwise.

- A survey of estate agents' services boldly suggested that you have a go at selling for yourself for a couple of weeks. If at the end of that time you have had no joy, you should give it to an agent, they say.

Surely, if what agents say is true, and they have national link-ups and buyers hanging on the back of the door, the best way is to let them have a go for a fortnight, and if their computers, books and door-hooks are bare, then settle down to the board and advertising routine for yourself.

- Most solicitors will provide your purchase file. Don't fret if they won't. Content yourself by asking them what they have to hide, but if you think there is something in it that is really necessary for you to have, an alternative source could be your lender's records. Keep in mind; the house is yours. The deeds are yours, and those deeds are only deposited with the lender as security for the loan.

- Vendors, do not get too involved with a prospective purchaser's solicitor, until a mortgage offer has been issued. Deposits subject to contract are paid today and back tomorrow. £100 paid as a survey fee is lost forever, and therefore more binding.

- Mortgage offer - if the purchase is to be funded by a loan not only never exchange till you have seen and accepted it, but read it very carefully to make sure you can comply with any conditions that appear in the offer. They come in all shapes and sizes and are often long-winded, turgid and badly worded. Also make sure the lender's solicitor is happy with the title, searches and other papers. If you exchange and find you cannot meet a requirement, or he does not like the look of your papers, you will have a serious problem. Remember also the role of the lender's solicitor is to act as the lender's insurer. If the money is advanced and it all goes wrong, he compensates them. One the one hand he will know that. On the other he is probably being paid peanuts to deal with the job, so do not be too surprised he is not going to take any risks or waste too much time helping you out.

- You are in a chain. Your vendor can't complete to contracted date. Write a nice letter to your purchaser, giving the new date. If in reply you receive a snotty letter use it as a model for a similar one to your vendor, but add a covering note saying where you got the idea from.

- Solicitors sometimes refer to a Land Registry Cover. To be precise – they mean a form for dealing, such as an AP1.

- If a conveyancing clerk asks you for a 'fully attested, certified, adjusted engrossed memorandum free of scrotage, together with vesting and singlet assent to reversion of entailed combination by teazle', ask him for a draft of the wording that would satisfy.

When you pay your last payment to your lender, write asking for:

- Registered property: the Charge Certificate and sealed form DS1 or DS3. You can send it all to the Land Registry (no other form required) and in return you will receive your Land Certificate. No need for a solicitor. The Land Registry makes no charge, and neither should your erstwhile lender.

- Unregistered property: ask for your deeds and check that the legal charge has something like, 'received all the monies intended to be secured herein' signed and sealed on it. Check that the conveyance to you is in the parcel and that it has been stamped by the Inland Revenue.

- Masterly controlled inactivity: just because you get a letter with an official heading, be it from Town Hall or Skinner and Hall, it doesn't mean that you have to answer it immediately, if at all.

- If you are told that there is a delay with the searches, phone the council and find out how long they are taking nowadays to deal with them.

16 Forms

Some of the main forms mentioned in this Guide are listed below, with completed examples included for guidance on following pages. You can obtain your forms from HM Land Registry, at their website www.landreg.gov.uk, or from legal stationers, such as Oyez, website www.oyez.co.uk.

Fig 16.1   *Completed Example 94A*
                Application by Purchaser for an Official Search

Application by Purchaser[a] for Official Search with priority of the whole of the land in either a registered title or a pending first registration application

HM Land Registry

Form 94A

Land Registration (Official Searches) Rules 1993

District Land Registry [b]

EDENSHIRE
PARKSIDE WAY
BLOSSOMTON
EDENSHIRE EH8 3TG

Small raised letters in **bold** type refer to explanatory notes overleaf.

Please complete the numbered panels

1 Title number (one only per form) - enter the title number of the registered land or that allotted to the pending first registration.

EDN 999707

2 Registered proprietor(s) / Applicant(s) for first registration[c] - enter FULL name(s) either of the registered proprietor(s) of the land in the above title **or** of the person(s) applying for first registration of the land specified in panel 8.

SURNAME / COMPANY NAME: SMART

FORENAME(S): CLINT

SURNAME / COMPANY NAME: SMART

FORENAME(S): CONSTANCE

3 Search from date - for a search of a **registered title** enter in the box a date falling within (a) of the definition of search from date in rule 2(1).[d] Note: If the date entered is not such a date the application may be rejected. In the case of a **pending first registration** search, enter the letters 'FR'.

16 March 1995

4 Applicant(s) - enter FULL name of each purchaser, **or** lessee **or** chargee.

MR. THOMAS BOLD

MRS. PRUDENCE BOLD

5 Reason for application - I certify that the applicant(s) intend(s) to:- (enter X in the appropriate box)

[X] [P] purchase   [ ] [L] take a lease of   [ ] [C] take a registered charge on

(enter X in the appropriate box)

[X] the **whole** of the land in the above registered title **or**

[ ] the **whole** of the land in the pending first registration application referred to above.

6 Enter the key number[e] (if any) and the name and (DX) address of the person lodging the application (**use BLOCK LETTERS**).

Key number: [ ][ ][ ][ ][ ][ ]

Name: MR THOMAS BOLD

DX No: DX Exchange:

Address including postcode (if DX not used):

1 PROSPECT AVENUE,
ORCHARD VALE,
BLOSSOMTON, EDENSHIRE

Reference: [f]

7 Enter, using BLOCK LETTERS, the name and either address (including postcode) OR (if applicable) the DX No and exchange of the person to whom the result is to be sent. (**Leave blank if result is to be sent to the address in panel 6.**)

Reference: [f]

8 Property details Administrative area [g]   EDENSHIRE

Address (including postcode) or short description:

14 PLEVNA PLACE
BLOSSOMTON ED2 8JD

9 Type of search (enter X in the appropriate box)

[X] **Registered land search**
Application is made to ascertain whether any adverse entry[h] has been made in the register or day list since the date shown in panel 3.

[ ] **Pending first registration search**
Application is made to ascertain whether any adverse entry has been made in the day list since the date of the pending first registration application referred to above.

10   **PAYMENT OF FEE** [i]

Please enter X in the appropriate box.

[X] The Land Registry fee of £4-00 accompanies this application; **or**

[ ] Please debit the Credit Account mentioned in panel 6 with the appropriate fee payable under the current Land Registration Fees Order.

Note: If the fee is not paid by either of the above methods the application may be rejected.

Signature   *Thomas Bold*

Date   1 Nov. 2001   Telephone (01234) 567890

Reproduced by Law Pack Publishing with the permission of the Controller of HMSO

Fig 16.1   Completed Example 94A
Application by Purchaser for an Official Search, continued

Explanatory Notes

(a) 'Purchaser' means any person who, in good faith and for valuable consideration, acquires or intends to acquire a legal estate in land, and includes a lessee or a chargee but not a depositee of a land or charge certificate. An official search made by such depositee or by any person other than a 'purchaser', as so defined, should, provided the land is registered, be made in Form 94C.

(b) The application must be sent to the district land registry serving the area in which the land is situated.

(c) The name(s) of the registered proprietor(s) of the land must be entered as set out in the register of the title. If there are more than two registered proprietors/applicants for first registration, enter the first two only.

(d) The statement printed on an office copy of the register contains the date on which the entries shown on the copy were subsisting (subsisting entries date). The statement will in future also show the date on which the copy was issued.

Where a person accesses a register on-line from the registrar's computer (under rule 4A of the Land Registration (Open Register) Rules 1991) a date (on-line subsisting entries date) is shown which has the same function as the subsisting entries date.

The search from date must be either:

(i) a subsisting entries date taken from an office copy issued not more than twelve months before the day on which the search application will be deemed to be delivered at the Registry; or

(ii) an on-line subsisting entries date shown on register entries transmitted by the registrar's computer system not more than twelve months before the day on which the search application will be deemed to be delivered at the Registry.

The date stated in a Land or Charge Certificate as the date on which the Certificate was officially examined with the register cannot be used.

For the definition of "search from date" see rule 2(1) of the Land Registration (Official Searches) Rules 1993.

For official use only

Record of Fee paid

(e) Where a key number has been allocated it should be used. If you wish the result to be issued to an address different from that associated with the key number, enter your key number and a reference but otherwise leave the remainder of panel 6 blank. Complete panel 7 instead.

(f) Any reference should be restricted to a maximum of 25 characters including oblique strokes and punctuation.

(g) Please enter the administrative area (county and district, county, county or London borough etc.) in which the property is situated.

(h) Any entry made in the register since the search from date of this application but subsequently cancelled will not be revealed.

(i) For the fee payable and the debiting of credit accounts see the current Land Registration Fees Order. Either enclose a cheque for the fee payable (made out to "H M Land Registry") or, if you hold a credit account with the Land Registry/Land Charges Department, ensure that the key number for that account has been entered in panel 6. If you hold a credit account but do not request it to be debited, and no cheque is enclosed, the registrar may nevertheless debit your account.

(j) Fuller information about the official search procedure is contained in Practice Advice Leaflet No. 5, entitled 'Searches of Registered Land and Land Subject to a Pending First Registration Application', and Practice Leaflet No. 7, entitled 'Development of Registered Building Estates' which are obtainable free of charge from any district land registry.

FOR OFFICIAL USE ONLY

1996 Edition 8.97 F34149
5061693

OYEZ The Solicitors' Law Stationery Society Ltd, Oyez House, 7 Spa Road, London SE16 3QQ

Fig 16.2   Completed Example Form 109
            Application for Office Copies of Register

Application for Office Copies of Register/Title Plan; a certificate in Form 102

HM Land Registry

Form 109

(Rule 2 Land Registration (Open Register) Rules 1991)

EDENSHIRE _____ District Land Registry
PARKSIDE WAY
BLOSSOMTON
EDENSHIRE EH8 3TG

Please complete the numbered panels on this form in typescript or **BLOCK LETTERS.**
No covering letter is necessary.
Applications for office copies of specified documents must be made on Form 110.
Use one form per title.

For official use only

Record of Fees paid

Fee Debited   £

1
Title Number (if known)   EDM999707   (Use one character per box)

2
Flat No., if applicable   **Property Description**

Postal number or description   17, PLEVNA PLACE

Name of road

Name of locality   BLOSSOMTON

Town

Administrative area (including district or borough if any)   EDENSHIRE

Post code   ED2 8JD

3 Application
I   THOMAS BOLD
(enter here name and address of person or firm making the application)
of   1 PROSPECT AVENUE
ORCHARD VALE
EDENSHIRE ED5 7AB

apply for

[X] office copy(ies) of the **register** of the above mentioned property;

[ ] office copy(ies) of the **title plan** of the above mentioned property;

[ ] a certificate in Form 102 in which case, either:-

[ ] an Estate Plan has been approved and the Plot Number is
or
[ ] no Estate Plan has been approved and a certificate is to be issued in respect of the land shown _____ on the attached plan and copy.

4   PAYMENT OF FEE

Please enter X in the appropriate box:-

[X] the Land Registry fee of £4.00 accompanies this application,
or
[ ] please debit the Credit Account mentioned below with the appropriate fee payable under the current Land Registration Fees Order.

FOR COMPLETION BY APPLICANTS WHO ARE CREDIT ACCOUNT HOLDERS

YOUR KEY NUMBER:-

YOUR REFERENCE:- (See over)

5 Please enter X in the appropriate box:-

[ ] I am, or act for, either the registered proprietor, or an intending purchaser or mortgagee.

[ ] The above does not apply.

Note: This information is requested for statistical purposes only.

6 Where the title number is NOT quoted in Panel 1 please enter X in the appropriate box(es):-
As regards this property, I am interested in the

[ ] Freehold estate.

[ ] Leasehold estate.

7 In case there is an application for registration pending against the title, please enter X in the appropriate box:-

[ ] I require an office copy back dated to the day prior to the receipt of that application,
or
[ ] I require an office copy on completion of that application.

Signature of applicant:- *Thomas Bold*   Date 15/11/01   Daytime telephone No:- (01234) 567890

8 Reference
THOMAS BOLD
1 PROSPECT AVENUE
ORCHARD VALE
EDENSHIRE ED5 7AB

Please enter above using BLOCK LETTERS the name and either address (including postcode) OR (if applicable) the DX number of the person to whom the office copies are to be sent.

Where you have requested that the fee be paid by Credit Account the appropriate fee has been debited.

Reproduced by Law Book Publishing with the permission of the Controller of HMSO

Fig 16.2   *Completed Example Form 109*

Application for Office Copies of Register, continued

Notes for guidance of applicants

a) The application must be sent to the district land registry serving the area in which the land is situated. A list of addresses of the district land registries is set out in Explanatory Leaflet No. 9 which is obtainable free from any land registry office.

b) Please enter the administrative area (county and district, county, county or London borough etc.) in which the property is situated.

c) Where application is made for a certificate in Form 102 and no estate plan has been approved a plan must be lodged in duplicate. It should be drawn to a suitable scale (generally not less than 1/2500) and must show by suitable markings the extent of the land affected and, where necessary, figured measurements to fix the position of the land by tying it to existing physical features depicted by firm black lines on the plan of the registered title.

d) If there is a pending application and you are applying for an office copy in connection with a further transaction, it is possible for negotiations to proceed on the strength of a back-dated office copy of the register which can be brought up-to-date in effect by making a non-priority official search in Form 94C in which the date of that office copy is entered as the date for the commencement of the search. The certificate of the result of search will reveal details of the pending application for registration and will state whether or not it has yet been approved for entry on the register. If negotiations proceed on this basis, and assuming that your prospective transaction is a transfer, lease or charge, the normal search in Form 94A or 94B can be made as usual immediately before the completion of the transaction.

If a back dated office copy is not required, see panel 7 overleaf, your application for office copies will be returned to you and you will be informed when the pending application has been completed. You should relodge your application for office copies at that time.

e) Full information on all aspects of applications for office copies is set out in Practice Leaflet No. 13 which is obtainable free from any land registry office.

f) If paying fees by cheque or postal order, these should be crossed and made payable to "HM Land Registry".

g) Any reference should be limited to 25 characters (including oblique strokes and punctuation).

For official use only	
Office Copies to be dated: Register ————————	Title Plan ———————
	Date ———————
Authorised by :- ———————————	
Other action —————————	
	—————————
Despatched by :- —————————	Date ———————

Crown Copyright (ref: LR/HQ) 6/97 (Internet)

Fig 16.3   *Completed Example K15*

Application for an Official Search (Unregistered Land)

Form K15

Land Charges Act 1972

Payment of fee

Insert a cross (X)
in this box
if the fee is
to be paid through a
credit account
(see Note 3 overleaf)

APPLICATION FOR AN OFFICIAL SEARCH

NOT APPLICABLE TO REGISTERED LAND

Application is hereby made for an official search in the index to the registers kept pursuant to the Land Charges Act 1972 for any subsisting entries in respect of the under-mentioned particulars.

IMPORTANT: Please read the notes overleaf before completing this form

For Official Use only			NAMES TO BE SEARCHED (Please use block letters and see Note 4 overleaf)	PERIOD OF YEARS (see Note 5 overleaf)	
STX				From	To
		Forename(s)	*CLINT* 1980	*2000*	
		SURNAME	*SMART*		
		Forename(s)	*CONSTANCE* 1980	*2000*	
		SURNAME	*SMART*		
		Forename(s)			
		SURNAME			
		Forename(s)			
		SURNAME			
		Forename(s)			
		SURNAME			
		Forename(s)			
		SURNAME			
		Forename(s)			
		SURNAME			

COUNTY (see Note 6 overleaf)   *EDENSHIRE*

FORMER COUNTY

DESCRIPTION OF LAND (see Note 7 overleaf)

FORMER DESCRIPTION

Particulars of Applicant (see Notes 8, 9 and 10 overleaf)		Name and Address (including postcode) for despatch of certificate (Leave blank if certificate is to be returned to applicant's address)
KEY NUMBER	Name and address (including postcode)	
	MR. THOMAS BOLD *1 PROSPECT AVENUE* *ORCHARD VALE* *EDENSHIRE* *ED5 7AB*	

Applicant's reference: *PLEV0014*	Date *7/11/01*	FOR OFFICIAL USE ONLY

Fig 16.3   Completed Example K15

Application for an Official Search (Unregistered Land), continued

NOTES FOR GUIDANCE OF APPLICANTS

The following notes are supplied for assistance in making the application overleaf. Detailed information for the making of all kinds of applications to the Land Charges Department is contained in a booklet entitled "Computerised Land Charges Department: A practical guide for solicitors" which is obtainable on application at the address shown below.

1. **Effect of search.** The official certificate of the result of this search will have no statutory effect in relation to registered land (see Land Registration Act 1925, s. 59 and Land Charges Act 1972, s. 14).

2. **Bankruptcy only searches.** Form K16 should be used for Bankruptcy only searches.

3. **Fees** must be paid by credit account or by cheque or postal order made payable to "HM Land Registry" (see the guide referred to above).

4. **Names to be searched.** The forename(s) and surname of each individual must be entered on the appropriate line of the form. The name of a company or other body should commence on the forename line and may continue on the surname line (the words "Forename(s)" and "Surname" should be crossed through). If you are searching more than 6 names, use a second form.

5. **Period of years to be searched.** The inclusive period to be covered by a search should be entered in complete years e.g. 1968-1975.

6. **County names.** This must be the appropriate name set out in the Appendix to Land Charges Practice Leaflet No. 3. Searches affecting land within the Greater London area should state "Greater London" as the county name. ANY RELEVANT FORMER COUNTY SHOULD ALWAYS BE STATED (see the Appendix to Land Charges Practice Leaflet No. 3 which lists county names).

7. **Land description.** It is not essential to provide a land description but, if one is given, any relevant former description should also be given (see the guide referred to above).

8. **Key number.** If you have been allocated a key number, please take care to enter this in the space provided overleaf, whether or not you are paying fees through your credit account.

9. **Applicant's name and address.** This need not be supplied if the applicant's key number is correctly entered in the space provided overleaf.

10. **Applicant's reference.** Any reference must be limited to 25 characters, including any oblique strokes and punctuation.

11. **Despatch of this form.** When completed, send this application to the address shown below, which is printed in a position so as to fit within a standard window envelope.

THE SUPERINTENDENT,
LAND CHARGES DEPARTMENT,
SEARCH SECTION,
BURRINGTON WAY,
PLYMOUTH PL5 3LP.
DX 8249, PLYMOUTH 3

(see Note 11 above)

2.98 F34716
5064154
· ★★★

OYEZ The Solicitors' Law Stationery Society Ltd, Oyez House, 7 Spa Road, London SE16 3QQ

Fig 16.4   Completed Example LLC1
Requisition for Search of Local Land Charges

Form LLC1. (*Local Land Charges Rules 1977 Schedule 1, Form C*)

Official Number_____
(*To be completed by the registering authority*)

The duplicate of this form must also be completed:
a carbon copy will suffice.

For directions, notes and fees see overleaf.

Insert name and address of registering authority in space below

EDENSHIRE COUNTY COUNCIL
HIGH STREET
BLOSSOMTON
ED4 9LJ

Register of local land charges

Requisition for search and official certificate of search

Requisition for search
(*A separate requisition must be made in respect of each parcel of land except as explained overleaf*)

An official search is required in *Part(s)*____1-12____of[1] the register of local land charges kept by the above-named registering authority for subsisting registrations against the land [defined in the attached plan and][2] described below.

fold

Description of land sufficient to enable it to be identified

14 PLEVNA PLACE
BLOSSOMTON
EDENSHIRE ED2 8JD

Name and address to which certificate is to be sent

THOMAS BOLD
1 PROSPECT AVENUE
ORCHARD VALE
EDENSHIRE ED5 7AB

Signature of applicant (*or his solicitor*)

Thomas Bold
Date
20/11/01
Telephone number
(01234) 567890
Reference

Enclosure
Cheque/Money Order/Postal Order/Giro

Official certificate of search

It is hereby certified that the search requested above reveals no subsisting registrations[3]

or the_____registrations described in the Schedule hereto[3] up to and including the date of this certificate.

Signed ....

On behalf of ....[4]
Date

To be completed by authorised officer

1 Delete if inappropriate. Otherwise insert Part(s) in which search is required.

2 Delete if inappropriate. (A plan should be furnished in duplicate if it is desired that a copy should be returned.)

3 Delete inapplicable words. (The Parts of the Schedule should be securely attached to the certificate and the number of registrations disclosed should be inserted in the space provided. Only Parts which disclose subsisting registrations should be sent.)

4 Insert name of registering authority.

Reproduced by Law Pack Publishing with the permission of the Controller of HMSO

Fig 16.4   Completed Example LLC1
          Requisition for Search of Local Land Charges, continued

Directions and notes

1 This form and the duplicate should be completed and sent by post to or left at the office of the registering authority.

2 A separate requisition for search should be made in respect of each parcel of land in respect of which a search is required except where, for the purpose of a single transaction, a certificate is required in respect of two or more parcels of land which have a common boundary or are separated only by a road, railway, river, stream or canal.

3 'Parcel of land' means land (including a building or part of a building) which is separately occupied or separately rated or, if not occupied or rated, in separate ownership. For the purpose of this definition an owner is the person who (in his own right or as trustee for any other person) is entitled to receive the rack rent of land, or, where the land is not let at a rack rent, would be so entitled if it were so let.

4 The certificate of the result of an official search of the register refers to any subsisting registrations, recorded against the land defined in the application for search, in the Parts of the register in respect of which the search is requested. The Parts of the register record:

Part 1	General financial charges.
Part 2	Specific financial charges.
Part 3	Planning charges.
Part 4	Miscellaneous charges.
Part 5	Fenland ways maintenance charges.
Part 6	Land compensation charges.
Part 7	New towns charges.
Part 8	Civil aviation charges.
Part 9	Opencast coal charges.
Part 10	Listed buildings charges.
Part 11	Light obstruction notices.
Part 12	Drainage scheme charges.

5 An office copy of any entry in the register can be obtained on written request and on payment of the prescribed fee.

Fees

Official search (including issue of official certificate of search)	
in any one part of the register	£1.90
in the whole of the register	£5.00
and in addition, but subject to a maximum additional fee of £13.00, in respect of each parcel above one, where several parcels are included in the same requisition (see notes 2 and 3 above) whether the requisition is for search in the whole or any part of the register	80p
Office copy of any entry in the register (not including a copy or extract of any plan or document filed by the registering authority)	£1.40
Office copy of any plan or other document filed by the registering authority	Such reasonable fee as may be fixed by the registering authority according to the time and work involved.

All fees must be prepaid

OYEZ   The Solicitors' Law Stationery Society Ltd, Oyez House, 7 Spa Road, London SE16 3QQ

5.98 F35122
5063019
* * *

LLC1

Fig 16.5   *Completed Example Con 29*
              Enquiries of Local Authority

CON. 29 (1994)
To be submitted in duplicate

ENQUIRIES OF LOCAL AUTHORITY
(1994 EDITION)

Please type or use BLOCK LETTERS

Search No......................................
The Replies are given on the attached sheet(s)

Signed .... Proper Officer

Date......................................

A.
To
EDENSHIRE COUNTY COUNCIL
HIGH STREET
BLOSSOMTON
EDENSHIRE EH7 9IJ

B.
Property

14 PLEVNA PLACE
BLOSSOMTON
EDENSHIRE
ED2 8JD

C. Other roadways, footpaths and footways

N/A

A. Enter name and address of District or Borough Council for the area. If the property is near a Local Authority boundary, consider raising certain Enquiries (e.g. road schemes) with the adjoining Council.

B. Enter address and description of the property. A plan in duplicate must be attached if possible and is insisted upon by some Councils. Without a plan, replies may be inaccurate or incomplete. A plan is essential for Optional Enquiries 18, 37 and 38.

C. Enter name and/or location of (and mark on plan, if possible) any other roadways, footpaths and footways (in addition to those entered in Box B) for Enquiry 3 and (if raised) Enquiries 19 and 20.

D. Answer every question. Any additional Enquiries must be attached on a separate sheet in duplicate and an additional fee will be charged for any which the Council is willing to answer.

E. Details of fees can be obtained from the Council or The Law Society.

F. Enter name and address of the person or firm lodging this form.

G. Tick which Optional Enquiries are to be answered.

PLEASE READ THE NOTES ON PAGE 4.

D.
A plan in duplicate is attached	YES/NO
Optional Enquiries are to be answered (see Box G)	YES/NO
Additional Enquiries are attached in duplicate on a separate sheet	YES/NO

E.
Fees of £   are enclosed.
          100

Signed : *Thomas Bold*

Date :   15/11/01

Reference :
PLEVNA

Tel. No. : (01234) 567890

F. Reply to
THOMAS BOLD
1 PROSPECT AVENUE
ORCHARD VALE
BLOSSOMTON
EDENSHIRE ED5 7AB

G. Optional Enquiries

	17.	Road proposals by private bodies
	18.	Public paths or byways
	19.	Permanent road closure
	20.	Traffic schemes
✓	21.	Advertisements
	22.	Completion notices
	23.	Parks and countryside
	24.	Pipelines
	25.	Houses in multiple occupation
	26.	Noise abatement
	27.	Urban development areas
	28.	Enterprise zones
	29.	Inner urban improvement areas
	30.	Simplified planning zones
	31.	Land maintenance notices
	32.	Mineral consultation areas
	33.	Hazardous substance consents
	34.	Environmental and pollution notices
	35.	Food safety notices
	36.	Radon gas precautions
	37.	Sewers within the property
	38.	Nearby sewers

LAW SOCIETY COPYRIGHT
9.97 F34273 5033379

OYEZ The Solicitors' Law Stationery Society Limited, Oyez House, 7 Spa Road, London SE16 3QQ
Conveyancing 29(1994)

Reproduced by Law Pack Publishing with the permission of the Controller of HMSO

Fig 16.5   *Completed Example Con 29*

Enquiries of Local Authority, continued

PART I—STANDARD ENQUIRIES
(APPLICABLE IN EVERY CASE)

DEVELOPMENT PLANS PROVISIONS

Structure Plan([1])

1.1.1 What structure plan is in force?

1.1.2 Have any proposals been made public for the alteration of the structure plan?

Local Plans([1])([2])

1.2.1 What stage has been reached in the preparation of a local plan?

1.2.2 Have any proposals been made public for the alteration or replacement of a local plan?

Old Style Development Plan

1.3 What old style development plan is in force?

Unitary Development Plan([1])

1.4.1 What stage has been reached in the preparation of a unitary development plan?

1.4.2 Have any proposals been made public for the alteration or replacement of a unitary development plan?

Non-Statutory Plan

1.5.1 Have the Council made public any proposals for the preparation or modification of a non-statutory plan?

1.5.2 If so, what stage has been reached?

Policies or Proposals for the Property

1.6 Do any of the above plans (including any proposed alterations or replacements) indicate:

(a)   a designation of primary use or zoning for the property or the area, or

(b)   a specific proposal which includes the property?

Land required for Public Purposes

1.7 Is the property included in any of the categories of land specified in Schedule 13 paras 5 and 6 of the T&CP Act 1990?

DRAINAGE

Foul Drainage

2.1.1 To the Council's knowledge, does foul drainage from the property drain to a public sewer?([3])([4])

2.1.2 If yes, does the property drain into the public sewer through:

(a)   a private drain alone, or

(b)   a private drain and then a private sewer?([3])([4])([5])

Surface Water Drainage

2.2.1 To the Council's knowledge, does surface water from the property drain to:

(a)   a public sewer, or

(b)   a highway drain?([3])([4])([5])

2.2.2 If the answer to 2.2.1(a) or (b) is yes, does the surface water drain to it through:

(a)   a private drain alone, or

(b)   a private drain and then a private sewer?([3])([4])([5])

Statutory Agreements and Consents

2.3.1 Is there in force an agreement under s.22 of the Building Act 1984 for drainage of any part of the property in combination with another building through a private sewer?

2.3.2 Except as shown in the Official Certificate of Search, is there in force an agreement or consent under s.18 of the Building Act 1984 for the erection of a building or extension of a building over or in the vicinity of a drain, sewer or disposal main?([4])

Adoption Agreement

2.4.1 To the Council's knowledge, is any sewer serving, or which is proposed to serve, the property the subject of an agreement under s.104 of the Water Industry Act 1991 for the sewer to become vested in the sewerage undertaker?([5])([6])

2.4.2 If so, is such an agreement supported by a bond or other financial security?([6])

Sewerage Undertaker

2.5 Please state the name and address of the sewerage undertaker.

MAINTENANCE OF ROADS ETC.

Publicly Maintained

3.1 Are all the roadways, footpaths and footways referred to in Boxes B and C on page 1 maintainable at the public expense within the meaning of the Highways Act 1980?([7])

Resolutions to make up or adopt

3.2 If not, have the Council passed any resolution to:

(a)   make up any of those roadways, footpaths or footways at the cost of the frontagers, or

(b)   adopt any of them without cost to the frontagers?

If so, please specify([7]).

Adoption Agreements

3.3.1 Have the Council entered into any subsisting agreement relating to the adoption of any of those roadways, footpaths or footways? If so, please specify([6]).

3.3.2 Is any such agreement supported by a bond or other financial security?([6])

ROAD SCHEMES

Trunk and Special Roads

4.1.1 What orders, draft orders or schemes have been notified to the Council by the appropriate Secretary of State for the construction of a new trunk or special road, the centre line of which is within 200 metres of the property?

4.1.2 What proposals have been notified to the Council by the appropriate Secretary of State for:

(a)   the alteration or improvement of an existing road, involving the construction, whether or not within existing highway limits, of a subway, underpass, flyover, footbridge, elevated road or dual carriageway, the centre line of which is within 200 metres of the property, or

(b)   the construction of a roundabout (other than a mini-roundabout([8])), or the widening of an existing road by the construction of one or more additional traffic lanes, the limits of construction of which are within 200 metres of the property?

Other Roads

4.2 What proposals of their own([9]) have the Council approved for any of the following, the limits of construction of which are within 200 metres of the property:

(a)   the construction of a new road, or

(b)   the alteration or improvement of an existing road, involving the construction, whether or not within existing highway limits, of a subway, underpass, flyover, footbridge, elevated road, dual carriageway, the construction of a roundabout (other than a mini-roundabout([8])), or the widening of an existing road by the construction of one or more additional traffic lanes?

Road Proposals Involving Acquisition

4.3 What proposals have the Council approved, or have been notified to the Council by the appropriate Secretary of State, for highway construction or improvement that involve the acquisition of the property?

Road Proposals at Consultation Stage

4.4 What proposals have either the Secretary of State or the Council published for public consultation relating to:

(a)   the construction of a new road indicating a possible route the centre line of which would be likely to be within 200 metres of the property, or

(b)   the alteration or improvement of an existing road, involving the construction, whether or not within existing highway limits, of a subway, underpass, flyover, footbridge, elevated road, dual carriageway, the construction of a roundabout (other than a mini-roundabout([8])), or the widening of an existing road by the construction of one or more additional traffic lanes, the limits of construction of which would be likely to be within 200 metres of the property?

OUTSTANDING NOTICES

5. What outstanding statutory notices or informal notices have been issued by the Council under the Public Health Acts, Housing Acts, Highways Acts, Building Acts([10]) or Part III of the Environmental Protection Act 1990?

(This enquiry does not cover notices shown in the Official Certificate of Search or notices relating to matters covered by Enquiries 13 or, if raised, 31, 34 or 35.)

BUILDING REGULATIONS

6. What proceedings have the Council authorised in respect of an infringement of the Building Regulations?

---

(1)   The present development plan system requires structure plans by the County Council in the non-metropolitan areas, as well as local plans by District Councils. County Councils also deal with minerals and waste plans. In Greater London and the metropolitan areas, Unitary Development Plans are prepared by the relevant London Borough or metropolitan district council.

(2)   Local plan includes action area plan.

(3)   Any reply will be based on the statutory sewer map provided to the Council by the sewerage undertaker and any other records which the Council may hold.

(4)   If the reply is "Not Known", the enquiry should be raised directly with the sewerage undertaker.

(5)   The sewerage undertaker is not responsible for the maintenance of private drains or private sewers connecting a property to the public sewer.

(6)   An adoption or vesting agreement requires adoption or vesting to take place only when the developer complies with his obligations under that agreement and the enquirer should make separate enquiries as to such compliance and should satisfy himself as to the adequacy of any bond or other financial security for such compliance.

(7)   An affirmative answer does not imply that the public highway directly abuts the boundary of the property.

(8)   A mini-roundabout is a roundabout having a one-way circulatory carriageway around a flush or slightly raised circular marking less than 4 metres in diameter and with or without flared approaches.

(9)   This enquiry refers to the Council's (including where appropriate the County Council's) own proposals but not those of any other bodies or companies; the latter are covered by Enquiry 17 in Part II.

(10) For property in Greater London, this includes the London Building Acts.

Fig 16.5   *Completed Example Con 29*

Enquiries of Local Authority, continued

PLANNING APPLICATIONS AND PERMISSIONS

Applications and Decisions

7.1 Please list:
- (a) any entries in the Register of planning applications and permissions,
- (b) any applications and decisions in respect of listed building consent, and
- (c) any applications and decisions in respect of conservation area consent.

Inspection and Copies

7.2 If there are any entries:
- (a) how can copies of the decisions be obtained?
- (b) where can the Register be inspected?

NOTICES UNDER PLANNING ACTS

Enforcement and Stop Notices

8.1.1 Please list any entries in the Register of enforcement notices and stop notices.

8.1.2 If there are any entries:
- (a) how can copies of the notices be obtained?
- (b) where can that Register be inspected?

Proposed Enforcement or Stop Notice

8.2 Except as shown in the Official Certificate of Search, or in reply to Enquiry 8.1.1., has any enforcement notice, listed building enforcement notice, or stop notice been authorised by the Council for issue or service (other than notices which have been withdrawn or quashed)?

Compliance with Enforcement Notices

8.3 If an enforcement notice or listed building enforcement notice has been served or issued, has it been complied with to the satisfaction of the Council?

Other Planning Notices

8.4 Have the Council served, or resolved to serve, any breach of condition or planning contravention notice or any other notice or proceedings relating to a breach of planning control?

Listed Building Repairs Notices, etc.

8.5.1 To the knowledge of the Council, has the service of a repairs notice been authorised?

8.5.2 If the Council have authorised the making of an order for the compulsory acquisition of a listed building, is a "minimum compensation" provision included, or to be included, in the order?

8.5.3 Have the Council authorised the service of a building preservation notice?[11]

DIRECTIONS RESTRICTING PERMITTED DEVELOPMENT

9. Except as shown in the Official Certificate of Search, have the Council resolved to make a direction to restrict permitted development?

ORDERS UNDER PLANNING ACTS

Revocation Orders etc.

10.1 Except as shown in the Official Certificate of Search, have the Council resolved to make any Orders revoking or modifying any planning permission or discontinuing an existing planning use?

Tree Preservation Order

10.2 Except as shown in the Official Certificate of Search, have the Council resolved to make any Tree Preservation Orders?

COMPENSATION FOR PLANNING DECISIONS

11. What compensation has been paid by the Council under s.114 of the T&CP Act 1990 for planning decisions restricting development other than new development?

CONSERVATION AREA

12. Except as shown in the Official Certificate of Search, is the area a conservation area?

COMPULSORY PURCHASE

13. Except as shown in the Official Certificate of Search, have the Council made any order (whether or not confirmed by the appropriate Secretary of State) or passed any resolution for compulsory acquisition which is still capable of being implemented?[12]

AREAS DESIGNATED UNDER HOUSING ACTS ETC.

Clearance

14.1 Has any programme of clearance for the area been:
- (a) submitted to the Department of the Environment, or
- (b) resolved to be submitted, or
- (c) otherwise adopted by resolution of the Council?

Housing

14.2 Except as shown in the Official Certificate of Search, have the Council resolved to define the area as designated for a purpose under the Housing Acts? If so, please specify the purpose.

SMOKE CONTROL ORDER

15. Except as shown in the Official Certificate of Search, have the Council made a smoke control order or resolved to make or vary a smoke control order for the area?

RAILWAYS

16. What proposals have been notified to the Council, and what proposals of their own have the Council approved, for the construction of a railway (including light railway or monorail) the centre line of which is within 200 metres of the property?

PART II—OPTIONAL ENQUIRIES
(APPLICABLE ONLY AS INDICATED ON PAGE ONE)

ROAD PROPOSALS BY PRIVATE BODIES

17. What proposals by others[13] have the Council approved for any of the following, the limits of construction of which are within 200 metres of the property:
- (a) the construction of a new road, or
- (b) the alteration or improvement of an existing road, involving the construction, whether or not within existing highway limits, of a subway, underpass, flyover, footbridge, elevated road, dual carriageway, the construction of a roundabout (other than a mini-roundabout[9]), or the widening of an existing road by the construction of one or more additional traffic lanes?

PUBLIC PATHS OR BYWAYS

18. Is any public path, bridleway or road used as a public path or byway which abuts on[7] or crosses the property shown in a definitive map or revised definitive map prepared under Part IV of the National Parks and Access to the Countryside Act 1949 or Part III of the Wildlife and Countryside Act 1981? If so, please mark its approximate route on the attached plan[14].

PERMANENT ROAD CLOSURE

19. What proposals have the Council approved for permanently stopping up or diverting any of the roads or footpaths referred to in Boxes B and C on page 1?

TRAFFIC SCHEMES

20. In respect of any of the roads referred to in Boxes B and C on page 1, what proposals have the Council approved, but have not yet put into operation, for:
- (a) waiting or loading restrictions,
- (b) one-way streets,
- (c) prohibition of driving,
- (d) pedestrianisation, or
- (e) vehicle width or weight restrictions?

ADVERTISEMENTS

Entries in Register

21.1.1 Please list any entries in the Register of applications, directions and decisions relating to consent for the display of advertisements.

21.1.2 If there are any entries, where can that Register be inspected?

Notices, Proceedings and Orders

21.2 Except as shown in the Official Certificate of Search:
- (a) has any notice been given by the Secretary of State or served in respect of a direction or proposed direction restricting deemed consent for any class of advertisement?
- (b) have the Council resolved to serve a notice requiring the display of any advertisement to be discontinued?
- (c) if a discontinuance notice has been served, has it been complied with to the satisfaction of the Council?
- (d) have the Council resolved to serve any other notice or proceedings relating to a contravention of the control of advertisements?
- (e) have the Council resolved to make an order for the special control of advertisements for the area?

COMPLETION NOTICES

22. Which of the planning permissions in force have the Council resolved to terminate by means of a completion notice under s.94 of the T&CP Act 1990?

---

(11) The Historic Buildings and Monuments Commission also have power to issue this type of notice for buildings in London Boroughs, and separate enquiry should be made of them if appropriate.

(12) This enquiry refers to the Council's own compulsory purchase powers and not those of other bodies.

(13) This enquiry refers to proposals by bodies or companies (such as private developers) other than the Council (and where appropriate the County Council) or the Secretary of State.

(14) A plan of the property must be supplied by the enquirer if this enquiry is to be answered.

Fig 16.5   *Completed Example Con 29*

Enquiries of Local Authority, continued

PARKS AND COUNTRYSIDE

Areas of Outstanding Natural Beauty

23.1 Has any order under s.87 of the National Parks and Access to the Countryside Act 1949 been made?

National Parks

23.2 Is the property within a National Park designated under s.7 of the National Parks and Access to the Countryside Act 1949?

PIPELINES

24. Has a map been deposited under s.35 of the Pipelines Act 1962, or Schedule 7 of the Gas Act 1986, showing a pipeline laid through, or within 100 feet (30.48 metres) of, the property?

HOUSES IN MULTIPLE OCCUPATION

25. Is the property included in a registration of houses scheme (houses in multiple occupation) under s.346 of the Housing Act 1985, containing control provisions as authorised by s.347 of that Act?

NOISE ABATEMENT

Noise Abatement Zone

26.1 Have the Council made, or resolved to make, any noise abatement zone order under s.63 of the Control of Pollution Act 1974 for the area?

Entries in Register

26.2.1 Has any entry been recorded in the Noise Level Register kept pursuant to s.64 of the Control of Pollution Act 1974?

26.2.2 If there is an entry, how can copies be obtained and where can that Register be inspected?

URBAN DEVELOPMENT AREAS

27.1 Is the area an urban development area designated under Part XVI of the Local Government Planning and Land Act 1980?

27.2 If so, please state the name of the urban development corporation and the address of its principal office.

ENTERPRISE ZONES

28. Is the area an enterprise zone designated under Part XVIII of the Local Government Planning and Land Act 1980?

INNER URBAN IMPROVEMENT AREAS

29. Have the Council resolved to define the area as an improvement area under s.4 of the Inner Urban Areas Act 1978?

SIMPLIFIED PLANNING ZONES

30.1 Is the area a simplified planning zone adopted or approved pursuant to s.83 of the T&CP Act 1990?

30.2 Have the Council approved any proposal for designating the area as a simplified planning zone?

LAND MAINTENANCE NOTICES

31. Have the Council authorised the service of a maintenance notice under s.215 of the T&CP Act 1990?

MINERAL CONSULTATION AREAS

32. Is the area a mineral consultation area notified by the county planning authority under Schedule 1 para 7 of the T&CP Act 1990?

HAZARDOUS SUBSTANCE CONSENTS

33.1 Please list any entries in the Register kept pursuant to s.28 of the Planning (Hazardous Substances) Act 1990.

33.2 If there are any entries:
(a) how can copies of the entries be obtained?
(b) where can the Register be inspected?

ENVIRONMENTAL AND POLLUTION NOTICES

34. What outstanding notices or informal notices have been issued by the Council under the Environmental Protection Act or the Control of Pollution Act?
(This enquiry does not cover notices under Part III of the EPA, to which Enquiry 5 applies).

FOOD SAFETY NOTICES

35. What outstanding statutory notices or informal notices have been issued by the Council under the Food Safety Act?

RADON GAS PRECAUTIONS

36.1 Is the property in an area where radon precautions are required for new dwellings?

36.2 If so, are full or secondary precautions required?

SEWERS WITHIN THE PROPERTY [3][14]

37. Does the statutory sewer map show, within the boundaries of the property as depicted on the attached plan, a public sewer or disposal main, a sewer in respect of which a vesting declaration has been made but which has not yet come into force, or a drain or sewer which is the subject of an agreement under s.104 of the Water Industry Act 1991?

NEARBY SEWERS [3][14]

38. Please either:
(a) state whether the statutory sewer map shows public foul and surface water sewers within 100 feet (30.48 metres) of the property ([15]), or
(b) supply a copy extract from the statutory sewer map showing any public sewers in the vicinity of the property([16]).

[15] The sewer map does not show the relative levels of the sewers and the property.

[16] If the Council supplies an extract from the sewer map, the notation should be carefully checked and any queries should be clarified with the Council or the sewerage undertaker.

GENERAL NOTES

(A) Unless otherwise indicated, all these enquiries relate to the property as described in Box B on page 1, and any part of that property, and "the area" means any area in which the property is located.

(B) References to "the Council" include references to a predecessor Council and to a Committee or Sub-Committee of the Council acting under delegated powers, and to any other body or person taking action under powers delegated by the Council or a predecessor Council. The replies given to certain enquiries addressed to District Councils cover knowledge and actions of both the District Council and the County Council.

(C) References to an Act, Regulation or Order include reference to (i) any statutory provision which it replaces and (ii) any amendment or re-enactment of it.

(D) References to any Town and Country Planning Act, Order or Regulation are abbreviated, eg "T&CP Act 1990".

(E) The replies will be given after the appropriate enquiries and in the belief that they are in accordance with the information at present available to the officers of the replying Council(s), but on the distinct understanding that none of the Councils, nor any Council officer, is legally responsible for them, except for negligence. Any liability for negligence shall extend for the benefit of not only the person by or for whom these Enquiries are made but also a person (being a purchaser for the purposes of s.10(3) of the Local Land Charges Act 1975) who or whose agent had knowledge, before the relevant time (as defined in that section), of the replies to these Enquiries.

(F) This form of Enquiries is approved by The Law Society, the Association of County Councils, the Association of District Councils and the Association of Metropolitan Authorities and is published by their authority.

Fig 16.6　　*Completed Example 28B*

　　　　　　Requisitions on Title

These requisitions are copyright and may not be reproduced

─── OYEZ ───

REQUISITIONS

ON TITLE

(For use where Enquiries before Contract have already been answered)

Please strike out any requisitions not applicable.

Short description of the property　re...

Parties　　...

　　　　to...

1.　PREVIOUS ENQUIRIES

If the enquiries before contract replied to on behalf of the Seller were repeated here, would the replies now be the same as those previously given? If not, please give full particulars of any variation.

2.　OUTGOINGS AND APPORTIONMENTS

(A) On completion the Seller must produce receipts for the last payments of outgoings, of which either he claims reimbursement of an advance payment or arrears could be recovered from the Buyer.

(B)　(i) In the case of a leasehold property or property subject to a legal rentcharge, the receipt for rent due on the last rent day before the day of completion, as well as the receipt for the last fire insurance premium, must be produced on completion.

　　(ii) Does the former receipt contain any reference to a breach of any of the covenants and conditions contained in the lease or grant?

(C) Please send a completion statement.

3.　TITLE DEEDS

A.　*Unregistered land*

　　(i) Which abstracted documents of title will be delivered to the Buyer on completion?

　　(ii) Who will give to the Buyer the statutory acknowledgment and undertaking for the production and safe custody of those not handed over?

　　(iii) Why will any documents not handed over be retained?

B.　*Registered land*

　　(i) If the Land Registry has approved an estate lay-out plan for use with official searches of part of the land in the title, on what date was it approved?

　　(ii) If the Seller's land certificate is on deposit at the Land Registry, what is the deposit number?

4.　MORTGAGES

(A) Please specify those mortgages or charges which will be discharged on or before completion.

(B) In respect of each subsisting mortgage or charge:

　　(i) Will a vacating receipt, discharge of registered charge or consent to dealing, entitling the Buyer to take the property freed from it, be handed over on completion?

　　(ii) If not, will the Seller's solicitor give a written undertaking on completion to hand one over later?

　　(iii) If an undertaking is proposed, what are the suggested terms of it?

Fig 16.6   *Completed Example 28B*
          Requisitions on Title, continued

5. POSSESSION

(A) (i) Vacant possession of the whole of the property must be given on completion.

    (ii) Has every person in occupation of all or any part of the property agreed to vacate on or before completion?

    (iii) What arrangements will be made to deliver the keys to the Buyer?

Or

(B) The Seller must on completion hand over written authorities for future rents to be paid to the Buyer or his agents.

6. NOTICES

Please give the name and address of any solicitor, residential tenant or other person to whom notice of any dealing with the property must be given.

7. COMPLETION ARRANGEMENTS

Please answer any of the following requisitions against which X has been placed in the box.

☐ (A) Where will completion take place?

☐ (B) We should like to remit the completion monies direct to your bank account. If you agree, please give the name and branch of your bank, its sort code, and the title and number of the account to be credited.

☐ (C) In whose favour and for what amounts will banker's drafts be required on completion?

☐ (D) Please confirm that you will comply with the Law Society's Code for Completion by Post (1998 edition).

The right is reserved to make further requisitions which may arise on the replies to the above, the usual searches and enquiries before completion, or otherwise.

Note. — Requisitions founded on the title or contract must be added to the above.

DATED

DATED

Buyer's Solicitor.

Seller's Solicitor.

1998 Edition
7.98   F35399
5032056
★ ★

© 1998 **OYEZ** The Solicitors' Law Stationery Society Ltd, Oyez House, 7 Spa Road, London SE16 3QQ

Conveyancing 28B

Reproduced by Law Pack Publishing with the permission of The Solicitors' Law Stationery Society Ltd.

Fig 16.7   *Completed Example TR1*
          Transfer of Whole of Registered Title(s)

**Transfer of whole
of registered title(s)**

HM Land Registry **TR1**

(if you need more room than is provided for in a panel, use continuation sheet CS and staple to this form)

1. Stamp Duty

Place "X" in the box that applies and complete the box in the appropriate certificate.

[X] I/We hereby certify that this instrument falls within category [ ] in the Schedule to the Stamp Duty (Exempt Instruments) Regulations 1987

[ ] It is certified that the transaction effected does not form part of a larger transaction or of a series of transactions in respect of which the amount or value or the aggregate amount or value of the consideration exceeds the sum of

£

2. Title Number(s) of the Property *(leave blank if not yet registered)*

EDN999707

3. Property

14 PLEVNA PLACE
BLOSSOMTON, EDENSHIRE ED2 8JD

If this transfer is made under section 37 of the Land Registration Act 1925 following a not-yet-registered dealing with part only of the land in a title, or is made under rule 72 of the Land Registration Rules 1925, include a reference to the last preceding document of title containing a description of the property.

4. Date

5. Transferor *(give full names and Company's Registered Number if any)*

MR. CLINT SMART and MRS. CONSTANCE SMART

6. Transferee for entry on the register *(Give full names and Company's Registered Number if any; for Scottish Co. Reg. Nos., use an SC prefix. For foreign companies give territory in which incorporated.)*

MR. THOMAS BOLD and MRS. PRUDENCE BOLD

Unless otherwise arranged with Land Registry headquarters, a certified copy of the transferee's constitution (in English or Welsh) will be required if it is a body corporate but is not a company registered in England and Wales or Scotland under the Companies Acts.

7. Transferee's intended address(es) for service in the U.K. *(including postcode)* **for entry on the register**

1 PROSPECT AVENUE
ORCHARD VALE
EDENSHIRE ED5 7AB

8. The Transferor transfers the property to the Transferee.

9. Consideration *(Place "X" in the box that applies. State clearly the currency unit if other than sterling. If none of the boxes applies, insert an appropriate memorandum in the additional provisions panel.)*

[X] The Transferor has received from the Transferee for the property the sum of *(in words and figures)*
£155,000   ONE HUNDRED FIFTY FIVE THOUSAND POUNDS

[ ] *(insert other receipt as appropriate)*

[ ] The Transfer is not for money or anything which has a monetary value

Fig 16.7   Completed Example TR1

    Transfer of Whole of Registered Title(s), continued

10. The Transferor transfers with *(place "X" in the box which applies and add any modifications)*

[X] full title guarantee   [ ] limited title guarantee

11. Declaration of trust *Where there is more than one transferee, place "X" in the appropriate box.*

[X] The transferees are to hold the property on trust for themselves as joint tenants.

[ ] The transferees are to hold the property on trust for themselves as tenants in common in equal shares.

[ ] The transferees are to hold the property *(complete as necessary)*

12. Additional Provision(s) *Insert here any required or permitted statement, certificate or application and any agreed covenants, declarations, etc.*

13. The Transferors and all other necessary parties should execute this transfer as a deed using the space below. Forms of execution are given in Schedule 3 to the Land Registration Rules 1925. If the transfer contains transferees' covenants or declarations or contains an application by them (e.g. for a restriction), it must also be executed by the Transferees.

Signed as a deed by   CLINT SMART

in the presence of:

Signature of witness

Name

Address

George Ross

GEORGE ROSS

6 The Willows

Blossomton

Edenshire EH78 12A

1.98 F34697
5061088

OYEZ The Solicitors' Law Stationery Society Ltd, Oyez House, 7 Spa Road, London SE16 3QQ

17 District Land Registries

Areas served

Administrative area	District Land Registry
England	
Bath and North East Somerset	Plymouth
Bedfordshire	Peterborough
Blackburn with Darwen	Lancashire
Blackpool	Lancashire
Bournemouth	Weymouth
Bracknell Forest	Gloucester
Brighton and Hove	Portsmouth
Bristol	Gloucester
Buckinghamshire	Leicester
Cambridgeshire	Peterborough
Cheshire	Birkenhead (Rosebrae)
Cornwall	Plymouth
Cumbria	Durham (Boldon House)
Darlington	Durham (Southfield House)
Derby	Nottingham (West)
Derbyshire	Nottingham (West)
Devon	Plymouth
Dorset	Weymouth
Durham	Durham (Southfield House)
East Riding of Yorkshire	York
East Sussex	Portsmouth
Essex	Peterborough
Gloucestershire	Gloucester

Areas served

Administrative area	District Land Registry
GREATER LONDON (London Borough)	
Barking & Dagenham	Stevenage
Barnet	Swansea
Bexley	Croydon
Brent	Harrow
Bromley	Croydon
Camden	Harrow
City of London	Harrow
City of Westminster	Harrow
Croydon	Croydon
Ealing	Swansea
Enfield	Swansea
Greenwich	Telford
Hackney	Stevenage
Hammersmith & Fulham	Birkenhead (Rosebrae)
Haringey	Swansea
Harrow	Harrow
Havering	Stevenage
Hillingdon	Swansea
Hounslow	Swansea
Inner & Middle Temples	Harrow
Islington	Harrow
Kensington & Chelsea	Birkenhead (Rosebrae)
Kingston upon Thames	Croydon
Lambeth	Telford
Lewisham	Telford
Merton	Croydon
Newham	Stevenage
Redbridge	Stevenage
Richmond upon Thames	Telford
Southwark	Telford

Areas served

Administrative area	District Land Registry
Sutton	Croydon
Tower Hamlets	Stevenage
Waltham Forest	Stevenage
Wandsworth	Telford
Greater Manchester	Lytham
Halton	Birkenhead (Rosebrae)
Hampshire	Weymouth
Hartlepool	Durham (Southfield House)
Herefordshire	Telford
Hertfordshire	Stevenage
Isle of Wight	Portsmouth
Isles of Scilly	Plymouth
Kent	Tunbridge Wells
Kingston-Upon-Hull	Kingston-Upon-Hull
Lancashire	Lancashire
Leicester	Leicester
Leicestershire	Leicester
Lincolnshire	Kingston-Upon-Hull
Luton	Peterborough
Medway Towns	Tunbridge Wells
Merseyside	Birkenhead (Old Market)
Middlesbrough	Durham (Southfield House)
Milton Keynes	Leicester
Norfolk	Kingston-Upon-Hull
North East Lincolnshire	Kingston-Upon-Hull
North Lincolnshire	Kingston-Upon-Hull
North Somerset	Plymouth
North Yorkshire	York
Northamptonshire	Peterborough
Northumberland	Durham (Southfield House)

Areas served

Administrative area	District Land Registry
Nottingham	Nottingham
(East) Nottinghamshire	Nottingham (East)
Oxfordshire	Gloucester
Peterborough	Peterborough
Plymouth	Plymouth
Poole	Weymouth
Portsmouth	Portsmouth
Reading	Gloucester
Redcar and Cleveland	Durham (Southfield House)
Rutland	Leicester
Shropshire	Telford
Slough	Gloucester
Somerset	Plymouth
South Gloucestershire	Gloucester
South Yorkshire	Nottingham (East)
Southampton	Weymouth
Southend-on-Sea	Peterborough
Staffordshire	Birkenhead (Old Market)
Stockton-on-Tees	Durham (Southfield House)
Stoke-on-Trent	Birkenhead (Old Market)
Suffolk	Kingston-Upon-Hull
Surrey	Durham (Boldon House)
Swindon	Weymouth
Thurrock	Peterborough
Torbay	Plymouth
Tyne and Wear	Durham (Southfield House)
Warrington	Birkenhead (Rosebrae)
Warwickshire	Gloucester
West Berkshire	Gloucester
West Midlands	Coventry
West Sussex	Portsmouth

Areas served

Administrative area	District Land Registry
West Yorkshire	Nottingham (West)
Wiltshire	Weymouth
Windsor and Maidenhead	Gloucester
Wokingham	Gloucester
Worcestershire	Coventry
Wrekin	Telford
York	York

Wales/Cymru

All Areas	Wales/Cymru

Postal addresses and telephone numbers

England

HM Land Registry Headquarters

Lincoln's Inn Fields
London WC2A 3PH

Website: www.landreg.gov.uk
Tel: 020 7917 8888
Fax: 020 7955 0110

Birkenhead

The address for titles in Cheshire, Halton and Warrington and the London Boroughs of Kensington and Chelsea/Hammersmith and Fulham is:

The Birkenhead (Rosebrae) District Land Registry
Rosebrae Court
Woodside Ferry Approach
Birkenhead
Merseyside CH41 6DU

Tel: 0151 472 6666
Fax: 0151 472 6789

The address for titles in Merseyside, Staffordshire and Stoke-on-Trent is:

The Birkenhead (Old Market) District Land Registry
Old Market House
Hamilton Street
Birkenhead
Merseyside L41 5FL

Tel: 0151 473 1110
Fax: 0151 473 0251

Coventry

The Coventry District Land Registry
Leigh Court
Torrington Avenue
Tile Hill
Coventry CV4 9XZ

Tel: 024 7686 0860
Tel: 024 7686 0864 (Enquiries)
Fax: 024 7686 0021

Croydon

The Croydon District Land Registry
Sunley House
Bedford Park
Croydon CR9 3LE

Tel: 020 8781 9100
Tel: 020 8781 9103 (Enquiries)
Fax: 020 8781 9110

Durham (Boldon House)

The Durham (Boldon House) District Land Registry
Boldon House, Wheatlands Way
Pity Me   Tel: 0191 301 2345
Durham DH1 5GJ   Fax: 0191 301 2300

Durham (Southfield House)

The Durham (Southfield House) District Land Registry
Southfield House
Southfield Way   Tel: 0191 301 3500
Durham DH1 5TR   Fax: 0191 301 0020

Gloucester

The Gloucester District Land Registry
Twyver House, Bruton Way   Tel: 01452 511111
Gloucester GL1 1DQ   Fax: 01452 510050

Harrow

The Harrow District Land Registry
Lyon House, Lyon Road   Tel:. 020 8235 1181
Harrow, Middx. HA1 2EU   Fax: 020 8862 0176

Kingston-Upon-Hull

The Kingston-Upon-Hull District Land Registry
Earle House, Portland Street   Tel: 01482 223244
Hull HU2 8JN   Fax: 01482 224278

Lancashire

The District Land Registry for Lancashire
Wrea Brook Court, Lytham   Tel: 01772 836838 (Enquiries)
Warton   Tel: 01772 836700
Preston PR4 1TE   Fax: 01253 840013

Leicester

Leicester District Land Registry   Tel: 0116 265 4000
Westbridge Place   Tel: 0116 265 4001 (Enquiries)
Leicester LE3 5DR   Fax: 0116 265 4008

Lytham

The Lytham District Land Registry   Tel: 01253 849849

Birkenhead House, East Beach   Tel: 01253 840012 (Enquiries)

Lytham St. Annes, Lancs. FY8 5AB   Fax: 01253 840001

Nottingham (East)

The Nottingham (East) District Land Registry

Robins Wood Road   Tel: 0115 906 5353

Nottingham NG8 3RQ   Fax: 0115 936 0036

Nottingham (West)

The Nottingham (West) District Land Registry

Chalfont Drive   Tel: 0115 935 1166

Nottingham NG8 3RN   Fax: 0115 935 0038

Peterborough

The Peterborough District Land Registry

Touthill Close

City Road   Tel: 01733 288288

Peterborough PE1 1XN   Fax: 01733 280022

Plymouth

The Plymouth District Land Registry

Plumer House   Tel: 01752 636000

Tailyour Road   Tel: 01752 636123 (Enquiries)

Crownhill, Plymouth PL6 5HY   Fax: 01752 636161

Portsmouth

Portsmouth District Land Registry   Tel: 023 9276 8888

St Andrew's Court, St Michael's Road   Tel: 023 9276 8880 (Enquiries)

Portsmouth, Hampshire PO1 2JH   Fax: 023 9276 8768

Stevenage

The Stevenage District Land Registry   Tel: 01438 788888

Brickdale House, Swingate   Tel: 01438 788889 (Enquiries)

Stevenage, Herts. SG1 1XG   Fax: 01438 780107

Swansea

The Swansea District Land Registry
Ty Bryn Glas
High Street   Tel: 01792 458877
Swansea SA1 1PW   Fax: 01792 473236

Telford

The Telford District Land Registry
Parkside Court, Hall Park Way   Tel: 01952 290355
Telford TF3 4LR   Fax: 01952 290356

Tunbridge Wells

The Tunbridge Wells District Land Registry
Forest Court, Forest Road   Tel: 01892 510015
Tunbridge Wells, Kent TN2 5AQ   Fax: 01892 510032

Weymouth

The Weymouth District Land Registry
Melcombe Court
1 Cumberland Drive   Tel: 01305 363636
Weymouth, Dorset DT4 9TT   Fax: 01305 363646

York

The York District Land Registry
James House, James Street   Tel: 01904 450000
York YO10 3YZ   Fax: 01904 450086

Wales/Cymru

Cofrestrfa Tir Ddosbarthol Cymru/
The District Land Registry for Wales
Ty Cwm Tawe
Phoenix Way   Tel: 01792 355000
Llansamlet   Tel: 01792 355095 (Enquiries)
Swansea SA7 9FQ   Fax: 01792 355055

BUYING BARGAINS AT PROPERTY AUCTIONS

18 Auctions – the place to pick up a bargain

The main advantage to me of buying at auction has got to be the price. Compared with the prices going through high street estate agents I paid 33% less.

Don Lee, buyer of a residential property at auction.

The UK is awash with bargains

In two recent auction sales the following properties sold for prices that would not be found in any estate agent's window:

- A three-bed city flat in Birmingham sold for £10,500. Less than the price of a new car.

- A studio flat could be had in south London for only £16,000.

- £27,250 is all that was needed to obtain a two-bed flat in a Dower house within half a mile of the centre of Lincoln.

- A three-bed house in London with a private garden sold for less than £50,000.

These results demonstrate that there are plenty of bargain properties out there, if you only know where to look and how to go through the auction process.

What you will learn from this guide

What you will learn from this guide

In the following pages you will be shown:

- how auctions work;
- where to find auctions;
- how to spot a bargain;
- the price you should bid up to;
- the costs of buying at auction;
- how to handle the legal aspects of the purchase;
- how auctioneers operate;
- the best bidding tactics;
- how to sell at auction;

- what the pitfalls are;
- how to avoid losing a lot of money.

Auctioneer's Anecdote:

Repossessions at rock-bottom prices

Auctions are full of mystique, but with the help of this guide, you will be taken inside how the auction process really works. It will enable you to have a clear idea of how to approach a property auction and it gives you the opportunity to pick up a bargain, saving you thousands of pounds compared with making a purchase through conventional channels.

Early in 1993 was a period when many building societies were using the auction room to dispose of their large portfolio of repossessed houses and flats. At the time, most auction houses were reporting successful sales of between 60 per cent and 75 per cent of the properties they were offering, but certain auctioneers publicised that they were having virtually a 100% success rate in the sales of properties they were offering for one particular leading building society. To experienced auction dealers, this meant that many bargains were available and the reserve prices were set at attractive levels.

What types of auction are there?

Auctions fall into four categories according to their size:

- Large composite
- Medium composite
- Smaller composite
- Single lot

Figure 18.1 lists the relative sizes, the number of lots to expect, the size of the audience and where they may be held. A composite auction is one where a collection of different types of property are sold at the same auction.

Fig 18.1 Size of auctions

	Number of lots	Likely audience	Likely venue
Large composite	100+	300+	Hotel/conference centre, theatre, meeting rooms
Medium composite	5–100	200–500	Hotel/conference centre
Smaller composite	2–5	10–100	Hotel, church hall, pub, restaurant, sale room
Single Lot	1	10–75	Hotel, church hall, pub, restaurant

Large

Over the last 20 years there has been a move towards large and composite auctions, run not only in London, but also in the larger financial cities outside the capital. The auctions are generally run by one auction house although, on occasion, several firms may co-operate. These composite auctions run frequently on a regular published calendar and may contain up to 50 lots offered in just a morning or an afternoon right through to 300 or 400 lots offered over several days. The sales may be restricted to a special type of property, for example vacant possession houses, residential investments, retail investments, commercial investments, shops, factories, warehouses or land, or a blend of any or all of these types. Where there is a mixture, the different categories of property tend to be offered in consecutive lots sometimes with intervals between the various categories.

Advantages of composite auctions

Bringing together a number of lots in a composite auction produces economies of scale for the auction house. But from the seller's point of view a composite auction frequently generates more interest, a larger audience, more extensive marketing and generally a cheaper entry cost. If you are attending an auction for the first time, the scope of the catalogue and the size of the audience may seem somewhat forbidding. But by following the steps in this book, you will be able to refine your interest down to only a few lots and will learn how to exercise your presence as a bidder at the vital moments in a crowded room.

Auctioneer's Anecdote:

For any given lot, the higher the price the slower the bidding

Large composite auctions need to take place in rooms of sufficient size to cope with the expected audience which will probably exceed 300. For this reason, auction houses usually choose to use hotel or conference centres, theatres or meeting rooms which can be laid out in theatre style seating facing a single rostrum. A public address system with sufficient amplification is normal.

Medium

The medium composite auction is a smaller version of the larger composite auction, where either the lots will be restricted to a particular category, for example repossessed vacant houses and flats on behalf of finance houses or, alternatively, a mixture of lots from a single geographical region covered by the auction house. This can be a suburb where the auctioneers specialise or a regional city such as

Birmingham, Manchester, Liverpool or Edinburgh where there is a source of mixed lots available, but insufficient lots on offer at regular intervals to produce larger composite auctions.

This size of sale can still produce an audience of between 200 and 500 people depending upon the popularity of the lots being offered and the amount of marketing that has taken place. Therefore the auctioneers will choose a venue similar to that necessary for large composite auctions with similar facilities.

'Subject to planning' – Where a property has development or redevelopment potential but there is no actual planning consent granted for that work then a buyer will need to obtain such a consent afterwards. It may or may not be forthcoming. An intending bidder may, by discussion with the development control officer at the local planning authority, be able to resolve any doubts he may have.

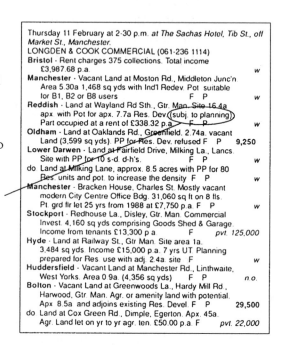

Thursday 11 February at 2-30 p.m. *at The Sachas Hotel, Tib St., off Market St.,* Manchester.
LONGDEN & COOK COMMERCIAL (061-236 1114)
Bristol - Rent charges 375 collections. Total income £3,987.68 p.a.   w
Manchester - Vacant Land at Moston Rd., Middleton Junc'n Area 5.30a 1,468 sq yds with Ind'l Redev. Pot. suitable for B1, B2 or B8 users   F   P   w
Reddish - Land at Wayland Rd Sth., Gtr. Man. Site 16.4a apx. with Pot for apx. 7.7a Res. Dev. (subj. to planning) Part occupied at a rent of £338.32 p.a.   F   P   w
Oldham - Land at Oaklands Rd., Greenfield. 2.74a. vacant Land (3,599 sq yds). PP for Res. Dev. refused F   P   9,250
Lower Darwen - Land at Fairfield Drive, Milking La., Lancs. Site with PP for 10 s-d. d-h's.   F   P   w
do. Land at Milking Lane, approx. 8.5 acres with PP for 80 Res. units and pot. to increase the density F   P   w
Manchester - Bracken House, Charles St. Mostly vacant modern City Centre Office Bdg. 31,060 sq ft on 8 fls. Pt. grd flr let 25 yrs from 1988 at £7,750 p.a. F   P   w
Stockport - Redhouse La., Disley, Gtr. Man. Commercial Invest. 4,160 sq yds comprising Goods Shed & Garage. Income from tenants £13,300 p.a.   F   pvt. 125,000
Hyde - Land at Railway St., Gtr Man. Site area 1a. 3,484 sq yds. Income £15,000 p.a. 7 yrs UT Planning prepared for Res. use with adj. 2.4a. site F   w
Huddersfield - Vacant Land at Manchester Rd., Linthwaite, West Yorks. Area 0.9a. (4,356 sq yds)   F   P   n.o.
Bolton - Vacant Land at Greenwoods La., Hardy Mill Rd., Harwood, Gtr. Man. Agr. or amenity land with potential. Apx. 8.5a. and adjoins existing Res. Devel. F   29,500
do. Land at Cox Green Rd., Dimple, Egerton. Apx. 45a. Agr. Land let on yr to yr agr. ten. £50.00 p.a. F   pvt. 22,000

Fig 18.2 Extract from Under the Hammer

Small

There are occasions when a smaller number of related lots are appropriate for being auctioned consecutively at the the same place and at the same time. This may be a number of adjoining building plots or retail or domestic investment properties or land and agricultural property in a particular vicinity.

Look out for special themes

Thus the small composite auction will generally follow a theme. It may contain lots which result from the 'break-up' of an individual estate. Examples of this are:

- A large agricultural investment estate where the owners have decided that the best prices can be obtained by offering portions of the estate in small lots.

- The owners of a portfolio of residential investments in one particular suburb or of a row of shops in a particular centre may decide that they will obtain the best price by offering the properties individually.

In such cases it is logical for the auction house to bring together its marketing and advertising and produce a single brochure, one set of advertisements and run just one auction session. The number of people attending is likely to be less than those attending a larger auction and therefore there is no need for the auction house to organise a sale in a large venue. The auction room may well be a smaller hotel, church, village hall or similar sized building.

The single lot

If a vendor (also called the seller) chooses to offer a single lot, it is often because the auctioneer believes there will be a tremendous demand for the property.

The costs of promoting a single lot sale will have been considerably higher than for a composite auction. This extra cost will be justified by the belief that the property is one for which there is a spectacular demand. The audience may only be between 10 and 75 people and the auction room will be of a corresponding size.

What properties are offered for sale by auction?

Thatched cottages

Some rural and suburban firms of auctioneers specialise in offering for sale by auction country cottages of which the 'thatched cottage' is the prime example. These are usually sold in single lots and occasionally in small, themed sales. Even when other types of auction during the 1950s were unpopular, the 'thatched cottage' sales were still held quite frequently, as both vendors and auction houses believed that considerable competition could be engendered between would-be-buyers, by offering this type of property for sale by auction. That belief was furthered by the belief amongst valuers that it was almost impossible to judge precisely what price such a property would realise.

From the owner's point of view, therefore, the possibility of a crowded auction in a hotel or public room one evening with bidders fighting to buy was irresistible. Although the romantic cottage exemplifies the type of property which vendors feel are best offered for sale by auction, it should not be forgotten that other types of property which are particularly attractive, for whatever reason, may also benefit from the 'thatched cottage' syndrome, and realise a high price in the auction room as a result of exceptional competition.

Why not pick up an exceptional property?

Other properties that might be exposed to this exceptional competition include:

- houses that are unique because of their historical associations or their exceptional position;

- building or development prospects which are in pockets of exceptional interest or demand;

- investment properties of a type which are particularly in vogue at the time;

- plots or buildings which hold the key to development or profit-making prospects;

- sites or buildings appropriate for uses which follow fashions of the time. (Over the years these have included post offices, launderettes, petrol stations, food take-aways, nursing homes, bowling alleys, multi-screen cinemas and docklands, to name a few.) Dealers and entrepreneurs who have spotted the next trend or vogue will already be combing the auction rooms for their future stock.

Properties that are almost unsaleable

Take care, however; the auction route has often proved more successful than the private treaty sale method in the disposal of properties that are nearly unsaleable. Presumably this is because at auctions there is an element in the audience who are able and willing to 'chance their arm', particularly if they feel that a lot is apparently a bargain.

The sale rooms have seen the successful disposal of various properties that have been:

- derelict;

- subject to compulsory purchase orders;

- subject to major disrepair or fabric failure;

- subject to local authority repair notices;

- subject to closing orders;

- offered with unsatisfactory legal titles;

- sold without access;

- sold with major fencing, paving, drainage or other similar responsibilities;

- sold subject to easements, covenants or restrictions which prevent their satisfactory use;

- in derelict or unpopular areas.

Auctioneer's Anecdote:

Read the particulars carefully

There is a long-standing joke in the auctioneers' profession that those auctioneers who sell land on behalf of Railtrack need long thin catalogues because of the long thin pieces of land which they have to offer. One particular piece, first offered by their Property Board, was near one of the conurbations and was three-quarters of a mile long but only several yards wide. It was disclosed in the catalogue and in the title for sale that the land had no access other than through other people's land, was being sold with no access from the railway line and the purchaser had to erect a new fence along the entire three-quarter mile length adjoining the line. These factors did not inhibit some enthusiastic bidding when the property was offered. No doubt the bidders felt that around the £1,500 mark they could 'not go wrong'. Three months later the auctioneer was approached by the successful buyer to re-offer the land because it had no access and because the fencing convenant was about to be enforced. The land sold a second time at a slightly lower price at auction. Over the next two years, the auctioneer was instructed to offer and succeeded in selling the land no fewer than five times in total and not always at steadily reducing prices. Presumably, the only parties to whom any of the transactions gave a satisfactory result were Railtrack and the auctioneers.

Repossessed houses

Fortunately for you, but unfortunately for their previous owner-occupiers, this category of property continues to feature considerably in many auctioneers' catalogues in the waves of repossessions that occur from time to time. Whilst feeling for those that have been dispossessed, there is no doubt that auction houses, speculators,

How much would you pay for a two-bed flat on the south coast? £50,000, £75,000 or £100,000? This one sold at auction for only £14,000.

LOT 52

First Floor Flat, 5 Victoria Road, Folkestone, Kent

HALIFAX

BY ORDER OF MORTGAGEES IN POSSESSION

A Leasehold First Floor Flat

TENURE
Leasehold. The property is held on a lease for a term of 99 years from 1st October 1987 (thus having approximately 93 years unexpired) at a current ground rent of £50 per annum.

LOCATION
The property is located on the west side of Victoria Road close to its junction with Broadmead Road in an established residential area close to Folkestone British Rail Station and within reach of the town centre.

DESCRIPTION
The property comprises a first floor flat situated within a mid terrace building.

ACCOMMODATION
Reception Room
Two Bedrooms
Kitchen
Bathroom with WC and wash basin

builders and new owner occupiers all benefit from such situations. The losses registered by the finance houses and the insurers may only be the result of a drastic domestic property revaluation or may also have been occasioned by the surfeit of vacant houses offered in the sale rooms because of a high level of repossesions at any one time.

But there is no doubt, there are some very good value-for-money properties to be purchased at auction. 'Repossession' is not to be considered synonymous with 'bargain'. You should still thoroughly research your target property.

Investment properties

Properties that are owned for the benefit of the income they produce are frequently included in auction catalogues. Investors cover a range of buyers from large pension funds and commercial investors at one end, through to medium-sized investment companies and smaller private pension funds, right down to individual investors, looking for a satisfactory return on their money.

The range of properties includes:

- office investments;

- shop investments;

- domestic investments (single houses, blocks of flats and portfolios of houses);

- ground and chief rents;

- investments in land;

- investments in easements;

- reversionary investments (where the investor is concerned with long term income or growth in it).

What affects the price of investment properties?

Prices paid for investments depend on many factors which include:

- security of the covenant of the payer of the rent;

- the quality and position of the property;

- the potential growth or variation of the income collectable;

- the frequency of rent reviews;

- the investor's view of the future of the money market and future interest levels;

- the investor's view of the yield which is appropriate for the type of property;

- the nature and responsibilities of the landlord;

- the nature and responsibilities of the tenant;

- other factors which could affect the future income of the property favourably or adversely.

A portfolio of lots being sold by property dealers

You should be aware that occasionally the same properties feature in different auctions at different times. A tenanted shop in Liverpool may first of all sell at an auction in that city and then some time later reappear at an auction in London. A vacant repossessed house may be sold at an auction just outside the capital and subsequently reappear in the hands of a local auctioneer in the town in which the property is situated. A portfolio of domestic investments may be offered 'en bloc' in the capital, appear in another auction in that city six months later broken up into smaller units and then perhaps 50 per cent of that portfolio will be represented in individual lots in, for example Manchester, Birmingham or Liverpool 12 months later.

Do not be totally discouraged from being interested in these dealing lots, but do watch out for them by combing auction advertisements frequently. If you see a property that interests you, approach it with care and only after thorough research.

The auction houses

The principal firms of property auctioneers are listed in the Appendix, with a great many firms offering their services throughout the country. There is no way you can monitor all their auctions, their results and their withdrawn lots. You will have to select the firms you examine acknowledging there are:

Select firms that cover your area

i)   varieties of specialist firms who only deal with particular types of property and who are generally London-based;

ii)   other auction houses in the capital who cover a wider range of properties, generally in composite auctions but occasionally in specialised ones as well;

iii) London-based firms who deal with property throughout the UK, sometimes only offering it in the capital but occasionally running sales in the regions;

iv) auction houses based upon the larger cities and towns throughout the country who run regular composite auctions, generally specialising in properties in their area rather than specialising in particular types of property; and

v)   local firms who run smaller auctions on demand.

Within these broad divisions, as you become acquainted with the auction field, you will discover that there are certain specializations and subspecialisations which various firms have developed through design or their past history and it is only by research that you will establish which auction houses to patronise, as a buyer or as a seller.

How to choose which firms to follow

1   Visit a few local auctions of any kind.

2   Decide upon the type of property in which you are interested.

3 Decide upon the geographical area you propose to cover.

4 Research auction advertisements in the property and local press.

5 Respond to those advertisements with specific requests for specific properties in which you are interested.

6 Subscribe to the mailing lists of firms who specialise in your type of property in your area.

7 Start visiting the auctions of your chosen firms on a regular basis.

By and large you will find that the sales of the majority of the firms are conducted in a similar manner. British auction houses are relatively traditional in their manner of offering with only minor variations in style, speed of selling, presentation and marketing.

> **KEY POINT:** *Whether you are a dreamer or a speculator, an entrepreneur or an investor, a would-be-owner occupier or a developer, an intending purchaser of many lots or only one, good luck in your hunt for bargains. Remember, they will only come with thorough research and plentiful experience. Follow the advice that follows and you should not go wrong.*

From a purchaser's point of view, I would have said you were going to get quite a good deal at auction, particularly in this climate.

Michael Kirby, Chartered Surveyor.

19 Clearing the contracts and arranging the finance before the auction

'You must ask why the property is going for sale at auction and what (if anything) is wrong with it and satisfy yourself that you are not buying a pig in a poke. You have got to be prepared to do your own research. For example, I had to check that I was not buying a property over a coal mine. I knew the reason for sale – that the property was foreclosed and put up for auction by a building society.'

Don Lee.

As soon as you have found your chosen property, you must take a careful look at the legal and financial issues to make sure you can finance the transaction and commit to exchanging contracts as soon as you succeed in your purchase. This chapter examines these issues and other pitfalls to watch out for in the run-up to attending the auction.

Your legal steps

You must be sure that they can move quickly since the time scale from when an auction is announced to when it occurs is often only three or four weeks.

What advice should I seek?

Hopefully, by the time you have absorbed half of the contents of this book, you will know as much as you need to know about contracts, conveyances and auction procedures. You should obtain an auction catalogue and look at the general and any special conditions of sale and check that the conditions do not contain any unusual or surprise clauses that could penalise you. As soon as you are reassured, you need to start researching the lot or lots in which you are interested. The conditions of sale are examined on page 227.

What information do you need to collect?

You will need detailed information about your prospective property including:

1 A copy of the auction catalogue.

2 A copy of all the conditions of sale.

3 Any further details of the lots you are interested in. For example:

Priors and posts bolster Erdman result

Erdman Lewis raised a total of £4.17m from its 21-lot auction at the Meridien Hotel in Piccadilly, W1, but only seven of the 16 successful lots were sold under the hammer.

Six were knocked down prior, raising £1.375m, and a further three went immediately after the auction, contributing £841,000.

Five out of six High Street shops, which are currently let to Foster Brothers Clothing, were snapped up, mainly by private investors, at net initial yields ranging from 8.14% to 10.53%. The one remaining lot was close to selling this week.

The properties are all let on leases of more than 20 years from August last year, when Foster Brothers completed a management buyout from Sears. Lot sizes ranged from £171,000 for 79 High Street, Bideford, Devon, to £300,000 for 17 Sheep Street, Bicester, Oxfordshire.

Auctioneer John Townsend commented that the good response to the shops meant that the company would be offering a further tranche in its June auction. The June catalogue will also contain 13 Barclays Bank sale and leasebacks, which have proved to be popular in previous sales.

The largest lot to go under the hammer at last week's sale was an Italian restaurant with flats above in Market Street, Brighton, East Sussex,

which fetched a price of £433,500. The annual income from the building is £43,600, reflecting a net initial yield of 9.79%.

A shop in Hampstead High Street, NW3, trading as Hobbs fashionwear, was knocked down prior, fetching approximately £600,000 — the same price that the vendor paid when he bought it at an Edward Erdman auction three years ago.

A freehold redevelopment opportunity in Princes Street, W1, went in the room for £385,000. The Grade II-listed building on basement, ground and three upper floors provides 3,790 sq ft of office accommodation.

Planning consents for the site, which is only 200 yards from Oxford Circus, exist for office, restaurant and residential uses.

Townsend said that there were signs of confidence among bidders which has been lacking for some time.

"Investors are obviously eager to pick up valuable properties and expect competition for them in the room," he said.

'Knocked down prior' – 'Knocked down' is a colloquial way of expressing the fall of the gavel and/or the exchange of contracts. 'Prior' is before the auction.

'Sale and leasebacks' – Owners of (generally commercial) properties occasionally wish to realise capital from that ownership whilst remaining in occupation. They do this by creating a lease back to themselves and then selling the freehold with the entitlements to collect the newly created rent on the new lease.

Fig 19.1
Estates Gazette report on an Erdman Lewis auction

LOT 80

Flat 1, 44 Elm Park Gardens, Chelsea, London SW10

HALIFAX

BY ORDER OF MORTGAGEES IN POSSESSION

A Leasehold Raised Ground Floor Flat

TENURE
Leasehold. The property is held on a lease for a term of 125 years from 29th September 1982 (thus having 113 years unexpired) at a current ground rent of £10 per annum.

LOCATION
Elm Park Gardens is situated off Fulham Road, midway between St Stephens Hospital and Brompton Hospital. Fulham Road provides access to Knightsbridge and a full range of shopping facilities.

DESCRIPTION
The property comprises a raised ground floor flat situated within a terraced house which overlooks the communal gardens of Elm Park. Access is from a communal entrance hall.

ACCOMMODATION
Reception Room with Integral Kitchen
Bedroom
Bathroom with WC

Would you like a flat in Chelsea without breaking the bank? You could have picked this one up for only £68,000

- a copy of the valuation/survey/builder's report;

- a copy of the lease (if possible);

- a copy of any further letters/details from the auctioneers;

- notes of answers to queries already put to the auctioneers;

- the name and address of the solicitors acting for the seller.

4 Who is making the purchase. For example:

- The full name and address of you and your partner.

- If a partnership is buying the property, then give partnership details.

- If a business or limited company is buying the property, then details of the business.

5 Financial arrangements:

- how the property is being paid for;

- name and address of the mortgage provider;

- your accountant and/or financial broker (if relevant);

- status of any sales or other assets which will be linked to the purchase.

What questions should you put to the vendor's solicitors?

Almost invariably the solicitors acting on behalf of the sellers are noted in the catalogue but, if not, the auctioneer's firm can advise you who is acting. You should then approach them with the appropriate questions covering in particular:

1. The quality of the title

As you know, the ownership of land in England is well catalogued and formulated. Most titles and their details are recorded at the Land Registry, who provide a log-book style document with a plan giving concise details of what a landowner holds. The log book should show:

- whether the title is freehold or leasehold (and its length);

- the current ownership;

- a brief history of the previous ownerships;

- covenants, restrictions or easements that affect the property and normally any major charge registered against the land.

Not all titles, however, are as thoroughly catalogued and ownership of land is not always as secure. It is not unusual for auctions to be used as places for the disposal of properties where the title may be questionable and where the vendor hopes that by submitting the property for sale in this manner, the purchaser will be less than thorough in making the necessary investigations. The possibility of such a problem should not stop you from considering buying properties at auction, but should encourage you to ensure that before buying, you check the title thoroughly.

How to own property without buying it!

As a rather extreme example of the sort of problem that can arise under English law, it is possible for someone who does not initially own a plot of land or property to become its owner by occupying it for at least 12 years without anyone – and particularly the true owner – raising any objection whatsoever during that period. After 12 years, the occupier usually becomes the landowner with an appropriate title to sell.

To obtain such a 'statutory title' (also sometimes known as a 'squatter's title'), the proper procedures must be followed meticulously for the title to be perfect. If, as a buyer of such a title, you have not had the process of development of ownership thoroughly checked, it could be possible that the possessory title is not supported by suitable affidavits or has not been created because of some inadequacies in the occupation. In such extreme circumstances, a buyer at auction may find that he has purchased a property and is subsequently unable to register his title or to defend it against an original and previous owner.

2. The nature of any covenants, restrictions or easements

Land is frequently subject to drains, culverts or water courses underneath it; electricity, gas or similar services running on, over or under it; rights of way, bridle paths, footpaths and roads running across it and many similar 'easements'. Occasionally, one hears of people discovering that rights of way exist that run right through their garden or even right through their property. It is an unlucky bidder who discovers only after a contract has been exchanged that his lot suffers such an impediment. Make sure you don't.

Can you use the property for the intended purpose?

Covenants and restrictions on use of land can be even more complicated. If you are buying a piece of building land to develop and do not research it adequately, it might result in your buying a piece which has covenants preventing the land from being developed for the intended purpose. For example, a buyer intending to erect a multi-storey block might find covenants preventing the erection of such a building. Alternatively, the buyer of a piece of land beside a railway line or road might discover they have acquired a responsibility to erect an expensive wall or fence.

3. Any adverse details revealed in the local search

As you know, the local search is a set of questions submitted to the local authority in which the property is situated. All sorts of planning (for example, highway and transport plans) may affect a lot. Building or planning regulations may not have been observed when the building on a lot was erected. The local authority environmental departments may be critical of items in the buildings or on the site which could have expensive repercussions after you have bought the property. All property is subject to detailed building and planning regulations under the auspices of the local authority. The local search should reveal if any problems are present.

Usually, the solicitor acting for the seller will have obtained a local search or be in the process of obtaining one prior to the auction. But it could be that the local search may not be available. If the local search has not been obtained, it would be wise for you to enquire with the relevant local authority, if there are any adverse proposals or notices affecting the property. Chapter 16 (page 188) reproduces the Enquiries of Local Authority form listing all the questions you will need to ask them about your target property. If any planning consents affecting the lot are of interest to you, the local authority will generally provide a copy at a nominal cost or, alternatively, make available for inspection at their offices the relevant planning register.

4. Any other appropriate legal points

If you are unsure in your bidding or if you have been unable to obtain any details before the auction itself, you should arrive early at the auction, to make whatever research is possible at the time and to assist you in your bidding when the lot comes up for sale.

> **KEY POINT:** *When you attend the auction, if you find the solicitor for the seller is present, check with him to see if there have been any subsequent alterations or changes and also to read through whatever literature he can provide.*

General Conditions of Sale applicable to all Lots insofar as they are not inconsistent with the Special Conditions of each Lot

1 (a) The property is sold subject to the following conditions ('The General Conditions') and to the Standard Conditions of Sale (3rd Edition) ('The Standard Conditions') so far as they are not inconsistent with the General Conditions and in the event of any conflict between the General Conditions and the Standard Conditions then the General Conditions shall prevail.

(b) Each Purchaser shall be deemed to purchase with full knowledge of all the conditions subject to which the property is sold.

(c) The Standard Conditions are amended as follows:-

(i) Reference in the Standard Conditions to 'the Seller' shall mean the Vendor' and to 'the Buyer' shall mean 'the Purchaser'.

(ii) The Contract rate referred to in Standard Condition 1.1.1(g) is 4% above Lloyds Bank Plc base lending rate from time to time.

(iii) The Standard Conditions 3.1.3, 3.3.2(c) and 4.3.2 shall not apply.

(iv) The Standard Condition 5.1 shall not apply and on and from the date of the Contract the property shall be at the sole risk of the Purchaser who shall insure it from such date in its full reinstatement value against all usual risks and perils with an insurance company of repute.

(v) The words 'without delay' shall be deleted from Standard Condition 3.2.2.(b).

(vi) In Standard Condition 7.3.4 the words 'if he does so he cannot claim compensation under Condition 7.3.1 as well' shall be deleted.

(vii) The words 'with an Absolute Title' shall be deleted from Standard Condition 8.2.4.

(viii) Standard Condition 8.3 shall not apply.

(d) Where the property transferred is leasehold the Transfer shall contain a declaration in the following terms "the covenant implied by the Transferor transferring in this deed with limited title guarantee" is varied as follows:- Section 4 of The Law of Property (Miscellaneous Provisions) Act 1994 shall not apply.

2 If a person attending the sale intends to bid on behalf of some other person or company, he shall before the sale commences hand the Auctioneer a note of the name and address of that other person or company failing which the Auctioneer shall be entitled, at any time prior to completion, to treat the bidder as the contractual purchaser whether or not the Auction Contract was signed for or on behalf of some other person or company.

3 On each Lot being knocked down the successful bidder must, upon being asked by the Auctioneer or the Auctioneer's Clerk, give his name and address or the name and address of the person or company on whose behalf he has been bidding and in default the Auctioneer shall be entitled to re-offer that property for sale as if it had not previously been knocked down.

4 (a) Bidding. All bids are to be made clearly. The Auctioneer reserves the right to regulate bidding and to refuse undesirable bids. The Vendor reserves the right to bid up to the reserve price or to authorise the Auctioneer to do so. In the event of any dispute in respect of the conduct of the auction the Auctioneer's decision is final.

(b) Each lot is offered subject to a reserve price unless otherwise stated.

(c) All bids are deemed to be exclusive of Value Added Tax.

5 The amount of the deposit shall be 10 per cent of the purchase price or £1500 whichever sum shall be the greater and shall be paid to the Auctioneers, Longden & Cook Commercial, as agents for the Vendor and Standard Condition 2.2 shall be varied accordingly.

6 If a cheque given for the payment of a deposit is dishonoured on presentation or if the successful bidder fails to pay such deposit, the Vendor shall be entitled (but shall not be bound) to treat such dishonour or failure as a repudiation of the Contract and to sell the property to some other person but without prejudice to the Vendor's right to claim against the successful bidder damages for repudiation of the Contract.

7 The date for completion of the purchase shall be on (or before) four weeks from the date of the contract at the offices of the Vendor's Solicitors or as they shall direct.

8 The tenure of each Lot and the estate or interest sold is as stated in the Particulars and Special Conditions of Sale for the Lot. In the case of land registered at HM Land Registry the title shall be deduced in accordance with section 110 of the Land Registration Act 1925. In the case of land not so registered the title shall be deduced as provided for in the Special Conditions of Sale. The Vendor sells as Beneficial Owner with full title guarantee unless otherwise provided.

9 Each Lot is believed to be and shall be taken as correctly described and any incorrect statement, error or omission found in the Auction Particulars or Special Conditions of Sale shall not annul the sale or entitle the Purchaser to rescind the Contract nor shall the Purchaser claim or be allowed any compensation in respect thereof.

10 The Purchaser shall be deemed to have made all searches and enquiries normally made by a prudent Purchaser and to have knowledge of all matters which would have been disclosed thereby and shall purchase subject to such matters. In particular the Purchaser shall buy subject to any existing or future notices claims acquisitions requisitions proceedings orders acts or requirements (whether registered or not) or any tribunal or local or other authority in relation to the property or any part thereof.

11 From the date of the Contract the property shall be at the sole risk of the Purchaser.

12 The Auctioneer reserves the right to hold the Memorandum of Contract or the Contract signed by them on behalf of the Vendor until the Purchaser's cheque for the deposit has been cleared.

13 No objection or requisition shall be raised as the permitted user of the property for the purposes of the Town and Country Planning Act or any Act or Acts for the time being amended or replacing the same.

14 The Purchaser acknowledge that (a) no statement or representation which may previously have been made to him or any person concerned on his behalf by or on behalf of the Vendor whether orally or in writing induced him to enter into this agreement (b) any such statement or representation does not form part of this agreement and (c) any liability of the Vendor in respect of any statement made to the Purchaser at law or in equity is hereby excluded to the extent authorised by the Misrepresentation Act 1967.

15 The Purchaser shall be deemed to purchase with full knowledge of the state of repair and condition of the Lot and notwithstanding anything in these General Conditions or in the Particulars and Special Conditions no representation,warranty or condition is made or shall be implied either as to the said state or condition of the Lot or any part thereof or as to whether the same is subject to any sanitary or Public Health Notice or notices, or intimation notice or notices or proposals under the Housing Acts or any of them. The Purchaser shall be deemed to purchase in all respects subject thereto whether or not he makes any enquiry and neither the Vendor nor the Auctioneers shall be required or bound to inform the Purchaser of any such matters whether known to them or not and the Purchaser shall raise no enquiry requisition or objection thereon or thereto.

16 Each Lot is sold (as mentioned in the Particulars and Special Conditions) either with vacant possession of the whole or part or subject to and with the benefit of the tenancies leases or other occupancies referred to in the Particulars and Special Conditions. The Purchaser shall take the Lot as he finds it and shall accept that Vacant Possession is given of the whole or any part offered with Vacant Possession notwithstanding that there may be furniture fittings or effects remaining therein and shall not be entitledto require the removal of any such furniture fittings or effects or object to taking the same on the ground that the existence thereof does not constitute Vacant Possession as such.

17 The fact (if such be the case) that the Lot is a house or part of a house which may not legally be used for immediate residential occupation shall not annul the sale or entitle the Purchaser to rescind the sale or claim damages or diminution in the price.

18 No representation is made that the rent payable in respect of any Lot or any part thereof is the rent properly chargeable under any Acts of Parliament or Statutory Instruments or Regulations regulating or controlling the same. The only representation made or intended to be implied by or from the Particulars and Special Conditions is that the rents referred to therein are the rents actually being paid by the Tenants to the Landlord and no objection or requisition shall be taken or made as to any matter arising under any such Acts Instruments or Regulations. The Purchaser shall not be entitled to raise any requisition or objection as to any rent limits or net rents or fair rents or the present or former regulated rents payable in respect of the property nor to the liability of the Vendor to produce copies of statutory notices of increase and notices to quit (if any) which may have been served. In the case of a regulated tenancy under the Rent Acts no objection shall be made on the grounds that the rent referred to is not the fair rent or that it may exceed the rent registered under the Rent Acts or that the rent has not been registered. No objection shall be taken by a Purchaser as to whether or not a notice of increase of rent has or has not been validly served or as to whether or not a Certificate of Disrepair has been obtained by the Tenant authorizing a reduction of rent nor shall the Purchaser object to the existence or terms of any counter-notice served upon or by a Tenant.

19 In the case of a Lot let, no representation is made as to whether or not there is any sub-tenant except where expressly stated in the Particulars and Special Conditions.

20 The Vendors shall not be required to assure the whole or any part of the property to any person other than the Purchaser and by one assurance.

21 The Vendor makes no representation as to the ownership of electric wiring and fittings and gas fittings and installations or central heating installations which may be on hire or hire purchase from the supply companies. In such case the Vendor accepts no liability for any payments that may be outstanding in respect thereof and the lot is sold subject thereto.

22 Each Lot is sold subject to Special Conditions of Sale of which each purchaser shall be deemed to have knowledge regardless of whether or not he has taken the opportunity that is available to inspect them or consult with the solicitors acting for the Vendor in each individual case. Wherever possible the Special Conditions of Sale will be available for inspection at the place of auction for at least three quarters of an hour before the sale.

23 Upon each Lot being knocked down, the successful purchaser shall as soon as practicable after the successful bid and in any event before leaving the auction room sign a form of contract or memorandum of the terms of the Contract at the table of the solicitors or that of the Auction Administrator. In default thereof, the Auctioneer shall be and is hereby authorised (but is not obliged) to sign on his behalf.

Fig 19.2   Auctioneer's general conditions

Note: The Royal Institution of Chartered Surveyors is close to completing a modernised version of these General Conditions which they hope will be used generally by solicitors shortly.

The following checklist illustrates the stages you should go through from initial instruction through to completion.

> ## YOUR LEGAL CHECKLIST:
> *Buying your property*
>
> 1 Request the contract, searches and replies to pre-contract enquiries plus auction catalogue. ☐
> 2 Check your financing of the transaction and reassess the pitfalls of buying at auction. ☐
> 3 Investigate title and raise any appropriate enquiries on that and any other matters and also raise such pre-contract and personal searches as may be necessary, for example, personal local search, British Coal search, etc. ☐
> 4 Establish your maximum bid and calculate the deposit amount you must take to the auction. ☐
> 5 A few days before the auction, see if there are any amendments with the seller's solicitors or auctioneers. ☐
> 6 Re-check the details received from the seller's solicitors and see if there are any amendments. ☐
> 7 Ensure the contract is signed correctly and exchange of contracts is recorded properly. ☐
> 8 Obtain signed contract from seller's solicitors, as normal, and then liaise with them up to completion. ☐

Conditions of sale

What are the conditions of sale?

These are the terms on which the successful bidder will buy the property. They regulate not only the bidding, but also any obligations the bidder must fulfil. They give a full and definitive description of the property and prescribe what happens after your bid is successful.

Check for onerous liabilities

If you are interested in bidding for a lot, you should ask to see these before doing so – otherwise you may end up buying something that is different from what you thought. You may be left with some heavy liabilities or the property may be subject to various covenants, for example a requirement to fence the borders of the property.

It is usual for an auctioneer to draw your attention to serious matters affecting the property, either in the auction catalogue itself and/or on the day in his introductory remarks. However, his remarks are very

Additional General Conditions of Sale

Additional General Condition of sale applicable to Lots specified insofar as it is not inconsistent with the Particulars and Conditions of Sales of each lot.

24 The Solicitors for the Vendors are:

25 General Condition 8 shall be read if:

(a) The words 'and the Purchaser shall not investigate or make any requisition or objection in respect of any earlier Title' had been added after the words or provided by the Special Conditions of Sale.

(b) Where the Lot is in a compulsory registration area under the Land Registration Acts or the Title is already registered at H.M. Land Registry the Vendor will nevertheless after completion of the purchase without expense to the Purchaser produce to the Chief Land Registrar all documents and do all acts and things required by the Registrar to enable him to accept the application of the Purchaser for registration of his Title to the Lot.

26 The purchaser shall execute and deliver to the Vendor within 14 days after completion of the purchase a duplicate of the Assurance of the Lot to the Purchaser such duplicate to be engrossed perused executed stamped and denoted by and at the expense of the Purchaser.

27 The Vendor shall not be required to execute more than one Assurance of the Lot.

28 (a) There are not included in the sale of any Lot (unless otherwise provided in the Particulars and Special Conditions of Sale):

(i) any mines or minerals under the property or any right of support from any mines or minerals whatsoever.

(ii) any easements of light air or support or other easements or right which would restrict or interfere with the free use by the Vendor or any person deriving Title under it for building or any other purpose of an adjoining or neighbouring land of the Vendor (whether intended to be retained or to be sold by it).

(b) There shall be reserved to the Vendor:

(i) the right at any time to erect of suffer to be erected any building or other erections and to alter any building or other erection now standing or hereafter to be erected on any part of its adjoining or neighbouring land in such a manner as to obstruct or interfere with the passage of light or air to any building which is or may be erected upon the Lot and any access of light and air over the adjoining land of the Vendor shall be deemed to be enjoyed by the licence or consent of the Vendor and not as of right;

(ii) the right of support from the Lot for the adjoining property of the Vendor;

(iii) the right to have maintain repair cleanse use reconstruct alter and remove any drains pipes wires cables and work on over or under the Lot now used for the benefit of the adjoining property of the Vendor;

(iv) full right and liberty for the Vendor and its Successors in Title with or without workmen and equipment at all reasonable times to enter upon the Lot for the purpose of exercising the right reserved by paragraph (iii) of this sub clause;

(v) full right and liberty for the Vendor and its Successors in Title with or without workmen and equipment at all reasonable times to enter upon the Lot for the purpose of maintaining repairing renewing reinstating altering or amending any fences walls or retaining walls and other works of the Vendor on its adjoining or neighbouring land, the Vendor making good any damage occasioned to the Lot by the exercise of the rights of entry reserved by paragraph (iv) and (v) of this sub-clause.

(c) Where under the Condition of Sale for any Lot of the Purchaser is required forthwith after completion or within a specified period thereafter to carry out any works to the Lot or its services or boundaries the Assurance of the Lot shall additionally reserve to the Vendor and its Successors in Title to its neighbouring land the right in the event of the Purchaser failing to carry out any such works by the due date to enter upon the property at any time within 10 years thereafter (after giving not less than six weeks notice in writing of its intention to exercise such right) for the purpose of carrying out any such works and the costs thereof shall be payable by the Purchaser on demand with interest thereon at the Contract rate.

(d) Exceptions reservations or declarations giving effect to the provisions of sub-clause (a) (b) and (c) of this Condition shall be incorporated in the Assurance to the purchaser.

29 Where under the Particulars and Special Conditions of Sale for any Lot a right of way is to be granted to the Purchasers over an adjoining roadway owned by the Vendor and reference is made to this condition in the Special Conditions the grant shall be in the following terms: 'The Vendor hereby grants in fee simple to the Purchaser and his Successors in Title to the property and his and their agents servants and licensees a right of way (in common with the Vendor and all others entitled) on foot or by vehicle at all times and for all purposes over and along the adjoining roadway of the Vendor coloured brown on the plan so as to enable access to be gained to the property and vice versa subject to the Purchaser or his Successors in Title observing and performing the covenants relating to the said roadway hereinafter contained'.

30 The Purchaser shall in the Assurance to him release the Vendor from all its obligations (if any) as to fencing and drainage in relation to the Lot and in addition covenant with the Vendor to indemnify it against its liability (if any) in respect of any such fencing and drainage.

31 The Assurance to the Purchaser shall contain the following declaration: 'it is hereby agreed by the Purchaser that the carrying on by the Vendor of its undertaking on its adjoining or neighbouring land in exercise of its powers and subject to its statutory and common law obligation shall not be deemed to be a breach of the covenant for quiet enjoyment implied herein by reason of the Vendor being expressed to convey as Beneficial Owner nor to be in derogation of its grant'.

32 The Assurance of the property shall contain a covenant by the Purchaser with the Vendor (by way of indemnity only) thenceforth to observe and perform the covenants (if any) subject to which the property is sold by virtue of the Particulars and Special Conditions (and including but without prejudice to the generality of the foregoing any covenants by the Vendor in its capacity as Landlord in relating to any of the tenancies leases or other occupancies referred to in the Particulars and Special Conditions of Sale) and to indemnify the Vendor against any actions costs claims expenses demands and liabilities brought against or occurred by the Vendor as a result of failure by the Purchaser of his Successors in Title to observe and perform the same.

33 Where the original of any agreement or counterpart of any lease or tenancy agreement subject to which the property is sold cannot be located by the Vendor the Purchaser shall accept in lieu a copy certified on the Vendors behalf as a true copy to the best of the Vendors knowledge.

34 Where in the Special Conditions of Sale for any Lot (or these General Condition as they apply to the Lot) reference is made to a plan this shall mean the plan forming part of the particulars in the copy of the special conditions held by the Auctioneer of the Lot in question.

35 IT IS HEREBY AGREED that except where the context forbids (a) words importing the singular number shall include the pluml and vice versa and (b) where there are two or more persons included in the expression "the Purchaser" covenants expressed to be made by the Purchaser shall be deemed to be made by such persons jointly and severally.

Fig 19.3   Auctioneer's additional general conditions

often only a summary. It is up to you to inform yourself and look at the conditions carefully. They will always be available from the auctioneer or from the owner's solicitors.

What types of conditions are there?

The bidder at auction will usually find up to four conditions to watch out for:

- the general conditions
- the additional general conditions
- the special conditions
- any other conditions under whatever name

These conditions may appear in several guises and in several places. You may find all the relevant conditions applicable to a lot are dealt with in the auction catalogue. Alternatively, you may find only some conditions in the catalogue, normally called 'General Conditions'. An example is shown in Figure 19.2.

Where an owner has a number of lots in an auction and he or his solicitor thinks it advisable to have certain conditions relating to all those lots or most of them over and above the general conditions, he can arrange for these to be printed in the catalogue and they will be headed 'Additional General Conditions' or something similar. An example is shown in Figure 19.3.

Watch out for hidden conditions

An owner's solicitor may need to draw up extra conditions to cover points that are not covered in the general conditions or additional general conditions, or he may find that the general conditions do not achieve what his client needs – in that case he will draw up special conditions.

Frequently, these will not be printed in the catalogue, as the catalogue will have been sent for printing before the owner's solicitor has even seen the title deeds. They will only be available from the auctioneer and the owner's solicitors. Figure 19.4 on page 230 shows an example of special conditions.

> **KEY POINT:** *You should always check to make sure that before you bid, you have seen and understand any conditions that apply to the purchase. All these conditions form the contract on which any lot is knocked down to you.*

SPECIAL CONDITIONS OF SALE

AS TO LOT 1

4a-18b Kenerne Drive, Barnet, Herts.

Solicitors: Taylor Walton, Hart House, 6 London Road, St. Albans, Herts. AL1 1NG Telephone: 01727 845245 (Ref. KNM).

1 The Property consists of:

   (1) FIRSTLY All that Freehold Property known as 4A and 4B and 6A and 6B Kenerne Drive Chipping Barnet in Greater London and

   (2) SECONDLY All that Freehold Property known as 8A 8B 10A and 10B Kenerne Drive Chipping Barnet Greater London and

   (3) THIRDLY All that Freehold Property known as 12A and 12B and 14A and 14B Kenerne Drive Chipping Barnet Greater London and FOURTHLY All that Freehold Property known as 16A and 16B 18A and 18B Kenerne Drive Chipping Barnet Greater London

2 Title to the Property FIRSTLY described is registered with Title Absolute under Title No. P162341 and Title to the Property SECONDLY described is registered at H.M. Land Registry with Title Absolute under Title No. NGL312988 and as to the Property THIRDLY described is registered at H.M. Land Registry with Title Absolute under Title No. NGL312776 and as to the Property FOURTHLY described at H.M. Land Registry with Title Absolute under Title No. NGL312777.

3 The Property FIRSTLY described is sold subject to and with the benefit of Entries Numbers 1 to 3 inclusive of the Charges Register of the said Title

and as to the Property SECONDLY described subject to Entries Numbers 1 to 3 of the Charges Register of the said Title

and as to the Property THIRDLY described subject to Entry No 1 of the Charges Register and as to the Property FOURTHLY described subject to Entry No 1 of the Charges Register of the said Title.

4.1 The Property FIRSTLY described is sold subject to and with the benefit of the following Leases:

   (i) 4A – a Lease dated 23 May 1967 made between Wodehouse Estates Limited (1) John Edward Green (2) for a term of 99 years from 25 March 1967 at a yearly rent of twelve pounds twelve shillings.

   (ii) 4B – a Lease dated 14 October 1966 made between Wodehouse Estates Limited (1) Sonia Elizabeth Pounds (2) for a term of 99 years from 25 March 1966 at a yearly rent of twelve pounds twelve shillings.

   (iii) 6A – a Lease dated 6 September 1989 made between Ronald John Cawley Roffe Richard Jeremy Golland (1) Grainne Cecilia Spain (2) for a term of 120 years from 25 March 1989 at an initial yearly rent of fifty pounds rising to four hundred pounds.

   (iv) 6B – a Lease dated 30 September 1971 made between Ronald John Cawley Roffe Jack Alexander Allerton (1) William George Edwards Marion Patricia Edwards (2) for a term of 99 years from 25 March 1970 at a yearly rent of fifteen pounds seventy five pence.

4.2.1 The Property SECONDLY described is sold subject to and with the benefit of the following Leases:

   (i) 8A – a Lease dated 24 May 1957 made between Frederick John Randall George Frederick Randall (1) John Porter Stretton (2) for a term of 99 years from 25 March 1957 at a yearly rent of five pounds five shillings.

   (ii) 10B – a Lease dated 22 June 1983 made between Ronald John Cawley Roffe Richard Jeremy Golland (1) Susan Elspeth Laithwaite (2) for a term of 99 years from 25 March 1983 at a yearly rent of twenty five pounds rising to seventy five pounds.

4.2.2 The Property SECONDLY described is sold subject to and with the benefit of the following Regulated Tenancies:

   (i) to L M Piper with a Registered Rent of £38.00 per week effective from 13 August 1990.

   (ii) to F L Harding with a Registered Rent of £33.00 per week effective from 13 August 1990.

4.3 The Property THIRDLY described as sold subject to and with the benefit of the following Leases:

   (i) 12A – a Lease dated 25 May 1984 made between Ronald John Cawley Roffe Richard Jeremy Golland (1) Paul Alexander Conway (2) for a term of 99 years from 25 March 1984 at a yearly rent of twenty five pounds rising to seventy five pounds.

   (ii) 12B – a Lease dated 21 May 1971 made between Ronald John Cawley Roffe Jack Alexander Allerton (1) Alan Bell (2) for a term of 99 years from 25 March 1970 at a yearly rent of fifteen pounds and seventy five pounds.

   (iii) 14A – a Lease dated 18 October 1965 made between Wodehouse Estates Limited (1) Martin Charles Curran and Patricia Curran (2) for a term of 99 years from 24 June 1965 at a yearly rent of twelve pounds twelve shillings.

   (iv) 14B – a Lease dated 26 April 1985 made between Ronald John Cawley Roffe Richard Jeremy Golland (1) Susan Carol St James (2) for a term of 99 years from 25 March 1984 at a yearly rent of fifty pounds rising to one hundred pounds.

4.4 The Property FOURTHLY described is sold subject to and with the benefit of the following Leases:

   (i) 16A – a Lease dated 14 August 1970 made between Ronald John Cawley Roffe Jack Alexander Allerton (1) Geoffrey Henry Howard and Jean Howard (2) for a term of 99 years from 25 March 1970 at a yearly rent of fifteen pounds fifteen shillings.

   (ii) 16B – a Lease dated 24 October 1977 made between Ronald John Cawley Roffe Richard Jeremy Golland (1) Trevor William Skinner and Angela Joy Booth (2) for a term of 99 years from 25 March 1970 at a yearly rent of fifteen pounds seventy five pence.

   (iii) 18B – a Lease dated 24 June 1991 made between Ronald John Cawley Roffe Richard Jeremy Golland (1) Nicola Le Moine and Raymond Vella (2) for a term of 125 years from 25 March 1989 at a yearly rent of seventy five pounds rising to four hundred pounds.

   AND

   18B – a Regulated Tenancy to J H Simpson with a Registered Rent of £33.00 per week effective from 13 August 2000.

5 The Vendor's Solicitors are Messrs Taylor Walton of Hart House 6 London Road St Albans Herts. AL1 1NG Telephone No 01727 845245 reference KNM. Copies of the Title Deeds, recent Local Authority Search Certificate and replies to Standard Form Enquiries before Contract are available for inspection at the offices of the Vendor's Solicitors in accordance with General Condition X.

6 Vacant Possession of the Property will not be given on completion.

7 The Vendor is not aware of any written Tenancy Agreements in respect of the Regulated Tenancies and the Purchaser shall not raise any objection or requisition thereto but shall accept as conclusive evidence a copy of the Rent Register which is available for inspection at the offices of the Vendor's Solicitors.

8 The Vendor has served no notice of disposal on the Tenants in accordance with Section 5 of the Landlord & Tenant Act 1987 and the Purchaser takes subject to the Tenant's rights under such Act. The Purchaser shall not raise any objection or requisition thereto but shall complete the Purchase of the Property notwithstanding that the Vendor has not served such Notices. Forthwith after Completion of the Purchase the Purchaser shall give Notice to all Tenants in accordance with Section 3 of the Landlord & Tenant Act 1985 (as amended by Section 50 of the Landlord & Tenant Act 1987) and shall indemnify the Vendor against any damages costs claims or other liabilities falling upon the Vendor by virtue of any delay or failure to do so.

9 The Purchaser shall in the Transfer (which shall be executed in duplicate) covenant with the Vendor to observe and perform the covenants and conditions contained in the Leases on the part of the Landlord and to keep the Vendor's estate and effects fully and effectually indemnified from all future costs claims demands and expenses in respect of any breach or non-observance thereof and if the Purchaser shall be a limited company it shall procure that at least one director of good financial standing personally covenants with the Vendor in the manner aforesaid.

AS TO LOT 2

75 Ashurst Road, North Finchley, London N12

Solicitors: Taylor Walton, Hart House, 6 London Road, St. Albans, Herts. AL1 1NG Telephone: 01727 845245 (Ref. KNM).

1 The Property consists of FIRSTLY All that Freehold Property known as 75 Ashurst Road Friern Barnet in the London Borough of Barnet and SECONDLY the Freehold passageway at the rear of 75/91 (odd numbers) Ashurst Road Friern Barnet in the London Borough of Barnet.

2 Title to the Property FIRSTLY described is registered at H.M. Land Registry with Freehold Title Absolute under Title No. MX193617 and as to the Property SECONDLY described Title to the Property is registered at H.M. Land Registry with Title Absolute under Title No. MX318831.

3 The Property FIRSTLY described is sold subject to and with the benefit of Entries Numbers 1 and 2 of the Charges Register of the said Title and as to the Property SECONDLY described subject to the Entries Numbers 1 to 10 inclusive of the Charges Register of the said Title.

4 As to the Property SECONDLY described the Purchaser shall raise no requisition or objection regarding the absence of the Conveyance dated 13 January 1970 referred to in Entry No 1 of the Charges Register.

5 The Property FIRSTLY described is sold subject to and with the benefit of a Regulated Tenancy to P E Watson with a Registered Rent of £210.00 per month effective from 13 August 1999.

Fig 19.4   *Auctioneer's special conditions*

What do the general conditions mean?

The general conditions (as shown in Figure 19.2) will usually cover the following:

1 **Incorporate most of the current Law Society Standard Form of Contract for sale of property but often with variations in the owner's favour!**

The main points in the Law Society's Standard Form to note are:

(a) the seller sells the property subject to any matters affecting it whether they are discoverable or not, either on inspection or through local search against the property.

For example, if the property has dry rot and you buy it, you are presumed to know about that rot. If the property has a compulsory purchase order against it, which is something that shows up on a local search, even if the vendor does not know about it, then you are presumed to know about it.

(b) A deposit of 10 per cent is payable on exchange of contracts. The general conditions will usually specify a minimum figure. For example: 10 per cent or a fixed sum – usually £1,500 – whichever is the greater.

(c) Risk of deterioration/disrepair should be the seller's responsibility, but the general conditions will usually alter this so the purchaser has to insure the property from the date when contracts are exchanged.

Hidden terms are no excuse to cancel a contract

(d) The purchaser is presumed to have investigated title prior to exchange of contracts. If the title has an oddity in it, which you discover after contracts have been exchanged, then you cannot use this to cancel the contract. You are presumed to have examined the title documents and know about the peculiarity. Examples of peculiarities that can arise are: someone other than the owner is claiming title to a part of the property or there is a covenant preventing you developing the site without consent from a third party.

(e) There is a timetable laid down for completion. For example: no later than 2.30pm on a working day four weeks after the contract has been exchanged.

A house in the heart of Kent for only £17,000

LOT 186
119 Corporation Road, Gillingham, Kent
BY ORDER OF MORTGAGEES IN POSSESSION

A Freehold Mid Terrace House

TENURE
Freehold.

LOCATION
The property is situated on the east side of Corporation Road, in an established residential area to the north east of the town centre which is within walking distance.

DESCRIPTION
The property comprises a mid terrace house arranged over ground and first floors beneath a pitched roof with a rear garden.

ACCOMMODATION

Ground Floor	First Floor
Reception Room	Three Bedrooms
Kitchen Area	
Bathroom with WC and wash basin	

(f) The purchase price must be paid by cleared funds, so a personal or building society cheque is not acceptable, whereas a banker's draft is.

2 Conditions about the bidding and formal paperwork.

(a) The owner can bid for his own lot up to (or beyond) the reserve or the auctioneer can do this on his behalf.

(b) The formalities a bidder is to complete before and after bidding. For example:

- completing a form giving your name and address;

- signing the Memorandum of Contract which is a record of the terms on which the purchaser has bought at the fall of the gavel. (The memorandum of contract is discussed in greater detail on page 257 and an example is shown in Figure 20.4 on page 256.)

(c) Bids are exclusive of Value Added Tax.

(d) If the bidder fails to sign the Memorandum of Contract then the auctioneer may do this on his behalf.

What do the special conditions mean?

The special conditions deal with the following:

1 The owner's identity and whether the property is being sold with or without vacant possession as owner, trustee or mortgagee.

2 The identity of the property. Strictly speaking, this will be found under the heading 'Particulars' but 'Particulars' tend to be presented with 'Special Conditions'.

3 Any new covenants the purchaser is to enter into with the owner (or any other party) on completion. You are most likely to come across this where a lot forms part of a larger piece of land owned by the vendor.

Special conditions imposed by a vendor

For example: A private landowner owns fields to the rear of his house. He puts these in an auction hoping that a builder will buy them. However, he wishes to protect his own comfort and so the special conditions provide that whoever buys the site must:

• erect a large fence and fast tall-growing conifers to screen off the development;

• only build private houses of a type to be approved by him;

• not use the new buildings other than as private residences.

4 Any tenancies affecting the lot.

5 Any rights the owner reserves.

Taking the same example as in 3 above of a sale of land for development, the owner would probably want to reserve all rights of light and air so his house enjoys the level of sunshine it currently has.

Where an owner has a number of similar lots with similar concerns, many of these points may be covered in the catalogue as 'Additional Conditions'.

Are these special conditions not unlawful?

The Unfair Contract Terms Act 1977 prevents a person drawing up an agreement from inserting terms which are unfair. However, this Act does not apply to contracts for the sale of land so, **no matter how onerous the contract is, the purchaser and the owner are obliged to abide by its terms.** There are two exceptions to this principle:

1 If an interest rate or penal arrangement for payment of the price is too onerous, it may be struck out by a court as being contrary to rules in equity on penalty clauses. These are separate from the 1977 Act and are unlikely to apply to most auction contracts you will come across.

Circumstances that may allow you to cancel a contract

2 If a seller makes a misrepresentation about the property prior to the contract and then in the contract itself disclaims any liability for that misrepresentation, the disclaimer may be unlawful. You may be able to withdraw from the contract if you have placed reliance on the misrepresentation the seller has made, or sue for damages. It depends on how the disclaimer is phrased.

For example, an owner advises a purchaser that the property has planning permission for six semi-detached buildings. In fact, the planning permission is for two detached houses. In the information pack available in the auction room, there is a copy of the planning permission. There is also a set of replies to standard enquiries which a purchaser would normally make before exchanging contracts and these reiterate that the property enjoys planning permission for six semi-detached houses. The successful bidder does not bother to read any of the information pack, nor does he speak with the auctioneer or the owner's solicitors before bidding.

Can you withdraw from the contract

The bidder may be able to withdraw in the following circumstances:

(a) If the special conditions do not refer to the planning permission or indicate the purchaser is presumed to buy with knowledge of the property or its use.

(b) If the special conditions do not refer to the planning permission but state:

The purchaser acknowledges that it has not entered into this agreement in reliance upon representations made by or on behalf of the vendor other than such written representations as the vendor's solicitor may have made and then save only as to such (if any) as were not susceptible of independent verification by inspection and survey of the property, by enquiry of the local authority, the local planning authority and any other competent authority of by inspection of documents made available to the purchaser before this agreement (whether or not the purchaser has made such inspection survey search or enquiry).

In this case the owner has misrepresented information but this clause tries to prevent the purchaser claiming he has relied on that.

Does this clause work and is it lawful? The property world believes it does work and is legitimate. Usage of this clause (and similar) is widespread – bidders beware!

Damages will not be payable   In this example, the estate agent or auctioneer may be criminally liable under the Property Misdescriptions Act 1991 for making a misleading statement. But do remember, this does not give you any right to damages.

If you can't stand the heat, get out of the kitchen!

At this stage, before the auction, the owner is making all the rules. The buyer has no opportunity to change them and no alternative but to purchase under the conditions that are laid down.

> **KEY POINT:** *If the conditions make the property 'too hot', whatever sort of bargain it appears, don't bid at the auction.*

Before bidding, every potential purchaser should make very sure that all the conditions (in whatever guise) have been read, checked and are acceptable. Since conditions are frequently clothed in 'legalese' you should consider very carefully the significance of any conditions – particularly those that appear at all unusual.

Some hidden pitfalls to watch out for

Major arrears

Frequently the sellers of tenanted properties find that their tenants do not pay as regularly as they should. Once they have sold a property, it is relatively difficult for them to press the tenant (with whom they no longer have regular contact) for outstanding arrears. It is therefore common for a vendor to provide in the contract of sale a clause stating that the purchaser pays a sum over at completion equal to any arrears outstanding.

Although this 'balances the books' for the seller, it leaves the buyer in the invidious position of having paid out money in full against the right to collect it back in arrears from the tenants. Those arrears may prove to be uncollectable or it may be necessary to spend a lot of time and money to retrieve from the tenant, the cash already paid over to the seller.

> **KEY POINT:** *Your responsibility to pay over outstanding arrears to the seller at completion may be revealed in the part of the catalogue that refers to the relevant lot or may only be mentioned in the conditions of sale.*

Counting the cost of collecting arrears

Before bidding on any property where this condition applies, you should make detailed enquiries to establish your chances (and costs) of collecting the outstanding money from tenants. Irregularity in payments may be reflected in the outstanding arrears and it should warn you to check on the past payment record. After such enquiries, you may decide that you should trim the size of your top bid accordingly. Alternatively, you may decide not to buy because the arrears are such that you can have no confidence in the future ability of the tenants you are about to acquire to pay their rent.

> **KEY POINT:** *In every case where you are buying a tenanted property, you should be positive before you buy that the actual tenant is in occupation of the property and has not 'done a moonlight flit'. An inspection just before the auction is always wise, whether the property is tenanted or not.*

Local authority charges, public health and other notices

Where the local search reveals a local authority charge against a property, you should expect the vendor to pay off that charge at completion. You should ensure that the conditions of sale provide for this. If they do not, reduce your highest bid by the amount of the charges that you will have to pay on owning the property.

Are you required to carry out repairs?

The local search may reveal other public health and similar notices which can range from requirements to carry out certain repairs, right through to closure or demolition notices. Auctioneers encourage their clients to reveal the existence of such notices. They are usually mentioned in the sale catalogue or amendment sheets or by the auctioneer (if he is aware of them) at the time of sale. Nevertheless, you should not rely on this. Instead, you should ensure by suitable enquiry to the local authority in which the property is situated that no notices or charges are outstanding.

They should reveal if any compulsory purchase orders are in existence or pending and indicate how the property is affected by any planning proposals, warning you of any similar drawbacks to the lot.

Do not take plan sizes for granted

As plans pass between owners, solicitors and auctioneers, they are often subjected to copying and re-copying. Sometimes, plans are deliberately shrunk to fit on pages for faxing, printing or other use.

Plans reproduced in the auctioneer's catalogue should never be relied upon to be accurate, even if a written scale is shown on the plan. Sometimes the auctioneer's catalogue includes a saving clause, indicating that plans may not be accurate. Omission of this clause from the catalogue does not mean the plan sizes can be relied upon. If you have an opportunity to check the actual size of any land or property that you are buying, you should do so or, at worst, take suitable measurements and make your own calculations from an original of the Ordnance Survey.

View, view and view again

> **KEY POINT:** *If a full inspection of your lot is reasonably feasible but is refused, you should be highly suspicious and make your decision whether or not to bid accordingly.*

Viewing any lot you are thinking of buying should not be difficult. Almost invariably the auctioneer's catalogue will indicate the viewing arrangements. Occasionally, specific days and times for viewing are shown where the lot particulars are printed. Alternatively, viewing may be by direct arrangement with the auctioneer's office or by collecting the keys where it is appropriate. Occasionally, the auctioneers can only arrange viewing subject to the consent of the tenants. Whatever means of inspecting the property is provided, you should take advantage of it.

Financing the purchase

Will I need an accountant's advice?

An accountant may be needed at the very early stages for more general than specific advice. It is not the purpose of this book to give detailed help on accountancy and taxation matters.

Nevertheless, you will need to make an early decision once you have become interested in a property, whether you are going to buy and sell personally or through a private company or whether, by appropriate planning, you can take advantage of schemes such as self-administered pension funds, overseas companies and other measures to reduce your tax liability.

The advice and assistance that an accountant can provide you with in terms of accountancy and taxation matters depends very much on the use to which the property is to be put.

Tax allowances for investment properties

If the property is to be rented then such income is taxable under Schedule A, unless the property is let as furnished accommodation in which case tax is charged under Schedule D, Case VI. A person is charged the tax under Schedule A by reference to the rents or receipts to which he becomes entitled in the tax year concerned. Payments that are actually made during the chargeable period may be deducted if they fall within the definition of 'permitted deductions'. These include maintenance repairs, insurance and other services that the owner was obliged to provide and for which he received no separate payment. As far as maintenance or repairs are concerned there is a whole host of types of expenditure which are normally allowable, including interior and exterior repairs and decorations, cleaning, upkeep of gardens and the costs of rent collection.

Capital allowances may also be claimed in respect of plant and machinery belonging to the landlord. These will include items of office equipment such as computers and machinery that has become part of the building, such as a lift.

Interest on a loan to purchase a property or carry out improvements may be set against Schedule A income. Where the qualifying interest exceeds the amount of Schedule A income, the excess may be carried forward and set against subsequent years' Schedule A income. Tax relief is available on interest paid on a loan to purchase an investment property provided that certain conditions are satisfied including:

- The property must be let at a commercial rent.

- In any 52-week period, the property must be let for more than 26 weeks and when not being let, the property must be available either for letting or prevented from being available because of construction work or repairs.

- The property must be situated in the United Kingdom or the Republic of Ireland.

Tax relief for holiday property

If the property being let represents furnished holiday accommodation, then it may be treated as a trade, provided certain conditions are satisfied, including the following:

- It must be let on a commercial basis.

- It must be let as furnished accommodation.

- It must be available for commercial letting to the public as holiday accommodation for at least 140 days in a 12-month period.

- It must be let for at least 70 such days.

- It must not normally be occupied by the same person for more than 31 consecutive days at any time during a period of 7 months within the 12-month period.

If a property is treated as being let as furnished holiday accommodation, then interest on loans used to purchase the property and finance the lettings will qualify as an expense. If this gives rise to a loss for tax purposes, it may be offset against other taxable income. In addition, equipment and furniture and fittings may attract capital allowances. Profits from furnished holiday lettings may qualify as 'relevant earnings' for the purposes of personal pension contributions and retirement annuity premiums. For capital gains tax purposes, roll over and retirement relief may also be available.

Double your exemption from capital gains tax

On disposal of the investment property, capital gains tax may be payable on the chargeable gains arising. However, an annual exemption can be deducted from the chargeable gains, which for the income tax year 2000/2001 was £7,200. If husband and wife jointly own the property, then each is entitled to this annual exemption against their proportion of the chargeable gain. It may, therefore, be advantageous to consider acquiring the property jointly between the husband and

This base in London could have been yours for only £16,000.

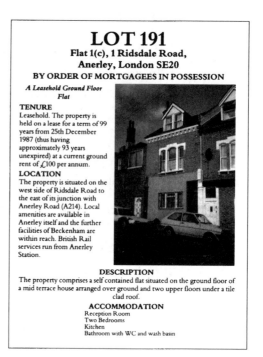

LOT 191
Flat 1(c), 1 Ridsdale Road,
Anerley, London SE20
BY ORDER OF MORTGAGEES IN POSSESSION

A Leasehold Ground Floor Flat

TENURE
Leasehold. The property is held on a lease for a term of 99 years from 25th December 1987 (thus having approximately 93 years unexpired) at a current ground rent of £100 per annum.

LOCATION
The property is situated on the west side of Ridsdale Road to the east of its junction with Anerley Road (A214). Local amenities are available in Anerley itself and the further facilities of Beckenham are within reach. British Rail services run from Anerley Station.

DESCRIPTION
The property comprises a self contained flat situated on the ground floor of a mid terrace house arranged over ground and two upper floors under a tile clad roof.

ACCOMMODATION
Reception Room
Two Bedrooms
Kitchen
Bathroom with WC and wash basin

wife to benefit from this exemption. One further advantage of this is that any rental income assessable is divided between the husband and wife for income tax purposes. As each spouse is assessed separately for tax purposes, then subject to any other taxable income, each is entitled to set their personal allowances against the rental income. Any remaining liability is subject to the 10 per cent or 22 per cent tax rate band with the remainder chargeable to higher rate tax at 40 per cent. In this way, personal allowances and lower rate tax bands can be utilised by both spouses.

The consequences of a company acquiring the property as an investment need to be examined carefully by your accountant, as there are significant differences in the taxation treatment of companies and individuals. For example, the annual exemptions for capital gains tax previously mentioned are not available to companies.

It is also possible for the property to be acquired by a small self-administered pension scheme which is linked to the company, provided certain criteria are met. The Inland Revenue requirements regarding such pension schemes will need to be discussed in detail with your accountant; however, they do offer the opportunities to mitigate the incidence of tax both on a corporate and personal level.

The VAT minefield

VAT on property is a minefield. At present, most properties are sold exclusive of VAT. However, the ramifications of this tax are extensive and if a property is expressed to be subject to VAT, this should be discussed in detail with your accountant at the earliest stage.

> **KEY POINT:** *The acquisition of property as an investment involves both tax planning opportunities and pitfalls. It is essential that you discuss the matter in detail with your accountant before undertaking the purchase.*

The deposit and balance

It is important to remember that on the day of the auction you will be required to make a deposit of 10 per cent of the purchase price or a minimum amount (whichever is the greater). You must ensure that you are able to pay both this deposit and the balance of the purchase price 28 days later. Figure 19.5 shows the different deposit amounts to be paid for sample purchase prices.

Fig 19.5   The purchase price, deposit and balance payable (minimum £1,500)

Price	Deposit	Balance
£350	£350	Nil
£500	£500	Nil
£1,000	£500	£500
£3,000	£1,500	£1,500
£5,000	£1,500	£3,500
£8,500	£1,500	£7,000
£12,000	£1,500	£10,500
£20,000	£2,000	£18,000
£30,000	£3,000	£27,000
£50,000	£5,000	£45,000
£100,000	£10,000	£90,000
£150,000	£15,000	£135,000
£250,000	£25,000	£225,000
£500,000	£50,000	£450,000
£1,000,000	£100,000	£900,000

If you are using a finance broker, bank or building society to provide the funds you should have the financing agreed, lot by lot, prior to the auction. The finance house will want to be satisfied that the valuation of the property is acceptable to them.

What other costs should I allow for?

You have already planned to meet professional fees for your valuer and your accountant. If your bid is successful and your purchase is above the relevant level, you will have the full Government Stamp Duty at one per cent of the purchase price for properties over £60,000.

Your cash flow is now fully prepared for the deposit payable at the auction, for the balance of the purchase price, plus VAT if it applies, 28 days later and for all your other costs. Figure 19.7 lists the possible total costs incurred for buying a property priced between £350 and £1,000,000. Depending on the individual property, there may be other costs to pay that are not mentioned here, but it gives a useful guide.

Figure 19.6 is a purchase costs checklist giving all the items for which you might have to budget.

Fig 19.6   Purchase costs checklist

- [ ] Deposit
- [ ] Balance
- [ ] VAT on purchase price
- [ ] Credit to vendor for tenants arrears
- [ ] Surveyor's fees and VAT
- [ ] Professional fees and VAT for attending at auction (if appropriate)
- [ ] Finance House commitment fee and VAT
- [ ] Local Search fees
- [ ] Stamp Duty (see left)
- [ ] Vendor's fees and costs (if charged)
- [ ] Repayment of grants
- [ ] Planning application fees
- [ ] Building regulation application fees
- [ ] Covenant buyout
- [ ] First insurance premium
- [ ] Contractor's bill for making secure/initial repairs
- [ ] Champagne celebration

Fig 19.7   *Total likely purchase costs*

The purchase price £	Deposit £	Balance £	VAT if payable on purchase price £	Surveyor's fees full structural £	Plus VAT auction incl VAT £	Stamp Duty £	Your expenses £	First insurance initial repairs £	Making secure £	Tenants' arrears fees £	Finance House £	Total £
£350	350	nil	61	–	–	nil	150	200	200	?	–	£961
£500	500	nil	88	–	–	nil	150	200	200	?	–	£1,138
£1,000	500	500	175	–	–	nil	150	200	200	?	–	£1,725
£3,000	1,500	1,500	525	200	35	nil	150	200	200	?	–	£4,310
£5,000	1,500	3,500	875	200	35	nil	150	200	200	?	–	£6,660
£8,500	1,500	7,000	1,488	250	44	nil	150	250	300	?	–	£10,982
£12,000	1,500	10,500	2,100	250	44	nil	250	250	300	?	150	£15,344
£20,000	2,000	18,000	3,500	300	53	nil	250	300	300	?	200	£24,903
£30,000	3,000	27,000	5,250	300	53	nil	250	350	400	?	300	£36,903
£50,000	5,000	45,000	8,750	400	70	nil	250	450	600	?	500	£61,020
£100,000	10,000	90,000	17,500	500	88	1,000	350	800	800	?	1,000	£122,038
£150,000	15,000	135,000	26,250	600	105	1,500	1,200	1,000	?	1,500		£182,155
£250,000	25,000	225,000	43,750	800	140	2,500	450	2,500	1,500	?	2,000	£303,640
£500,000	50,000	450,000	87,500	1,200	210	15,000	550	4,000	3,500	?	4,000	£615,960
£1,000,000	100,000	900,000	175,000	2,000	350	40,000	650	8,000	7,000	?	3,500	£1,236,500

Financial catches to watch out for

- Remember that finance houses frequently require a commitment fee, not to mention their interest charges and their capital repayments.

- As you interpret the conditions of sale, make sure you know what amount you could have to pay for items such as tenants' arrears.

- Ensure that you are aware of any outstanding local authority charges or grants. These can often be made the responsibility of the purchaser to repay.

- If you are hoping to explore the planning potential of your purchase, remember that planning and building regulation applications may require the payment of a fee to the local authority.

- Be sure that you have made allowance to buy out any covenants if such a procedure is appropriate. For example, if you are buying a site for development there could be covenants preventing you from carrying out your proposals until the person holding the benefit of these covenants has agreed to your proposals and been paid a sum for their amendment.

- Finally, always leave sufficient margin for the champagne celebration after you have successfully purchased a lot at your price.

20 Going for your bargain

I went to auction a couple of times before to get the feel for it and to see what the prices were like. I thought just before Christmas would be a good time to buy because people haven't got a lot of spare money and have other things on their mind and as it turns out I was proved right.

Don Lee, buyer of a residential property at auction.

Doing a dummy run

Get the feel for how an auction works

Although you can be armed with the information in this guide and be made aware of what happens in an auction, nothing can be better than experiencing several auctions before you go to the first one at which you intend to bid. Doing a 'dummy run' is highly recommended. Ideally, this should extend way beyond merely calling at one or two auctions to see how matters proceed. Earlier on in the previous chapter, you read the recommendation that you approach your accountant at an early stage and do your legal research. You could focus your research and enquiries by indicating a general interest in a lot in an auction during your dummy run. By doing so, you will be able to develop the enquiries and questions you will put to them when your 'run' is for real.

Key points for the dummy run

1. Choose a specific lot to focus your interest.

2. List and rehearse the questions you would wish to ask.

3. Visit your dummy property and make a thorough inspection as if you were intending to buy. (You may find that you can discuss it with a surveyor without charge, if you warn him that this is a dummy run but that you are looking to develop mutual business in the future.)

4. Ask the seller's solicitor all the necessary questions.

5. Look at a copy of the local search or ring the relevant local authority if the search is not available.

6. Read carefully the conditions of sale, general and additional conditions and auctioneer's conditions. This will prepare you for similar research when it really matters.

7. Contact the auctioneer's office. Consider having a trial negotiation with them to practise your negotiating skills. Your experience with them in such negotiations may cast a revealing light on their approach and the reality of their guideline figures.

'Chief Rents' – These rents are also known as perpetual annual rent charges which are payable by the owners of freehold land annually. In the main, the rents only exist in the Greater Manchester, Bristol and Channel Isles' districts. The period over which they can now be collected is restricted by statute.

'O.P.P.' – This is an acronym for 'Outline Planning Permission'.

FRANK R MARSHALL & CO at Nantwich, Apr 7	
Shavington — Green Bank Farm, B5071 Rd. Arable/pasture farm. Hse, 10 rms, 3 attic rms, tradn bdgs, loose boxes, stores, barns. 106.10 a. F, P	400,000
BIGWOOD at Birmingham, Apr 8	
Goostrey — Buckbean Way etc. Chief rents on 57 units at £1,140 pa.	6,000
Holmes Chapel — Danefield Rd etc. Chief rents on 80 units at £1,299 pa.	6,500
DENTON CLARK & CO at Rowton, Apr 14	
Ashton — Gable Cottage, Kelsall Rd. Terr cottage, 2 bed. F, P	66,500
Cuddington — Cuddington Barn, B5069 Rd. Barn with PP conversion to hse, 4 bed, adj cottage, 1 bed. Stables/store. 2.62 a. F, P	65,000
Marbury — School Hse, School Lane. Cottage, 3 bed. Adj bdg plot with OPP 1 dwelling. F, P	60,000
Tilston — Constabulary Cottage, Church Rd. Det cottage, 3 bed. F, P	66,000
Adj garden land, 110 ft x 50 ft. F, P	8,500
Apr 15	
Helsby — Off A56 Chester Rd. Accom pasture, 13.07 a. F, P	52,000
Accom pasture, 10.73 a. F, P	26,000
Accom pasture, 28.54 a. F, P	28,500
Paddocks, 2.99 a. F, P	5,000
Manley — Manley Rd, Riley Bank. Pasture/conservation land, 27.95 a. F, P	35,000
Morley Lane, Dunham Heath. Pasture, 10.02 a. F, P	20,000

Fig 20.1   Estates Gazette auction results

Cut out the competition and buy your bargain before auction

I always try to do a deal beforehand because you never know what opposition you are going to come up against at auction. But you should never show your hand in case it does go to auction. The vendor is generally only going to accept a higher price before the auction.

Michael Kirby, Chartered Surveyor.

Move in before the auction happens

Negotiating the purchase of a lot before auction is not at all unusual. Do remember that all the steps previously recommended should be undertaken. Before the day of the sale, you may feel confident enough to risk negotiating for the property. Lucky buyers can acquire bargains in this way but they do run the risk of 'disclosing their hand' to the auctioneers and they can be passing the initiative to them. Whether you take up such an initiative is undoubtedly a gamble. Only you can decide whether it is worthwhile in the light of your desire to buy the lot and to beat the competition that might take place on auction day. On the other hand, by revealing your interest so soon, you can lose what would otherwise be a strong position in your bidding at the auction.

Before you start such negotiations you will no doubt have decided how much you wish to pay for the property. If you are endeavouring to buy before auction, this must be either because you wish to buy the property noticeably cheaper than the amount you are ready to pay on auction day, or because you want the lot so badly that you do not want anybody else to have the opportunity to purchase and 'bid you up' on that day. The decision is entirely yours.

> **KEY POINT:** *By bidding before the auction you are likely to remove any opportunity of buying the property any cheaper than your pre-auction bid. But this has to be balanced against the advantages of cutting out the competition.*

Contracts must be exchanged quickly for pre-auction sales

If you decide to bid before the auction, you must be prepared to negotiate quickly and if your bid is successful, to sign a contract and pay your deposit even faster. The auctioneer will require you to exchange contracts before the auction (and probably by several days in advance). *You have an even greater need for speed.* If you have decided to buy before the auction, you must be aware that there could be other people who have a similar desire to buy early. You should not then plan to exchange contracts or memoranda in the normal course of 'legal' time. You should complete your enquiries at top speed and exchange contracts or memoranda as a matter of urgency. You will obviously have to provide your 10 per cent deposit at the time the exchange takes place and have your finance already organised.

> **KEY POINT:** *You must realise that a purchase prior to the auction does not change any of the procedures, responsibilities or actions detailed in this book other than those that relate to attending and bidding at the auction itself.*

Many auctioneers are willing to allow you to leave your deposit with them and to complete and exchange memoranda or contracts in their office. This will speed the passage of the sale but it is not recommended unless you are satisfied with your enquiries about the title and background to the property. Only those who want a lot so badly that they are prepared to risk irrevocably committing themselves to a purchase before they are satisfied, should proceed before then. Having exchanged, if you then decide to 'go back' on the purchase, legal sanctions (including loss of your deposit and other responsibilities to meet damages) will follow. The same sanctions apply if you succeed with a bid on the auction day itself and subsequently withdraw.

Buyer's timetable

For most auctions, you will have only three or four weeks from the initial advertisement to the auction itself to carry out all your preparations. The following timetable provides a useful guide for buyers on when you need to make the necessary arrangements prior to the auction.

Days prior to and after the auction	Action
21	See advertisement and apply for auctioneer's catalogue.
19	Receive catalogue
17	First inspection of property
	Check auctioneer's particulars
16	Instruct valuation surveyor
14	Read and understand the conditions of sale
13	Receive surveyor's report
12	Start legal checks
	Visit accountant
	Arrange finance
10	Second inspection of property

	Assess quality of tenants, if appropriate
6	Consider a pre-auction purchase
5	Be satisfied with the title
	Check availability of finance
3	Decide on your maximum bid
1	Final visit to property prior to the sale
Auction day	Attend auction
	Bid successfully,
	Exchange contracts or memoranda
	Pay deposit
1	Insure property immediately
	Revisit property
	Check security
	Meet tenants
1/3	If your lot was withdrawn on the day, negotiate to buy
21/28	Complete purchase
	Pay balance of purchase monies
	Pay stamp duty
	Relax and celebrate

Attending the auction

You always feel a little apprehensive before you go in. You go in with nothing and come home with something else.

Michael Roe, buyer of residential properties.

You have picked out your lots, you have done your research, you have spoken to your accountant and other advisers and your finance is arranged. You have settled in your own mind the maximum figure you are prepared to bid for the lots you are interested in. Now you are ready to go to your auction. The next sections address the atmosphere, the nature of the auction, details of the procedures you can expect to have to follow and suggests ways you might go about the purchase of your bargain lots.

The following checklist gives the key points you should watch out for at auction. Each one is discussed in depth below.

| AUCTION CHECKLIST: *For the bargain hunter* |

1   Wise to attend yourself. ☐

2   Check the etiquette. ☐

3   Follow any registration procedure. ☐

4   Choose a good vantage point. ☐

5   Pay attention. ☐

6   Listen to the auctioneer's speech. ☐

7   Check for any amendments. ☐

8   Watch out for VAT. ☐

9   Make your first bid loud and clear. ☐

10 Watch competitive bidders. ☐

11 Be aware the auctioneer rules the roost. ☐

12 Try to read the auctioneer. ☐

13 Subsequent bids should be obvious. ☐

14 Only bid enough to buy. ☐

15 Only bid up to your maximum. ☐

16 Concentrate on what is happening even if you have stopped bidding. ☐

17 Be aware of the lots you have bought. ☐

18 Sign the contract or memorandum before you leave the room. ☐

19 Expect to pay a 10 per cent deposit (subject to the stated minimum). ☐

20 An unsold lot could be a bargain – move in quickly to negotiate. ☐

How to attend

Although you may expect most buyers to attend an auction in person, this is not necessary. Methods of bidding without attending are given below. But if you are to have the best opportunities of securing a bargain you would be wise to be in the room so that you can weigh up the atmosphere, judge the approach of the auctioneer and, particularly, to outmanoeuvre your opposing bidders.

A three-bed city flat that fell under the hammer for less than the price of a new car. Ridiculous but true. It sold for only £8,500.

LOT 203
10 Darefield Walk, Highgate, Birmingham, West Midlands
BY ORDER OF MORTGAGEES IN POSSESSION

A Leasehold Ground and First Floor Maisonette

TENURE Leasehold. Please refer to the Vendor's Solicitor for further details.

LOCATION The property is situated on the west side of Darwin Walk to the south of its junction with Alcester Street. Local amenities are available in Highgate itself and the facilities of Birmingham city centre are within reach.

DESCRIPTION The property comprises a self contained maisonette arranged over the ground and first floors of a purpose built block.

ACCOMMODATION
Ground Floor
Reception Room, Kitchen
First Floor
Three Bedrooms, Bathroom, Separate WC

What will it be like?

As we saw earlier, auctions are of various types but by the time you attend you will have had every opportunity to judge the nature of the auction to which you will be going. Figure 20.2 lists different types of auction, the number of lots, the size of audience and probable venue you can expect. A large and composite auction in a central city venue will have had extensive advertising and a large, high quality catalogue. You can expect a crowded room with between 200 and 1,000 potential bidders and a thoroughly organised room and reception laid out in theatre seating. With luck, you might even be offered free coffee and refreshments. There is still likely to be only a single auctioneer on the rostrum but he will probably be supported by two or three 'spotters' alongside who are there to help him pick bidders out of the large audience. Beside the auctioneer is likely to be his clerk who will record all bids as an aide-memoire during the sale. In some auctions, part of the room will be allocated as an area where contracts are signed after successful bids have been received. In other auctions there will be an

Fig 20.2   Size of auctions

	Number of lots	Likely audience	Likely venue
Single lot	1	10–75	Hotel, church hall, pub, restaurant
Small composite sale room	2–5	10–100	Hotel, church hall, pub, restaurant, sale
Medium composite	5–50	50–200	Hotel
Large composite	50–100	200–500	Hotel/conference centre/theatre

area allocated for tables where solicitors, acting on behalf of owners, will be presiding with details of their clients' titles (and probably copies of local searches). They are there ready to exchange contracts if their clients have been successful in selling.

> **KEY POINT:** *You will have the choice to sit or stand but do find a position from which you are able to watch your competing bidders.*

Make your first bid obvious

In such a crowd, you can expect quite a hubbub with people moving around the room. The auctioneer will have amplification equipment to assist him, but it is very probable that you will need to make a large and obvious gesture, or even to call out to attract the auctioneer's attention at your first bid for each of your chosen lots.

The size of the auction audience often comes down as the scale of the auction reduces. A composite auction, where the number of lots on offer is between approximately 50 and 100, is likely to attract an audience of between 200 and 500 people. The room and atmosphere are similar to that of larger auctions, but it will probably be easier for the bidder to attract the auctioneer's attention. Because of the size of the audience, it is possible for you to make your bids discreetly. Where auctions of this size occur outside London, it is more usual for the sellers' solicitors to attend the auction.

At smaller auctions, the audience is also frequently smaller (unless the lots offered are of overwhelming interest) with between 10 and 100 people attending. For a smaller auction, the venue chosen is often a smaller sale room or hired room in a public house or local hall, instead of a large hotel or conference centre. At this size, the proceedings are a little less formal. The auctioneer does not need spotters and the sellers' solicitor frequently attends. The bidding is much more discreet and you will have more opportunity to see the quality and strength of any opposing bidders.

How to behave at auction

Listed below are the key points you need to know about auction room etiquette and behaviour:

1   The auctioneer and his staff welcome anyone who swells the crowd, who is dressed reasonably presentably, regardless of their intention to bid or not and who intends to behave reasonably quietly.

2 There is always a constant to-ing and fro-ing of people. You are welcome to arrive and leave whenever it suits you, although it is usual for the audience to avoid interfering with the enjoyment of the proceedings by other people while bidding on a lot is taking place.

3 Arriving late or leaving after the lot in which you are interested is not at all unusual, although it is unwise to miss the auctioneer's opening speech and announcements.

4 Auctioneers often seem to comment on vacant seats available at the front of the auction room, despite research showing that lots are no more expensive whether you are sitting at the front of the room or standing at the back. Don't hesitate to use empty seats if you are happy to do so, but it is a useful tactic to gain a vantage point from where you can observe opposing bidders.

5 Sitting or standing is left to the choice of the attenders. If you are intending to bid, you need to be in a position where you can see the auctioneer and he can see you easily.

Arrive early and make your final checks

6 Auction rooms usually open approximately one hour before the auction commences. Most of the audience turn up in the 20 minutes before proceedings start. Auctions often start approximately five minutes late, but do not rely on this. Amazingly, it is not unusual for 90 per cent or more of the audience never to bid. If you have questions to ask the auctioneer's staff or solicitors before the auction, it is wise to arrive 30 minutes before the auction starts, if you are to avoid a crush. This will give you an opportunity to speak to solicitors, inspect local searches, deeds and leases and whatever else is available for your viewing.

7 On arrival, always check :

- if there have been any additions or amendments to the lots and lot details;

- if the lot in which you are interested has already been sold or withdrawn;

- if the lots are to be offered in alphabetical or numerical order.

8 If the auctioneers have a registration procedure, it is polite to adopt it and complete appropriate forms at their request. You will not normally be asked for confidential information.

DATE: . . . .   NUMBER: . . . .

TO ALL THOSE ATTENDING THE
LONGDEN & COOK COMMERCIAL AUCTION:

To assist in your identification and to maintain privacy, please complete the details below and return this
sheet to one of our staff in exchange for a numbered bidding paddle.
When a Lot is sold to you, please advise the auctioneer of your number before going across to the
solicitors' table to complete the documents.

1   (a)   Your full names   . . . .
    (b)   Your address   . . . .
                                  . . . .
    (c)   Your telephone number(s) . . . .
2   (a)   Your Solicitors   . . . .
    (b)   Their address   . . . .
                                  . . . .
    (c)   The person acting   . . . .
    (d)   Solicitors' phone number . . . .

IF YOU ARE INTENDING to bid on someone else's behalf please indicate below:

3   (a)   That person's full name   . . . .
    (b)   Their address   . . . .
                                  . . . .
    (c)   Their telephone number   . . . .

4   Do you wish to go on our Mailing List for future auction catalogues?   Yes ☐   No ☐

I ACKNOWLEDGE RECEIPT of a bidding paddle or number sheet and acknowledge that by signing
this form I agree to participate in this auction on the basis of the Conditions of Sale published in this
Catalogue.

SIGNED: . . . .

PLEASE RETURN YOUR BIDDING PADDLE AT THE END OF THE AUCTION

Fig 20.3   Auctioneer's registration form

9 If the auctioneers publish in the catalogue or elsewhere any particular requirements, ensure you fulfil them in plenty of time.

10 If you are intending to bid, do not be shy about drawing the auctioneer's attention to your bid by an obvious gesture or by calling out loudly. Once you have attracted the auctioneer's attention, it is unlikely that you will need to attract his attention that obviously again for that particular lot. However, if it proves necessary, do not lose the opportunity to bid by being shy about repeating the obvious gesture or loud call.

11 Practices vary from auctioneer to auctioneer in the registration and identification of buyers. One of the more modern systems (said to have been first used at an auction of Beatles memorabilia) is the paddle system which is descibed in the next section.

Auctioneer's Anecdote:

A smoked salmon bomb!

On occasion, auctioneers are known to provide refreshments for their audience and a leading firm of London auctioneers decided to push the boat out with smoked salmon sandwiches which were particularly popular. At the end of the auction, they noticed a briefcase had been left behind in the refreshment area and feared it was a bomb. Curiosity overcame circumspection however and the briefcase was opened to reveal that it was absolutely full of smoked salmon sandwiches and a card identifying its owner. The auctioneer was delighted to note the owner's embarrassment when he telephoned him later to tell him that his briefcase had been retrieved.

How will the auctioneer know I am a bidder?

The paddle system is one method used to register prospective bidders. As the audience arrives, each person is invited (if they express interest in bidding) to complete a registration form (see Figure 20.3). This form will always include the name and address of the bidder or the name and address of the company or organization on whose behalf they are bidding. The information sheet is then exchanged for a numbered bidding paddle which is not necessarily used for bidding but which is shown to the auctioneer by the successful purchaser after the gavel has fallen.

This enables the auctioneer to identify the buyer immediately and to pass instructions for the preparation of contract. Other information useful to the auctioneer is frequently sought including the name of the solicitors – if any – acting for the bidder. It is not unusual for the form to be used by the auctioneer to collect statistical data, to find out where you saw the advertisement for the lot which interests you.

Auctioneers who do not use a registration system generally have more 'spotters' on their rostrum. These spotters identify the successful bidder with the help of the auctioneer and then approach him, asking him to complete a form which details the bidder's name, address and – if any – his solicitors. The form is collected so that the necessary contract or memoranda can be prepared. The same spotter returns later to the purchaser to take him over to the table for exchange of contracts.

The auction kit

Auction
15th November 2000
Memorandum of Contract

Contract Lot No. ....
Property ....
Price: £ .... Deposit: £ ....
I/We
of   do hereby acknowledge that I/we:
(1)   were the highest bidder(s) at the Sale by Auction this day of the lot detailed above.
(2)   was/were declared the Purchaser(s) thereof subject to the Particulars and Conditions and Special Conditions of Sale at the price detailed above.
(3)   have paid the deposit detailed above to the Auctioneers.
(4)   agree to complete the said purchase in all respects according to the Particulars, Conditions and Special Conditions of the Sale.

Purchase money .... £
Less Deposit paid .... £
Balance to be paid on completion .... £

AS WITNESS my/our/hand(s) this   day of   19

                                           Signed ....
                                           (for and on behalf of/the Purchaser(s))

We hereby confirm this sale and acknowledge receipt as agents for the vendor of the said deposit of £   ....   in accordance with the Particulars, Conditions and Special Conditions of Sale.

                                           Signed ....
                                           (signed on behalf of the Vendor(s))
Abstract of Title to be sent to . ...

Sample memorandum

Figure 20.4   Memorandum of Contract

Where the paddle system is used, it is usual for the bidder to be escorted over to the table for exchange of contracts immediately after the gavel has fallen. If a bidder wishes to bid on subsequent lots shortly after his successful purchase, he may need to defer attending the table for exchange.

Exchanging contracts or memoranda

The full contract

In every case, buyers have to sign and exchange contracts or memoranda before they leave the auction room at the end of the sale. If they fail to do so, the auctioneer has the right to sign the contract on their behalf. The contract is virtually identical to the contract which any purchaser signs to buy a property. It often follows a standard layout used by many solicitors throughout the country.

What the contract contains

- the names of the buyer and the seller;

- the price that is being paid (the final price of the successful bidder);

- deposit to be paid;

- the completion date;

- whether or not vacant possession is given;

- details of the property and its tenure;

- the status by which the seller will convey the property;

- brief details of the title;

- covenants that affect the property being sold;

- fixtures and fittings that are included;

- the general conditions of the published Law Society conditions referring to the relevant edition;

- the interest rate payable if the sale is delayed;

- other specific items worthy of notice.

The memorandum

The memorandum is a much briefer contract which is usually printed in the auction catalogue. An example is shown in Figure 20.4. Where full contracts are not available for signing by buyers, then the memorandum in the catalogue is used. This details:

- the contract lot number and the property;

- the price and the deposit payable;

- the name of the purchaser, declaring them the highest bidder at the sale.

The memorandum is not normally detached from the copy of the auction catalogue, so that the details of the property and its lot number are linked to the memorandum. A small table in the memorandum details the purchase money, the deposit paid and the balance to be paid on completion.

In the case of both the memorandum and the contract, one copy is signed and dated by the purchaser. The other copy is signed and dated on behalf of the vendors. The two documents are then 'exchanged' with the one received by the purchaser acting as a receipt for the deposit.

> **KEY POINT:** *When you have bid successfully and exchanged contracts or memoranda you need to arrange the usual steps towards completion.*

When a contract is created

It is an interesting feature of auction law that the moment of contract is the point at which the auctioneer bangs down his gavel. The exchange of contracts or memorandum that takes place afterwards is merely a recording of the existence of the contract. The auctioneer has the legal right to sign the contract on behalf of the vendor and also the right to sign on behalf of the purchaser provided the signature takes place in the environs of the auction room within a reasonable time of the sale having taken place. The right to sign on behalf of the vendor is frequently used, but it is most unusual for the auctioneer to sign on behalf of the purchaser. However, it does leave the auctioneer in a position where he can sign either part of a contract or memorandum prior to the exchange of the parts. This is a convenient arrangement where the owner of the property is not present at the sale or where the purchaser has sent in a written bid or is at the other end of a telephone.

> **KEY POINT:** *No purchaser or bidder should think they have an opportunity to renege on their bid, after the gavel has fallen, by leaving the room without completing their part of the memorandum or contract.*

Financial, legal and tax traps – a last-minute check

Will the owner's solicitors be present?

Across the country, the practice of solicitors attending auction varies. It appears to be a more usual practice in the north than the south that solicitors acting on behalf of the sellers attend the auction. An enquiry to the auction firm will always give you the answer.

> **KEY POINT:** *If the answer is yes, the vendor's solicitors are attending, you should nevertheless arrange to check the title to the property well before the sale.*

Check for late information

If the vendor's solicitors are at the auction, they may have some late information or be able to show you the results of a local search. They may ask you to look at this essential item if you have not had the opportunity and if you think it will be available on the day. The search may bring up questions that need to be put to the local authority to check that there are no adverse plans affecting the property. The vendor's solicitors may be holding other documents that you would like to see again. It is a good idea to check whatever are available and ask if any changes have occurred. These may include:

- plans of the lot being sold;

- leases and their actual wording;

- local searches;

- title details;

- a copy of the contract or memorandum;

- requirements to pay VAT.

It is not unknown for some bidders at auction to read through the catalogue as they arrive and recklessly decide to bid for a property unseen from the catalogue. If you are feckless enough to consider such a course, do at least check through whatever documents are available at the solicitor's table or at the auctioneer's clerk's table before you bid.

Auctioneer's Anecdote:

Unseen is unsafe

It is not as unusual as you would think for bidders to buy lots unseen. There are investors who will tell you 'I have always had my most

259

A three-bed house in the shires for a very reasonable £16,500

LOT 211
53 Queen Street, Desborough, Northamptonshire
BY ORDER OF MORTGAGEES IN POSSESSION

A Freehold Mid Terrace House

TENURE
Freehold.

LOCATION
Queen Street is located off Rushton Road, which in turn runs into Station Road. Local shops and amenities are within reach.

DESCRIPTION
The property comprises a mid terrace house arranged over ground and first floors beneath a pitched tile roof. The property benefits from a rear garden.

ACCOMMODATION

Ground Floor	First Floor
Two Reception Rooms	Three Bedrooms
Kitchen Area	
Bathroom with WC and wash basin	

successful deals where I never saw the property until after I bought it'. There are those who have walked up to the auctioneer afterwards and said "I liked the look of that lot on the slide, so I bought it. Can you tell me exactly where it is?'

There was a man with £30,000 (at 1995 values) burning a hole in his pocket who bought 27 properties in one lot at that figure in the belief that he could not go wrong getting those properties for that price. He did! They had subsided, were subject to various closure and repair notices and 15 of them were about to be purchased for clearance at a very small site value.

Watch the legal traps

Every buyer must be aware that the contract is created at the moment that the gavel comes down. The exchange of contracts or memoranda thereafter is only a documentation of the existence of that contract. As we have already seen, the auctioneer can sign on behalf of both sides certifying that the existing contract is satisfactorily documented by the written details.

All auctioneers are aware of the Sale of Land by Auction Act 1867 which prohibits vendor's bids being made by more than one method. In property auctions, the Sale of Goods Act 1979 is partially relevant, but more important are the Estate Agents Act 1979 and the Property Misdescriptions Act 1991. These Acts regulate the propriety and behaviour of the auctioneer and his employees and business colleagues. The Property Misdescriptions Act is intended especially to ensure that auctioneers' particulars are not misleading.

More important to the purchaser is the Auctions (Bidding Agreements) Acts 1927 and 1969. The main purpose of these Acts (as far as the bidder is concerned) is to ensure that you do not come to any agreement not to bid against anyone else at an auction unless the existence of such an arrangement and the parties to it have been declared in writing to the auctioneer before the sale begins.

> KEY POINT: *The Act makes it a criminal offence for a potential bidder, who is in business as a dealer, to offer an inducement to anyone else not to bid.*

Conditional contracts

A limited number of property auctioneers use a conditional contracts procedure which applies when the bidding just fails to reach the reserve price. The procedures do not apply if your final accepted bid is at or above the reserve price since then the normal contract exchange process will be used. The auctioneer will always indicate in the catalogue if the conditional contracts procedure will apply at the auction.

Vendors may decide not to accept your bid

The terms of the conditional contract normally provide for you to be committed to a purchase at your highest bid while the seller decides whether or not he wishes to accept a sale at the same sum below his reserve. The seller is usually given between 24 and 72 hours to decide. The terms of conditional contracts vary but are always published by the auctioneer. If you attend an auction where conditional contracts are used, you should read the terms particularly carefully. If the conditional procedure applies, it is unlikely that the auctioneer's gavel will fall, but the final bidder will be approached immediately after the lot has been withdrawn to sign the conditional contract.

'SC' –
Self-contained

'P' –
This is normally used as
an abbreviation for
'Vacant Possession' which
can also be noted as 'V.P.'

'L' –
Leasehold

'F' –
Freehold

'RUP' –
Residential upper part

'Mais' –
Maisonette

LONDON

STRETTONS of E1 at New Connaught Rms, WC2, Apr 19

E1 — 18 Pevensey Hse, Ben Johnson Rd. S/C mais, 4 rms. L, P	**30,000**
50 Cephas Ave. End terr hse, 6 rms. Closing order. F, P	**53,000**
37 New Rd. Terr w/shop bdg. 2 floors. Let £2,068 pa. 2 floors, 388 & 410 sq ft with P. F	**55,000**
E3 — 104 Fairfoot Rd. Bdg plot. PP 2 flats. F, P	**15,000**
111 Grove Rd. Terr hse, 5 rms. F, P	**54,000**
13 Grafton Hse, Wellington Way. 2nd floor, S/C flat, 3 rms. L, P	**17,500**
E5 — 5/7 Chatsworth Rd. 2 adj shops, RUP 2 S/C flats, 4 & 5 rms. Let £3,120 PAX. Closing Order. F	**40,000**
4 Cricketfield Rd. S/C flat, 2 rms. L, P	**25,500**
19 Elderfield Rd. End terr hse, 9 rms. PP flat, mais, 2 garages. Closing order. F, P	**43,000**
30 Glenarm Rd. 2nd floor, S/C studio flat. L, P	**15,500**
103 Mount Pleasant Lane. S/C flat, 3 rms. L, P	**23,000**
E6 — 132 Charlemont Rd. RUP S/C flat, 2 rms. L, P	**20,500**
58 Dickens Rd. End terr hse, 3 bed. F, P	**35,000**
130 Masterman Rd. Terr hse, 2 bed. F, P	**36,500**
St Andrews Hall, Roman Rd. Derelict hall, site 0.10 a. Planning brief for 2 hses. F, P	**31,000**
E7 — 165 Capel Rd. Corner bdg, 6 rms, part used as clinic. PP 2 hses & garages on rear land. F, P	**66,500**
7 Neville Rd. End terr bdg as 3 S/C flats. 1 LGR, 1 studio flat & 1 x 3 rms with P. For completion. F	**36,500**
75 Pevensey Rd. Terr hse as 2 flats, 3 rms. F, P	**38,000**
7 Reginald Rd. Corner shop, rear rm. RUP 3 rms. F, P	**35,000**
21 Shaftesbury Rd. Terr hse, 2 bed. F, P	**35,500**
E8 — 234 Dalston Lane. 4 storey hse, 10 rms, 2 store rms. F, P	**55,000**
376C Kingsland Rd. RUP S/C mais, 3 rms. L, P	**22,000**
113 Shacklewell Lane. Shop, rear rm. S/C mais, 3 rms. P	**28,500**
E10 — 287 High Rd. Shop, rear rm, basement, mais, 4 rms, garage. F, P	**60,000**
E12 — 32 Salisbury Rd. Terr hse, 3 bed. F, P	**36,500**
E13 — 198 Balaam St. S/C flat, 3 rms. L, P	**18,000**
163 Grange Rd. Terr hse, 6 rms. F, P	**34,500**
50 London Rd. S/C flat, 2 rms. L, P	**14,000**
31 Maud Rd. Terr hse as S/C flat, 3 rms & S/C mais, 3 rms. F, P	**41,000**
Tabernacle Ave. Site 0.16 a. Planning brief for development. F, P	**16,000**

Fig 20.5   *Estates Gazette auction results*

> **KEY POINT:** *Where conditional contracts do apply, intending bidders should read the details specified in the catalogue or the auctioneer's terms carefully.*

How and when is the deposit paid?

Immediately the gavel has fallen, the purchaser is due to exchange his memorandum or contract and to pay over the deposit. Usually the payment is 10 per cent of the purchase price, subject to a specified minimum. The amount due is indicated in the auctioneer's catalogue, generally somewhere in the conditions of sale. It is not unusual for these terms to be displayed on the walls of the sale room as well as in the catalogue and it may also be referred to in the auctioneer's opening remarks.

Be ready to hand over your money

Most auctioneers will accept a normal cheque drawn upon a recognised bank or building society. Cash is only accepted by certain auctioneers; if you intend to pay this way, check before the sale. No auctioneer has yet indicated that he will accept payment by credit card.

Certain auctioneers require certified or guaranteed cheques or banker's drafts. Personal or building society cheques are not acceptable. This does create a slight problem, since you will need to arrange for the cheque or draft to be prepared before the auction and you will not know how much the purchase price is going to be and therefore, how much the cheque should be. The only way of covering this is to ensure that the amount specified on the draft is at least 10 per cent of the maximum bid proposed – and maybe a little higher to allow for a touch of indulgent bidding. It is normally sufficient for the payment order to be made out to the auctioneer's firm but, on occasion, the catalogue may specify different instructions. Where auctioneers have a practice of inviting the solicitors acting on behalf of the vendor to attend the sale, then sometimes (but not very often) the solicitors for the vendor ask for the cheque to be made payable in their name. In a few instances, where sales are being conducted for government or local authority departments or quangos, cheques are occasionally requested to be payable to them. Cheques are normally only payable to the vendor if it is a reputable and well-known body.

> **KEY POINT:** *The destination of this deposit cheque, and the way in which the money is held, is very important to both parties to the transaction between contract and completion.*

The conditions of sale usually indicate whether the deposit money, after the exchange of contracts, is held by:

- a stakeholder on behalf of the vendor;

- a stakeholder on behalf of the purchaser;

- a stakeholder on behalf of both sides;

- the vendor.

Insist on an indemnity bond

A stakeholder can be any person, but they must be acceptable to both parties. The auctioneers or vendor's solicitors often act as the stakeholder. If the money is held on behalf of the vendor, a purchaser should insist, before exchanging contracts, that the money is covered by an insurance bond, to be held by the auctioneers or the solicitors and require that the vendor is prohibited from having access to the money until completion. The bond will protect the purchaser's money in the event of fraud or insolvency of the auctioneers or solicitors.

If the money is held on behalf of the purchaser, then there is no need to restrict control of the money further, although it is still wise to ensure that the money, whilst in the hands of professionals, is covered by an insurance bond. Virtually all auctioneers and solicitors indicate the arrangements made. Once paid, the purchaser will not have access to the deposit unless the contract is cancelled.

Where the money is held by a stakeholder it is usually in the control of the auctioneers or solicitors who have been so nominated to hold it on behalf of both vendor and purchaser until completion. Again, it is wise that this money should be covered by an insurance bond and you should be satisfied that the amount is paid into an appropriate client account.

Who keeps the interest?

Where big deposit sums are payable or the period between purchase and completion is longer than usual and the amount of interest earned on the money in this period is significant, then it is important that everyone is clear who receives the interest. Normally, the interest is retained by:

- the auctioneers; or

- the solicitors; or occasionally

- the vendor; or very occasionally

- the purchaser (and then only by special agreement).

However, if the interest to be earned is large, discuss the matter with the auctioneers at least several days prior to the sale. You would be wise to make arrangements with the auctioneer's and vendor's solicitors for the interest to be credited to your benefit, making it a condition of your bidding that such an arrangement must be entered into. Alternatively, if you cannot make such arrangements, allow for loss of interest when calculating the amount of your final bid.

Bids by phone require deposit payments in advance

If you intend to bid by telephone, fax, internet or letter then you will have to make arrangements with the auctioneer to pay the deposit before the sale. Unless you are well known to the auctioneer, he will invariably require you to pay the deposit by banker's draft, building society or personal cheque, which will have to be cleared before the sale begins. The amount will be equal to or higher than 10 per cent of your proposed maximum sum, subject to a specified minimum. It is wise to make such arrangements well in advance of the auction, giving the auctioneer at least a week's notice.

It is imperative that funds are available to cover any cheque issued for a deposit. If a cheque or financial instrument issued to cover the deposit fails to provide the necessary funds, the vendor will exercise his rights under the conditions of sale permitting him to:

- cancel the sale at his option; and

- take civil proceedings against the purchaser for any loss or costs.

The vendor is not required to re-offer the lot by auction, but can take any reasonable steps chosen to re-sell the lot. Before taking proceedings to recover any loss or costs the seller must show that reasonable endeavours have been made to re-sell at a proper price.

If a deposit cheque bounces, this could open up criminal proceedings. Such an offence does not remove the seller's rights to a civil claim.

> **Lot 20**
>
> **VACANT OFFICE PREMISES OFFERED WITH A RESERVE OF £77,500**
>
> | | |
> |---|---|
> | **Situation:** | A-Z B1 84. Off Waterloo Road, Middle Hillgate |
> | **Construction:** | Brick and slate |
> | **Tenure:** | Freehold |
> | **Accommodation:** | The offices have been thoroughly refurbished. |
> | *Ground floor:* | Entrance hall, 4 large offices, kitchen and storage. |
> | *First floor:* | Two offices, large showroom fronting to Canal Street, toilet facilities. |
> | *Exterior:* | Car parking at rear. |
> | **General:** | The showroom area has an open ceiling revealing the original roof beams which have been polished and provide a most attractive feature. This building of character is a former public house which has recently undergone a comprehensive refurbishment. The offices are carpeted throughout and have double glazed windows, full gas fired central heating, suspended ceilings with recessed lighting on the ground floor. |
> | **Approximate Total Floor Area:** | 1950 sq ft |
> | **Viewing & Co-agents:** | Edwards & Co (N M Hunter), 20 Albert Square, Manchester, M2 5BE. Tel: 061-833 9991. |
> | **Vacant Possession:** | On completion |
>
> **Solicitors: Gabbie & Co, 60 Talbot Road, Manchester, M16 0GB. Tel: 061-872 5363.**

Fig 20.6   *Auction catalogue illustrating an upset price. This was a property where the vendor had the building on the market for quite a long time before the auction, at an asking price noticeably higher than the upset price quoted. She felt that by publishing the upset price, it would be an indication to people who had previously been interested that the vendor would be willing to sell at a noticeably lower figure than had previously been asked in the market. As it happened the property offered still did not sell at the auction.*

CHECKLIST: *Paying the deposit*

1 How much is payable?   ☐

2 Who is it to be paid to?   ☐

3 When is it required?   ☐

4 Do they require cleared funds?   ☐

5 Who receives the interest?   ☐

6 Can the interest be paid into my account?   ☐

7 Is the vendor prohibited from receiving
   the moneys until completion?   ☐

8 Is there an indemnity bond?   ☐

9 Is there an insurance bond?   ☐

10 Are the moneys being paid into client accounts?   ☐

Value Added Tax

In certain circumstances VAT is payable on property or land purchases. Where a property has been registered as subject to VAT, then the purchaser will have to pay at completion VAT at the going rate in addition to the purchase price. The purchaser will receive a VAT receipt and may be entitled to reclaim that tax or part of it. Nevertheless, the incidence of the payment may well affect cash flow, financing and, possibly, the legal vehicle in which the property is bought. Appropriate advice should be taken as long as possible before the auction.

Almost invariably, the auction catalogue will disclose if VAT is payable. If not, the auctioneer should publish it in the amendment sheet. He may also mention it in his opening speech and will undoubtedly mention it at the time he offers the lot.

Timing of VAT payments

VAT is almost always paid at completion of the purchase. Unless announced otherwise, the VAT will always be in addition to the price bid at the time the gavel falls.

Lot 26

23 Vale Street, Clayton
AT NO RESERVE

VACANT SEMI DETACHED HOUSE IN NEED OF COMPLETE RESTORATION

Situation: A-Z 2F 51. Off North Road, Ashton New Road (A662)
Tenure: Long leasehold subject to a ground rent of £4 pa.
Accommodation: *Ground floor:* Hall, lounge, kitchen. *First floor:* 3 bedrooms, bathroom/wc *Exterior:* Gardens front and rear, space for car
Viewing: Keys available from the auctioneers
Note: The property is boarded up. The entire property is in need of thorough overhauling and refurbishment.
Vacant Possession: On completion
Solicitors: Davies Wallis Foyster
(Mr I Osborne) 37 Peter Street, M2 5GB

Fig 20.7   An auction lot offered at no reserve

How to find out if VAT is payable

Is VAT mentioned:

1. in the conditions of sale?

2. in the general preamble at the beginning of the catalogue?

3. in the description of the lot in the catalogue?

4. in any memoranda published in the catalogue?

5. in the auctioneer's amendment sheet?

6. in the auctioneer's opening speech?

7. at any time during the offering of the lot?

8. just before the gavel is brought down?

9. where the property on offer gives a rental income to the owner and VAT is paid by the tenants in addition to their rent?

> **KEY POINT:** *If VAT is not mentioned in any of these contexts then you may rest assured that it is not payable in addition to the gavel price.*

How can I find out the reserve price?

Most owners are unwilling to sell their properties below a fixed figure. This is the amount which they indicate to the auctioneer as the reserve. The gavel is not brought down to create a contract for sale for any lot until there is a bid equal to or larger than the reserve figure. The auctioneer will of course encourage bidders to bid up to that price, so that he then has a sale. Usually he provides in the conditions of sale for the right to put in bids below the reserve amount on behalf of the owner who is selling.

> **KEY POINT:** *The reserve is a highly confidential amount and it is most unusual for it to be disclosed to the public or to any intending bidders.*

It is not unusual for public bodies to put the reserve in a sealed envelope which the auctioneer only opens as he goes onto the rostrum, although it is quite possible that he will have discussed an appropriate

Fig 20.8   Opening bids, reserves and increments

Reserve	Likely opening increments with responsive bidding	Possible opening bid with unresponsive bidding	Possible opening bid
£10,000	£1,000	£6,000	£4,000
£20,000	£1,000	£15,000	£10,000
£30,000	£2,500	£20,000	£15,000
£50,000	£5,000	£30,000	£20,000
£100,000	£10,000	£60,000	£50,000
£200,000	£10,000	£150,000	£100,000
£300,000	£25,000	£200,000	£150,000

amount with his client beforehand. Some owners even refuse to disclose their final reserve to their own auctioneer and sit in the audience giving a pre-arranged signal when the bidding has reached a level at which the auctioneer can sell. This practice is discouraged by auctioneers because of the uncertainty it creates for them.

Reserves that are published

Only on a limited number of occasions – particularly where owners are thinking of selling at a low price – do auctioneers publish their reserve as part of their marketing campaign. This is done deliberately to create interest and the figure is usually published in the auction catalogue and often put into advertisements. It may be described as an *'upset price'* (see Figure 20.6). This practice is frequently adopted where the instructions to sell have come from liquidators and receivers.

A published reserve puts you in the driving seat

To the auctioneer, having his reserve disclosed is rather like playing a poker hand face upwards on the table. Immediately the price at which he can sell is disclosed, then everyone in the audience is aware of whether the bids have reached a point at which the auctioneer can sell or not. He is not in a position to put pressure on people in the room to bid by going through the offering procedure on a 'mock' basis as if he was about to sell. This procedure is examined later in this chapter.

Without reserve

Very occasionally, lots are offered 'without reserve' and this literally means that if only one (even if it is excessively low) bid is received, the auctioneer has to sell. Anyone attending an auction where a property is offered at no reserve would be perfectly entitled to start the bidding at £1.

The vagaries of human nature are such that it is not at all unusual for properties offered with no reserve to attract a lot of attention and for bidders to get carried away but it is a brave owner who would offer his property on this basis thinking he will sell at a high sum. It is a practice used more often for properties for which there is little demand or where there are large liabilities for structural repairs or other costs.

> **KEY POINT:** *Properties offered without a reserve are not always the bargain which they may seem and should be approached with considerable care.*

A cautionary tale

Mr Black is after a cheap property that he can 'do up and rent out' to bring him a small income. He calculates that if he buys something under £5,000, refurbishes it for £10,000 and then rents it out at £4,000 a year, this would represent a really good investment.

Don't get carried away by 'no reserves'

He is delighted to see a property at a local auction at no reserve. It looks a little run-down in the picture but does not seem too bad and he dashes to the auction without doing any checking. Before Mr Black had even collected his wits at the auction, the bidding had started at only £5 for the lot which interested him and seemed to be going fast and furious until it slowed down at £2,700. He quickly jumped in with £2,800 and was delighted when the gavel fell on his first bid, particularly since he felt he had saved himself £2,200 already.

His solicitor's charges of £500 seemed rather expensive and he was even less pleased on seeing the property for the first time the day after the auction to discover that it suffered from subsidence, rising damp, was infected with woodworm and had suffered from an arson attack which had burnt out the back of the building. A surveyor estimated it would take around £35,000 to put it right.

The local council, having had their attention drawn to the property by the auction publicity, sent around their building inspector, who condemned it. Mr Black failed to respond to the request that he demolish it and they carried out the work for him submitting a bill for £3,200 including 15 per cent establishment expenses plus VAT.

Mr Black still owns an empty site which cost him over £7,600 and no-one wants to buy but upon which a lot of people seem to want to 'fly-tip' rubbish, which has to be cleared away at his expense.

In Figure 20.7, the derelict nature of the property is obvious and, furthermore, was spelt out in the auctioneer's description. Defects in properties offered at no reserve are not always so obvious.

Disclosing when the reserve has been reached

Auctioneers will go to great lengths to prevent the audience from realising which bids are made on behalf of the sellers and which bids have been made by people in the room. Therefore, there is usually no obvious indication when the auctioneer 'reaches' or 'passes' the reserve. Thereafter, certain auctioneers like to disclose that the bidding is higher than the reserve and will use such phrases as 'the property is in the market' or 'at this price I shall sell if I receive no higher bid' or simply indicate that the reserve has been reached. Other auctioneers only disclose this information on certain lots where they feel it will encourage the bidding.

> **KEY POINT:** *Many auctioneers never disclose that the reserve has been reached and it is only known when either the gavel falls for the sale or the gavel does not fall and the lot is withdrawn.*

Discovering the reserve price

If you are able to discover, by fair means or foul, the level of the reserve, you are in a stronger position than other bidders competing against you. To discover reserves, bidders must resort to their ingenuity. In most cases, the reserve figure will be known to the auctioneer and to some of his senior and junior staff who may be led into disclosing the actual figure. Close acquaintanceship with the auctioneer might or might not help but, undoubtedly, a 'quick peek' at his auction catalogue (if he has an unguarded moment) could reveal the figure.

Can I tell what the reserve is from the starting price?

There is no fixed theory about the relationship between the price that the auctioneer first asks for, the figure at which he takes the first bid and the reserve price. It is worth considering the psychology of the auctioneer and weighing up his style and practice as the auction proceeds. There are several factors in his mind:

- On the papers in front of him for each lot, he will have the reserve 'writ large'. His note of the reserve figure will not only be in large numerals but also in a bright colour so he cannot miss it. He is striving to encourage the bidding to reach this reserve figure. As he starts off each lot, this amount will be uppermost in his mind as his target. It is not unusual that the first figure he mentions in seeking the opening bid could well be that reserve amount.

- The auctioneer likes to receive bids in the room and be seen to be taking them. On the other hand, if he has a considerable number of lots to sell and is in a hurry to complete the sale, he will wish to start the bidding not too far below the reserve. Figure 20.8 illustrates possible opening bids and increments against given reserve prices.

- If the auction is going well, and the auctioneer is receiving responsive bidding from the floor, then he is likely to start the bidding closer to his reserve than otherwise. If there is very little response and not many bids forthcoming, he may try a starting bid that is particularly low to encourage enthusiasm from the audience. Unfortunately, there is no proven formula; but as you become used to your auctioneer's style you may be able to spot a pattern in his behaviour.

The auction itself was run very well. I had been before so I knew they were good and entertaining – it's the best bit of free entertainment in Manchester.

Don Lee, buyer of a residential property at auction.

Author's modesty prevents the identity of the auctioneer being disclosed!

21 'We bought at auction' – what buyers have to say

How have others fared with the auction process? To give you a flavour of what it is like, the following people's experiences illustrate what they thought and felt about buying a property at auction.

1. Caroline Titley bought two semi-detached Victorian houses for her business

Caroline Titley, runs her own business in Ashton-under Lyme. She needed a property for her business and decided it would be more advantageous to buy than to rent, as it was cheaper.

'I found the property from an estate agent, not the auctioneer. It is a Victorian property comprising two semi-detached houses and is around 150 years old. We bought the whole property and inhabit one half for our business and have a tenant in the other half. This was the first property that my partner and I had bought at auction and we made the bids ourselves. We had been to an auction before, so we were familiar with the process.

It was originally offered for sale in one auction but failed to receive a single bid and was withdrawn. The agent said the owner was seeking an asking price of £85,000 and that it was going to auction again in three weeks' time. We thought we might get it cheaper at auction rather than negotiating the sale there and then.

At the second auction, I asked how much the reserve price was and was given a guideline figure of £70,000 to £75,000. We thought that given the lack of interest in the property at the first auction, if we bid up to the guideline then no one would bid any higher. The bidding process went smoothly. I wasn't too apprehensive about it and I had my business partner with me although he did not want to do the actual bidding when it came to it. It started at £70,000. I was so surprised when someone bid against me. It was all over in a matter of minutes, but I was equally surprised that just before the property reached £85,000 the other bidder dropped out.

'We didn't go over what we could afford.'

'We didn't go over what we could afford'

In the end, we got it for the price we were prepared to pay and we didn't go over what we could afford. I was really pleased that we had acquired the property and I would certainly purchase commercial property at auction again and recommend others to use an auction to do the same.'

2. Don Lee paid 33 per cent less buying his house at auction

Don Lee lives in Manchester and has bought two residential houses at separate auctions.

'I was living in Manchester and noticed there was a number of run-down properties in the inner city part of Manchester. They had been built as private houses in 1982/3 and there had been problems with them simply because the people who had bought them could not pay their mortgage. They were quickly vandalised and went down in value like the rest of the property market.

I noticed that the auctioneers had managed to get hold of a few of these properties and they were going for about £14,000 which was pretty good even then. I waited for the best of the houses to come along which was an end one overlooking a public space with a pleasant view. I went to auction a couple of times before to get the feel for it and to see what the prices were like. I thought just before Christmas would be a good time to buy because people haven't got a lot of spare money and have other things on their mind and as it turns out I was proved right.

'I was surprised they did not go for more.'

There was a certain tension at the auction. However, the property failed to reach its reserve and was withdrawn at auction. I negotiated a price of £12,000 for it after the auction and it only needed another £1,000 to put it into liveable condition. I was surprised they did not go for more.

The auction itself was run very well. I had been before so I knew they were good and entertaining (it's the best bit of free entertainment in Manchester). I did all the legal side myself and the conveyancing.

'I paid 33 per cent less.'

The main advantage to me of buying at auction has got to be the price. Compared with the prices going through high street estate agents I

'Closing Order' –

Where the local authority feels that a property is unsuitable for occupation, they issue a 'Closing Order' which prevents the property being used. It is often possible to agree a schedule of repairs with the local authority, upon completion of which they will allow the property to be used for occupation once more.

'Planning Brief' –

Certain planning authorities for particular sites or areas often prepare a 'brief' for that area indicating the type and nature of development which they will be inclined to permit.

Fig 21.1. Estates Gazette auction results

LONDON

STRETTONS of E1 at New Connaught Rms, WC2, Apr 19

E1 — 18 Pevensey Hse, Ben Johnson Rd. S/C mais, 4 rms. L, P	30,000
50 Cephas Ave. End terr hse, 6 rms. Closing order. F, P	53,000
37 New Rd. Terr w/shop bdg. 2 floors. Let £2,068 pa. 2 floors, 388 & 410 sq ft with P. F	55,000
E3 — 104 Fairfoot Rd. Bdg plot. PP 2 flats. F, P	15,000
111 Grove Rd. Terr hse, 5 rms. F, P	54,000
13 Grafton Hse, Wellington Way. 2nd floor, S/C flat, 3 rms. L, P	17,500
E5 — 5/7 Chatsworth Rd. 2 adj shops. RUP 2 S/C flats, 4 & 5 rms. Let £3,120 PAX. Closing Order. F	40,000
4 Cricketfield Rd. S/C flat, 2 rms. L, P	25,500
19 Elderfield Rd. End terr hse, 9 rms. PP flat, mais, 2 garages. Closing order. F, P	43,000
30 Glenarm Rd. 2nd floor, S/C studio flat. L, P	15,500
103 Mount Pleasant Lane. S/C flat, 3 rms. L, P	23,000
E6 — 132 Charlemont Rd. RUP S/C flat, 2 rms. L, P	20,500
58 Dickens Rd. End terr hse, 3 bed. F, P	35,000
130 Masterman Rd. Terr hse, 2 bed. F, P	36,500
St Andrews Hall, Roman Rd. Derelict hall, site 0.10 a. Planning brief for 2 hses. F, P	31,000
E7 — 165 Capel Rd. Corner bdg, 6 rms, part used as clinic. PP 2 hses & garages on rear land. F, P	66,500
7 Neville Rd. End terr bdg as 3 S/C flats. 1 LGR, 1 studio flat & 1 x 3 rms with P. For completion. F	36,500
75 Pevensey Rd. Terr hse as 2 flats, 3 rms. F, P	38,000
7 Reginald Rd. Corner shop, rear rm. RUP, 3 rms. F, P	35,000
21 Shaftesbury Rd. Terr hse, 2 bed. F, P	35,500
E8 — 234 Dalston Lane. 4 storey hse, 10 rms, 2 store rms. F, P	55,000
376C Kingsland Rd. RUP S/C mais, 3 rms. L, P	22,000
113 Shacklewell Lane. Shop, rear rm. S/C mais, 3 rms. P	28,500
E10 — 287 High Rd. Shop, rear rm, basement, mais, 4 rms, garage. F, P	60,000
E12 — 32 Salisbury Rd. Terr hse, 3 bed. F, P	36,500
E13 — 198 Balaam St. S/C flat, 3 rms. L, P	18,000
163 Grange Rd. Terr hse, 6 rms. F, P	34,500
50 London Rd. S/C flat, 2 rms. L, P	14,000
31 Maud Rd. Terr hse as S/C flat, 3 rms & S/C mais, 3 rms. F, P	41,000
Tabernacle Ave. Site 0.16 a. Planning brief for development. F, P	16,000
E14 — 46 Chapel House St. Terr hse, 3 bed. F, P	60,000

paid 33% less. That is perhaps a bit more than usual – I think 25 per cent is a bit nearer the mark. However, I realised I was buying a vandalised property and knew what I was getting. I didn't buy a pig in a poke – you can do that – there is always that risk.

I bought another house recently and was surprised when it was knocked down to me for £24,000 as I was expecting to pay up to £25,000. I did think at one stage that I might not get the property although I was prepared to bid £1,000 more than I paid for it. For this second house, similar properties are costing almost twice as much. I was surprised it went for what it did do. I was well pleased with it.

'I would definitely buy another property at auction.'

I would definitely buy another property at auction and have no hesitation recommending others to buy at auction provided they understand the risks and have no worries. You must ask why the property is going for sale at auction and what (if anything) is wrong with it and satisfy yourselves that you are not buying a pig in a poke. You have got to be prepared to do your own research. For example, I had to check that I was not buying a property over a coal mine. I knew the reason for the sale – that the property was foreclosed and put up for auction by a building society.'

3. Michael Kirby is a chartered surveyor who buys commercial property for clients

'The latest property I bought was a Railtrack goods yard which I was buying on behalf of tenants as an investment property. It was let to them on short leases. The property is used for open storage of coal, pallets and cars.

I have bought one or two properties before, on behalf of clients and I made all the bidding myself.

We did try to bid for the property beforehand. This was unsuccessful and it was suggested that we go to the auction where the price we got it for was slightly above what we originally bid beforehand. If you bid beforehand, you can open up a situation and show your hand so you must be careful.

I didn't start the bidding. There were one or two other bidders lower down. I let them have their say and then came in at the end. We bid twice and the second time it stopped, my bid being the highest bid. I thought the auctioneer might withdraw it because it was only slightly higher than we had bid before the auction. I thought it probably hadn't reached the reserve. But then the gavel came down and I knew it was ours.

From a purchaser's point of view, I would have said you were going to get quite a good deal at auction, particularly in this climate. It all depends on the day because you never know who else is going to bid. In our case we didn't think there would be anyone else interested, but there was. We assume that we bought it at the reserve.

'I always try to do a deal beforehand.'

I always try to do a deal beforehand because you never know what opposition you are going to come up against at auction. But you should never show your hand in case it does go to auction. The vendor is generally only going to accept a higher price before the auction.

For a house or a plot of land that is good you can be outbid if people get carried away. The professional who is buying property will not get carried away but the average punter can tend to get carried away quite easily.

You can sometimes get a better deal at auction especially from lots that get withdrawn. Once you have reached your highest price you hope

A south London family residence for under £50,000? This could have been yours for £46,000.

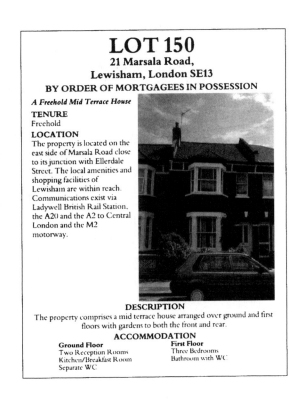

LOT 150

21 Marsala Road,
Lewisham, London SE13
BY ORDER OF MORTGAGEES IN POSSESSION

A Freehold Mid Terrace House

TENURE
Freehold

LOCATION
The property is located on the east side of Marsala Road close to its junction with Ellerdale Street. The local amenities and shopping facilities of Lewisham are within reach. Communications exist via Ladywell British Rail Station, the A20 and the A2 to Central London and the M2 motorway.

DESCRIPTION
The property comprises a mid terrace house arranged over ground and first floors with gardens to both the front and rear.

ACCOMMODATION

Ground Floor
Two Reception Rooms
Kitchen/Breakfast Room
Separate WC

First Floor
Three Bedrooms
Bathroom with WC

that the property hasn't reached the vendor's reserve and you can do a deal afterwards. You can get quite good deals that way.

Years ago it wasn't the done thing to buy property at auction but now it is more the norm especially on repossessions and investments. It's a quick way to buy a property. It gets the deal done.'

4. Michael Roe has bought two houses successfully at auction

'It is usually cheaper to buy property at auction.'

'I bought a two-up, two-down terrace. I saw the property originally from the auctioneer's catalogue and went to view it from that. I have bought three properties at auction and so I was fairly familiar with the procedures. The great advantage to me is that it is usually cheaper to buy property at auction.

I have bought properties that are in some state of disrepair. They always wanted modernising and bringing up to date. In deciding what price to bid I tend to take an overall view. I check local sale prices and work out how much it will cost me to bring it up to date. I am usually prepared to pay so much at auction and if it goes for that price, I will buy it.

You always feel a little apprehensive before you go in. You go in with nothing and come home with something else. It was a fair investment, but it wasn't a big enough sum to worry me very much. The ones I've gone for I've got. I didn't feel I was going to lose the property during the auction.

With the latest one, I waited until the other bids had been made and then came in at the end. I only made one bid, and that was the last bid that succeeded. I was pleased to get it.

Buying at auction is very straightforward. If I could see houses that were being sold at comparable prices in comparable areas I would buy privately. But buying at auction is a way of ensuring I don't have to pay more than I need to pay. You want to make sure you acquire your property at a bargain level and auctions are the way.'

Appendix – Principal property auctioneers

Allen & Harris
Auction Administration Centre for Wales
7a Heol-y-Deri, Rhiwbina, Cardiff CF4 6HA
Tel: 029 2062 5626 Fax: 029 2062 5632
Catalogue request line: 09069 118846
Results fax line (touchtone): 0991 118819
Results fax line (non-touchtone): 0660 222223
Website: www.rsaproperty.co.uk/auctions

Allen & Harris
Newfield House, Vicarage Lane
Blackpool, Lancashire FY4 4EW
Tel: 01253 607634 Fax: 01253 607777
Website: www.rsaproperty.co.uk/auctions

Allsop & Co (Residential Department)
100 Knightsbridge, London SW1X 7LB
Tel: 020 7494 3686 Fax: 020 7581 3058
E-mail: post@allsop.co.uk
Website: www.allsop.co.uk
Catalogue request line: 0906 5151510
Auction live link: 09003 411262
Audio guide price line: 09067 110450
Audio results line: 09067 110451
Results fax line: 09067 110200
Buyers' fax guide on: 09067 110201
Legal documents line: 020 7494 3686
Audio results: refer catalogue

Allsop & Co (Commercial Department)
27 Soho Square, London W1V 6AX
Tel: 020 7437 6977 Fax: 020 7437 8984

E-mail: post@allsop.co.uk
Website: www.allsop.co.uk
Catalogue request line: 0115 972 6222
Auction live link: 09003 411262
Guide prices & results fax line: 09067 110202
London & SE regional fax list: 09067 110203
SW, E & W Mids, E Anglia fax list: 09067 110204
Yorks, Humbs, NW, Wales, N, Scot fax list: 09067 110205
High yield prop fax line: 09067 110206

Andrews & Robertson
27 Camberwell Green, London SE5 7AN
Tel: 020 7703 2662 Fax: 020 7708 2453
Individual results phone line: 09067 110455
Auction results fax line: 09067 110235

Astley Samuel Leeder
49 Mansel Street, Swansea SA1 5TB
Tel: 01792 655891 Fax: 01792 476926

Athawes Son & Co
203 High Street, Acton, London W3
Tel: 020 8992 0056/0122 Fax: 020 8993 0511
Guide price & results fax line: 09067 110209

Bacons
71/73 St Peter's Avenue
Cleethorpes DN35 8HF
Tel: 01472 691905 Fax: 01472 691267
Website: www.bacons.co.uk
Also two offices in Grimsby
(Tel: 01472 351126/351127)

Barnard Marcus
Auction Office, Commercial House
64/66 Glenthorne Road
London W6 0LR
Tel: 020 8741 9990/9001
Fax: 020 8741 2188/2168
Audio guide prices: 09067 110460
Audio results: 09067 110461
Fax guide prices: 09067 110210
Fax results: 09067 110461
Catalogue hotline: 0906 5226631 (£1.50/min!)
Auction live link: 0900 3411262
E-mail: auctions.bm@rsaproperty.co.uk
Website: www.rsaproperty.co.uk/auctions/barnardmarcus

Bigwood
43a Calthorpe Road, Edgbaston
Birmingham B15 1TS
Tel: 0121 456 2200 Fax: 0121 456 4008
Auction Line: 0121 625 0489
Website: www.bigwoodassociates.uk.com

Bond Wolfe
Victoria House, 290-292 High Street
West Bromwich
West Midlands B70 8EN
Tel: 0121 525 0600 Fax: 0121 525 8660
Results faxline: 09067 110075

Boultons Harrisons
54 John William Street
Huddersfield HD1 1ER
Tel: 01484 515029 Fax: 01484 450025

Butters
49/53 Trinity Street
Hanley, Stoke-on-Trent ST1 5LX
Tel: 01782 261511 Fax: 01782 202159
Results faxline: 09067 110252
Website: www.charlesbutters.co.uk

Caxtons
5 Clarendon Place
King Street, Maidstone
Kent ME14 1BQ
Tel: 01622 609050
Auction results fax line: 09067 110 299

Clarke Hillyer
163/165 Hoe Street
Walthamstow, London E17 3AL
Tel: 020 8521 6121 Fax: 020 8521 0382

Colliers Conrad Ritblat Erdman
Milner House
14 Manchester Square
London W1A 1BA
Tel: 020 7935 4499 Fax: 020 7487 1810
London results fax line: 09067 110213
Manchester results fax line: 09067 110254

Cottons
361 Hagley Road, Edgbaston
Birmingham B17 8DL
Tel: 0121 247 2233 Fax: 0121 247 1233
E-mail: auctions@cottons.co.uk

Countrywide Property Auctions
144 New London Road
Chelmsford, Essex CM2 0AW
Tel: 01245 344133 Fax: 01245 358985
Catalogue request line (Local rate): 0870 240 1140
London results fax line: 09067 110214
Leeds results fax line: 09067 110215
Manchester results fax line: 09067 110216
Durham results fax line: 09067 110249
Birmingham results fax line: 09067 110250
Plymouth results fax line: 09067 110251

Darlows
Auction Department, 5 North Street
Newport NP20 1JZ
Tel: 01633 250485 Fax: 01633 220909

Website: www.darlows.co.uk
Auction results fax line: 0991 118804

Dedman Property Services
'Hillsboro', 377 Southchurch Road
Southend-on-Sea, Essex SS1 2PQ
Tel: 01702 467000 Fax: 01702 460929
Auction enquiry line: 01702 311010
E-mail: auctions@dedman.net
Website: www.auctioninfo.co.uk
Results fax line: 09067 110238

Drewery & Wheeldon
Rebrook House, 124 Trinity Street
Gainsborough, Lincolnshire DN21 1JD
Tel: 01427 616118 Fax: 01427 811070

Drivers & Norris
407-409 Holloway Road
London N7 6HP
Tel: 020 7607 5001 Fax: 020 7609 5031
Guides & results fax line: 09067 110217
E-mail: auction@drivers.co.uk
Website: www.drivers.co.uk

Eddisons
Pennine House, Russell Street
Leeds LS1 5RN
Tel: 0113 243 0101 Fax: 0113 242 1364
Results faxback line: 09067 110222
E-mail: property@eddcom.co.uk
Website: www.eddcom.co.uk
Offices in Bradford and Huddersfield

Edwin Evans
253 Lavender Hill
Battersea, London SW11 1JW
Tel: 020 7228 5864 Fax: 020 7223 7637
Guide price fax line: 09067 110218
Guide price audio line: 09067 110458
Results fax line: 09067 110219
Results audio line: 09067 110459
Catalogue request line: 09067 110590

Clive Emson
8 Cavendish Way, Bearstead
Maidstone, Kent ME15 8XY

Tel: 01622 630033 Fax: 01622 630036
Results fax line: 09067 110237
Results audio line: 09067 110454
Results by post: 09068 517744
E-mail: clive@emson.demon.co.uk
Website: www.auctioninfo.co.uk

Fox & Sons
HQ & Brighton Auction Centre
117/118 Western Road, Brighton
BN1 2AE
Tel: 01273 321300 Fax: 01273 204756
Covering East Sussex, West Sussex and bordering areas of Surrey and Kent.

Southampton Auction Centre
32-34 London Road
Southampton SO15 2TB
Tel: 023 80338066 Fax: 023 80225479
Covering Hampshire, Dorset, Wiltshire, the Isle of Wight and south-west Surrey.

Catalogue request line 09067 110582
Guide prices and entries
fax line: 09067 110246
Recent results (last two sales)
fax line: 09067 110247

Austin Gray
123-125 & 135-137 Dyke Road
Hove, East Sussex BN3 1TJ
Tel: 01273 232232 Fax: 01273 232233
Results faxline: 09067 110236
E-mail: property@austingray.co.uk

Chris Guttridge
20 High Street, Wath Upon Dearne
Rotherham, South Yorkshire S63 7QG
Tel: 01709 872247 Fax: 01709 877397

Frederick G Hair & Son
200 London Road, Southend on Sea
SS1 1PJ
Tel: 01702 432255 Fax: 01702 337846
Guides/Results fax line: 09067 110253
E-mail: hairandson@iclweb.com

Website:
www.propertylive.co.uk/hairandson
Website: www.auctioninfo.co.uk
Offices also in Westcliff-on-Sea,
Leigh-on-Sea and Thorpe Bay.

Halifax National Property Auctions
National Auction Division, Halifax
House
28 High Street, Kegworth
Derby DE74 2DA
Tel: 01509 680701 Fax: 01509
670888
Website: www.halifax.co.uk
Birmingham results fax line: 0906
5867173
Bolton results fax line: 0906
5867174
Bristol results fax line: 0906
5867175
Cardiff results fax line: 0906
5867176
Leeds results fax line: 0906 5867178
Catalogue request line: 09067
530166

Hamilton Osborne King
32 Molesworth Street, Dublin 2
Tel: 00 353 1 618 1300 Fax: 00 353
1 676 7066
E-mail: info@hok.ie
Website: www.hok.ie

Handleys
10 Blenheim Walk, Leeds LS2 9AQ
Tel: 0113 246 9090 Fax: 0113 246
9100
E-mail: auctions@handleys.com
Website: www.handleys-leeds.com

Harman Healy
340 Grays Inn Road
London WC1X 8BJ
Tel: 020 7833 5885 Fax: 020 7833
5995
Results fax line: 09067 110224
Auction Live Link: 09003 426507

Healey & Baker
29 St George Street
Hanover Square, London W1A 3BG
Tel: 020 7629 9292 Fax: 020 7514
2360
E-mail: jcornwell@healey-baker.com
Website: www.healey-baker.com
Guide prices faxline: 09067 110285

Results fax line: 09067 110221
Audio guide price lines: 020 7514
0745 to 0751

Mark Jenkinson & Son
8 Norfolk Row, Sheffield S1 2PA
Tel: 0114 276 0151 Fax: 0114 275
6370
Website: www.markjenkinson.co.uk

Jones Lang LaSalle
22 Hanover Square, London W1A
2BN
Tel: 020 7493 6040 Fax: 020 7399
5637
Guide price fax line: 020 7399 5399
Results fax line: 020 7399 5399
Catalogue request line: 020 7399
5399
E-mail:
uk.auctions@joneslanglasalle.com
Website:http://reach.joneslanglasalle.
com

Lambert & Foster
77 Commercial Road, Paddock
Wood
Tonbridge, Kent TN12 6DR
Tel: 01892 832325 Fax: 01892
834700
Website:
www.lambertandfoster.co.uk

Larards
33 Lowgate, Hull HU1 1PB
Tel: 01482 223311 Fax: 01482
618131

Longden & Cook Commercial and Edward Mellor
182 London Road
Hazel Grove
Stockport
Cheshire SK7 4DQ
Tel: 0161 230 1740 Fax: 0161 419
9933
E-mail: auction@auctioneers-
lcc.co.uk
Website: www.auctioneers-lcc.co.uk

D.J. Manning
Carriden, Bo'ness, West Lothian
EH51 9SF
Tel: 01506 827693 Fax: 01506
826495

Miller Metcalfe
56 Bradshawgate, Bolton BL1 1DW
Tel: 01204 535 353 Fax: 01204 362
945
Catalogue request line: 01204 525
150
Website: www.millermetcalfe.co.uk

Morgan Beddoe
147 Whiteladies Road, Clifton,
Bristol BS8 2QT
Tel: 0117 946 7100 Fax: 0117 946
7111
Website: www.morgan-beddoe.co.uk

Morgan Evans & Co
Head Office, 28-30 Church Street
Llangefni, Anglesey LL77 7DU
Tel: 01248 723303 Fax: 01248
750146
Property Office: 01248 716816
Website: www.property-
wales.uk/morganevans

Morton & Flanagan Ltd
Main Street, Words, Dublin
Tel: 00 353 1 840 4011 Fax: 00 353
1 840 4459

Nelson Bakewell
25 Sackville Street, London W1X
2HQ
Tel: 020 7544 2000 Fax: 020 7544
2222
Auction line: 020 7544 2244
Results fax line: 09067 110229
Catalogue request line: 0115 946
5715
E-mail: auction@nelson-
bakewell.com
Website: www.nelson-bakewell.com

Keith Pattinson
(Auction Office) 210 High Street
Newcastle upon Tyne NE3 1HN
Tel: 0191 213 0550 Fax: 0191 222
0314
Website: www.pattinson.co.uk

Royal & SunAlliance
Newfield House, Vicarage Lane
Blackpool, FY4 4EW
Tel: 01253 607600 Fax: 01253
607777
Website:
www.rsaproperty.co.uk/auctions

FPD Savills
139 Sloane Street, London SW1X
9AY
Tel: 020 7824 9091 Fax: 020 7824
9062
Results fax line: 09067 110220
Catalogue hotline: 0906 538 3458
(60p/min)
E-mail:
ccolemansmith@fpdsavills.co.uk
Website: www.fpdsavills.co.uk

FPD Savills
4 St Peter's Gate,
Nottingham NG1 2JG
Tel: 0115 934 8000 Fax: 0115 934
8001/2
Guide price & results fax line: 09067
110223
Catalogue hotline: 0906 863 3458
(60p/min)
E-mail:
ccolemansmith@fpdsavills.co.uk
Website: www.fpdsavills.co.uk

Seel & Co
The Crown House, Wyndham
Crescent
Canton, Cardiff CF11 9UH
Tel: 029 2034 2721 Fax: 029 2023
7544
Catalogue request line: 029 2034
2721
E-mail: property@seel-and-
co.demon.co.uk

Sherry FitzGerald
13 Merrion Row, Dublin 2
Tel: 00 353 1 661 6198 Fax: 00 353
1 661 3755
Website: www.sherryfitz.ie

Shonki Brothers
55 London Road, Leicester LE2 0PE
Tel: 0116 254 3373 Fax: 0116 258
4491

**Strettons (incorporating Stickley &
Kent)**
Auction Office, Central House
189-203 Hoe Street, Walthamstow
London E17 3AP
Tel: 020 8520 8383 Fax: 020 8520
7306
E-mail:auctions@strettons.co.uk
Website: www.strettons.co.uk

Results fax line: 09067 110230
Audio database: 09067 110453
Auction live link: 09003 411262
Recorded lot results: refer catalogue
Catalogue request line: 09003
424806

Sullivan Mitchell
36 St Thomas Street,
Lymington SO41 9NE
Tel: 01590 677555 Fax: 01590
677333
404–406 Garratt Lane, London
SW18 4HP
Tel: 020 8944 8899 Fax: 020 8944
8886
Auction results: 09067 110 231

SVA Property Auctions
3a St Vincent Street, Edinburgh EH3
6SW
Tel: 0131 624 6640 Fax: 0131 624
6630
E-mail: sva.auctions@cableinet.co.uk
Website: www.sva-auctions.co.uk

K. Stuart Swash
2 Waterloo Road, Wolverhampton
WV1 4BL
Tel: 01902 710626 Fax: 01902
428017

TOPS Property Services Ltd
15-17 Princes Street, Norwich NR3
1AF
Tel: 01603 767050 Fax: 01603
767567
Website: www.ITLhomesearch.com

Venmore Thomas & Jones
44 Stanley Street, Liverpool L1 6AL
Tel: 0151 236 6746 Fax: 0151 255
0403
Auction results fax line: 09067
110243
E-mail: liverpool@vtj.co.uk
Website: www.vtj.co.uk

Ward & Partners
136 Ashford Road, Bearsted
Maidstone, Kent ME14 4NH
Tel: 01622 736736 Fax: 01622
738738
Catalogue hotline: 0906 8020113
(60p/min)
Results faxline: 09067 110245

E-mail:
auction.dept@wardandpartners.co.uk
Website:
www.arunestates.co.uk/auctions

Weaving & Partners
20 Water Street, Liverpool L2 8TL
Tel: 0151 236 9090 Fax: 0151 236
1144
Results fax line: 09067 110244
E-mail: jmw@weaving.co.uk
Website: www.weaving.co.uk

Willmotts
Willmott House, 12 Blacks Road
Hammersmith, London W6 9EU
Tel: 020 8748 6644 Fax: 020 8748
9300
Results audio line: 09067 110452
Results fax line: 09067 110232

Wilsons Auctions
22 Mallusk Road, Newtownabbey
Belfast BT36 8PP
Tel: 028 9034 2626 Fax: 028 9034
2528
E-mail:
auctions@wilsons.attmail.com
Website: www.wilsons-auctions.com

Winkworth Auctions
23 Brighton Road, South Croydon
Surrey CR2 6EA
Tel: 020 8649 7255 Fax: 020 8666
0559
Website: www.winkworth.co.uk
North of England office: 01253
796260
Auction results fax line: 09067
110233
Addendum update line: 09067
110234
Auction live link: 09003 411292

Glossary

A–E

absolute title – highest and most unquestionable title.

abstract of title – a summary of documents proving title.

assent – the title of a legatee or devisee is not complete until the deceased's executor/personal representative has completed an assent which then becomes a good root of title.

assignment – transfer of benefit of lease.

attested – witnessed.

beneficial owner – person/s owning land for own benefit.

beneficiary – one who has the beneficial interest, i.e. receives the rent or is the occupier.

charge/legal charge – mortgage.

counterpart – lease signed by tenant – the part is signed by landlord.

conveyance – a written instrument of transfer of real property used when the land is not registered at HM Land Registry.

covenant – promise written in deed.

deed – is 'signed, sealed and delivered' all transfers of freehold and leasehold property must be.

devise – a gift by will of land or other real estate. A bequest is a gift by will of personal estate.

easement – right of one landowner to use other's land for right of way, water, drains, etc.

equity – (on redemption) the money owing to you after the loan has been paid off.

escrow – a deed delivered conditionally, it does not become effective until the condition is satisfied, e.g. other party signs his part

E–S

estate – (a) real: ownership of freehold/leasehold.
(b) personal: ownership of effects other than land.

execute – sign.

executor – person appointed in will of deceased person to carry out provisions of will. Probate proves entitlement to do so.

fee simple – freehold.

filed plan – the plan from which Land Registry identifies land.

flying freehold – (so called) applies to (a) upper parts of buildings. The soil is owned by another. (b) foreshores (c) interest in part of area of meadows allocated by annual drawing of lots

freehold – absolute ownership as opposed to leasehold.

incumbrance – a mortgage upon either real or personal estate.

indenture – deed made by more than one party. A conveyance used to be called an Indenture.

intestate – leaving no valid will.

joint and several – Two or more parties who render themselves liable to a joint action against all, as well as to a separate action against each in case the agreement or bond is not kept.

joint tenants – co-owners of land with or without buildings on it. Survivor takes all (see also tenants in common).

land – general real estate term, refers to land and all buildings that stand on it.

overriding interest – the rights of persons other than owners to occupy property. These rights do not have to be registered at the Land Registry to be effective.

parcels – the pieces a hitherto single plot has been split into.

private treaty – sale not by auction.

restrictive covenant – promise in a deed restricting use of land.

root of title – documents through which ownership is proved. (Will become archaic when all land registered.)

scrotage – A Bradshavian neologism.

S–V

seisen/seised – possessed of land as freeholders.

sitting tenant – tenant of house or flat. Usually, this term means a tenant who has acquired security of tenure and whose tenancy cannot be ended by the landlord giving notice.

specific performance – successful completion of contract.

stakeholder – holder of deposit which he does not pass to vendor without authority of buyer, or return to buyer without permission of vendor.

stamp duty – payable on some deeds and documents which cannot be used as evidence or registered at the Land Registry unless properly stamped with duty paid, or 'adjudicated' or 'particulars delivered'.

tenant for life – person entitled to benefit of real estate for term of his life, after which it will pass to others as determined by an existing will or trust.

tenants in common – the property is owned in shares and each owner can bequeath his part to whom he will.

tenure – The mode of holding or occupying lands. No person except the Sovereign can be the absolute owner of land in England. So the rest of us hold immediately of the crown (freehold) or mediated by a freeholder (leasehold). How far a tenure extends is called the tenant's estate, hence estate in fee simple, etc.

testimonium – formal introduction to the attestation clause in a deed.

title – evidence which signifies a person's right to enjoyment of land.

trust – created when property transferred to a person (trustee) to apply for benefit of another.

trustees for sale – where two or more people are entitled to the estate. Purchasers need receipt for purchase moneys on conveyance or Form 19 signed by at least two of them unless there are two joint tenants and only one survives. The survivor can then deal with the estate.

vacating receipt – Receipt written and signed on the Legal Charge showing all moneys intended to be secured by the deed to have been paid off.

Index

The index covers all chapters except listings. Terms categorise property auctions, buying, selling and conveyancing. **Bold** type within a sequence of page numbers indicates a more significant section; an 'i' after a page number indicates an illustration (or illustration and text); an 'f' after a page number indicates a figure (or figure and text).

H

heating 20
holiday properties 239
homes
    matrimonial *see* matrimonial homes
    properties as, drawbacks 12–13
    see also individual property headings
husbands, occupation rights 172

I

increments 269f
Inland Revenue, on stamp duty 135
instruments of transfer 165–6
insurance
    auctions, deposits 264
    NHBC 21–2
    restrictive covenants 102, 112
interests, registers 160–1
investments 214, 216–17, 276
    by companies 240
    last houses on developments 27
    properties as
        developments on 26
        impediments 25–6
    see also individual property headings;
bargains

J

job satisfaction 7
junk, disposal 51

K

K15 forms 157, 160
K16 forms 124, 157
knocked down prior 222f, **246–8**, 276, 277

knowledge, vs acumen **3–4**, 107, 168–9, 175 *see also* confidence; practice

L

Land Charges Department, The 91–2
Land Registry, The 92, 223
    Charges Register 93–4f, 96, 99–105, 160–1
        forms 4–5, 146–7
            TR1 forms 111
        Property Register 93f, 96, 97
        Proprietorship Register 93f, 96, 97–8
Land Registry Cover 177
last-time buyers
    questions 30
    reasons, drawbacks 29
leasehold properties 78–9, 112
    vs freeholds 97–8
        matrimonial homes 172
    sale and leasebacks 222f
leaseholders, freehold rights 172, 175
legalese 177–8, 235
lenders 24, 129
    debt recovery from 20–1
    final requests 178
    forms 139–40
    mortgages *see* mortgages
    questions from 137–8
    solicitors 133–4
        fees 141
        forms 166–7
    surveyors 20
let the buyer beware (*caveat emptor*) 4, 109
licensed conveyancers *see* solicitors
lighting 67
LLC1 forms 125, 126, 130–1, 158, 160

loans
>bridging 6, 39
>tax on 238–9

lots 221–3
>composite 210–13f, 251–2f
>single 210f, 213, 251f *see also*

individual property headings
>unseen 259–60
>>drawbacks 270–1
>withdrawn 273, 274, 277

M

markets
>buyers' 31, 32
>vendors' 31, 32

matrimonial homes 157–8, 171
>cautions 104, 173–4
>continuation orders 173
>forms 172–3
>freehold vs leasehold 172

Memoranda of Contract 232, 256f, 257–8

memory prompts, properties 11

modern properties
>cavity walls 14–15
>developments *see* developments,

properties
>NHBC 21–2, 23
>romantic appeal 27

modernisation, limitations 51–2

mortgages 102–3, 129, 131, 145–6, 156, **177**
>DS1 forms 136–8, 140, 147
>endowment 41
>fees 168
>narrow limits 40–1
>obligatory advice 137
>redemption for deeds 141
>second 161

widened limits 41

N

names
>of forms 8
>of owners 135
>of properties 54

National House Building Council (NHBC) 23
>builders
>>obligations 21
>>registration 22
>coverage 21–2
>insurance cover 21–2
>limitations 21, 22

negotiations
>agreements 72–3
>>estate agents' 37
>bargaining points 71
>commission, estate agents' 36
>final stands 71–2
>increased valuations 50
>opening
>>keenness in 70
>>reluctance in 69–71
>perseverance 71–2
>underselling 72–3
>viewing, locations 52

neighbours 113
>troublesome 12, 175–6

nervousness, bidding 278

networking, estate agents' 34–5

NHBC *see* National House Building Council (NHBC)

94a forms 139

96 forms 64–5, 156–7

noise 12

notices 236–7